Competitiveness in Small Developing Economies

Competitiveness in Small Developing Economies

Insights from the Caribbean

Alvin G. Wint

University of the West Indies Press
Barbados ● Jamaica ● Trinidad and Tobago

University of the West Indies Press
1A Aqueduct Flats   Mona
Kingston 7   Jamaica

07   5 4 3

The following chapters are revised from previously published articles and reprinted with permission.
Chapter 1: First published as "Competitive Disadvantages
and Advantages of Small Nations: An Analysis of Inter-
Nation Economic Performance", *Journal of Eastern Caribbean Studies* 27, no. 3 (2002).
Chapter 3: First published as "Anchoring a Programme of
Macroeconomic Stabilisation: Lessons from the Experience
of Barbados?", *Caribbean Journal of Public Sector Management* 1, no. 1 (1999).
Chapter 7: First published as "Enterprise Competitiveness
in a Small, Low Growth Developing Environment: Jamaican Experiences", *Caribbean Journal of Public Sector Management* 2, no. 2 (2001).
Chapter 9: First published as "International Competitiveness and Rare Tradeables: Assessing the Jamaican Health
System", *Social and Economic Studies* 51, no. 3 (2002).

CATALOGUING IN PUBLICATION DATA

Wint, Alvin G., 1959–
Competitiveness in small developing economies: insights
from the Caribbean / Alvin G. Wint
p. cm.
Includes bibliographical references and index.
ISBN: 976-640-132-2

1. Competition – Caribbean, English-speaking. 2. Competition, International –
Caribbean, English-speaking. 3. Investments, Foreign – Caribbean, English-
speaking. 4. Industrial promotion – Caribbean, English-speaking. I. Title.

HF1414.W57 2003   338.6

Book design by ProDesign Ltd, Red Gal Ring, Jamaica.
Cover design by Robert Harris.
Printed in Canada.

To Masie, Andrew and Adrian

Contents

Figures

Tables

Acknowledgements

It is the rare scholarly book that is not, in fact, a collaborative venture. Single-authored books may appear to be the work of a single author. Many are not. This one is certainly not. Many individuals have contributed significantly to the research that is reported on in this volume.

My collaborative work with two of my colleagues in the department of management studies at the University of the West Indies, Noel Cowell and Anne Crick, on the subject of workplace transformation and international competitiveness, is reported on in chapter 8 of this volume. Two of my former graduate students in the department's Master of Science in International Business programme, Claudius Emmanuel and Densil Williams, collaborated with me in research on exchange regime choice and determinants of foreign direct investment flows to developing countries. Our collaborative research in these areas is reported on in chapters 2 and 6 respectively. My work on the Jamaican health system, reported in chapter 9, developed out of a departmental project on research and training in health administration, supported by the Pan American Health Organization. I thank that organization for financial support of the project, Hilton McDavid, my colleague in the department of management studies, for conceiving of this project, and Tamika Haynes for providing research assistance in the early stages of the project.

I have concluded that competent librarians are a researcher's stress release valve. Several have gone beyond the call of duty in providing me with assistance in gathering information during the course of this multiyear, multination research project. Audrey Chambers and Norma Davis of the Sir Arthur Lewis Institute of Social and Economic Studies Documentation Centre have been extraordinarily gracious and efficient. I express a deep debt of gratitude to them. I also express my gratitude to the library staff of the University of Sydney, the University of Hawaii and the Baker Library at the Harvard Graduate School of Business Administration. In addition, I thank the staff of the World Bank's Foreign Investment Advisory Service Office in Sydney for allowing me access to their information resources. And I thank all those executives and policy makers who consented to be interviewed.

I thank the two reviewers of the first draft of this manuscript, both of whom provided very useful comments. Louis Wells's comments on the manuscript were sufficiently detailed that he could qualify as a coauthor. I thank him for his usual incisiveness. I thank Heidi Vernon and Sonia Jones for their tremendous support. I thank Linda Speth and her team at the University of the West Indies Press for their professionalism and support throughout the publication process.

I thank those who have provided support for me during this research exercise. The University of the West Indies study and travel grant programme provided important financial assistance. The research for, and writing of, this book took place during the five years that I have served as head of the department of management studies at the University of the West Indies. As the largest department, but one of the youngest departments, in the university, it presents particular administrative and leadership challenges. I am deeply grateful to my colleagues who have assisted me in the administration of the department during this period. These include Anne Crick, Michael Haughton, Jan Henry, Stanford Moore, Diaram Ramjeesingh, Asenath Sharpe and Carlene Wynter. Barrington Chevannes provided excellent overall support.

My friends at Unit Six of Andrews also provided critically important spiritual balance. I thank them also, as I do my colleagues at the University of the West Indies, my friends and my very supportive extended family. Finally, I am deeply grateful to my wife, Masie, and my sons, Andrew and Adrian, who are collaborators in all my ventures, and to whom I dedicate this book.

Abbreviations

DW	Durbin Watson statistic
CARICOM	Caribbean Community
CEO	Chief executive officer
CTUSAB	Coalition (later, Congress) of Trade Unions and Staff Associations of Barbados
DALE	Disability adjusted life expectancy
FDI	Foreign direct investment
GDP	Gross domestic product
GoInvest	Guyana Office for Investment
IMF	International Monetary Fund
JNIP	Jamaica National Investment Promotion Agency
JAMPRO	Jamaica Promotion Company
MES	Minimum efficient scale
MDCs	More developed countries
NIE	new institutional economics
OECD	Organisation for Economic Cooperation and Development
OECS	Organisation of Eastern Caribbean States
PPP	Purchasing power parity
Pro Panama	National Commission for the Promotion of Foreign Investments (Panama)
WHO	World Health Organization

Introduction

This book reports on research into efforts to improve standards of living, national productivity and firm-level competitiveness in small developing countries, using data drawn primarily from the small economies of the Caribbean region. The divergent experiences of these economies provide lessons for competitiveness enhancement efforts in other small developing countries. Indeed, these experiences may also provide lessons for efforts to enhance competitiveness in small countries of any income level, and in developing countries of any size.

Although issues of relative economic performance among countries and relative business performance among firms from different countries have long dominated the attention of economic and management scholars, these issues have taken on even greater prominence beginning in the last two decades of the twentieth century. This can be attributed primarily to the fact that these two decades saw the beginning of what many regard as a historically unprecedented convergence of markets for products, capital, labour and information. It was the evidence of the convergence of tastes across nations, leading to a demand for similar products in different parts of the world, which drew one of the earliest references to globalization in the academic literature.[1]

There are also those who suggest that the current trends towards market convergence are not unprecedented, positing that the trade, investment, capital and labour flows across borders are less significant as a proportion of global production and population today than they were between the mid-1800s and the early 1900s.

It is certainly true that the rapid fall in transportation costs, coupled with relatively open borders and the absence of capital controls, led to significant flows of goods, capital and people during this earlier period. But this comparison misses a key element of the current integration of markets around the world. The current integration is driven by dramatic reductions in telecommunication costs through the development of a confluence of computers, satellites, fibre-optic transmission cables and the Internet. The factor that is driving the current integration in markets is less the movement of goods[2] and people, and more the seamless flow of the most important characteristic of a market; that is, information.

The reduction in the cost of moving information around the world is likely to be far greater than the reduction in the cost of transporting goods that has fuelled the surge in merchandise trade. The Internet demonstrates the cost reduction possibilities. Estimates suggest that in current dollars, it cost US$300 to make a three-minute call between New York and London in 1930. Today that call could involve virtually no variable costs to the caller, courtesy of the Internet. In this context, it is acceptable to suggest that the reports of the "death of distance"[3] have not greatly exaggerated the probable and impending state of affairs, at least for certain types of activities.

Adding the freer flow of information to the advances in trade in goods and the relative mobility of capital creates both opportunities and challenges for small developing economies. The opportunities relate to the ability of these economies to tap into world markets for capital and information, and to gain market access for goods. The challenges, however, can easily seem unnerving. As markets increasingly integrate, cross-border competition among firms, and for factors of production, is likely to intensify.

Further, cross-border competition has historically been focused on physical goods. Obviously, in an age in which information is flowing ever more easily across borders, competition will intensify in services. Firms in developing countries, operating in industries such as health care, education and finance which have hitherto been relatively sheltered from global competition, will increasingly face similar competitive pressures to those faced by their counterparts competing in the production of physical goods.

Indeed, some two decades after Levitt's observation about the global convergence of tastes and products,[4] the debate is less about whether or not globalization has occurred at unprecedented levels in the recent past, and much more on the merits of the globalization that has taken place. In this latter regard, the cacophony of voices in the debate has reached fever pitch. Proponents of globalization point to the benefits that liberalized markets have created for the global economy as a whole, and for developed and developing countries independently,[5] while opponents from all regions suggest that globalization has contributed to worsening inequality between and within developed and developing countries.[6]

It could be argued that between 1998 and 2002 there were at least five inflexion points in the trend towards globalization. First, in 1998 there was successful opposition to the introduction of a multilateral agreement on investment (MAI). Second were the anti-globalization protests that coincided with, and had some impact on, the failed attempt to begin a new multilateral round of trade negotiations in Seattle in 1999–2000. Third, in September 2001 the world witnessed the terrorist attack on the United States. Fourth was the eventual agreement, including some acceptance by the developed world of the negotiating position of developing countries, to initiate a new round of trade negotiations in Doha, Qatar in November 2001. And fifth, in 2002 the United States imposed tariffs on imported steel and increased subsidies to farmers, to the consternation of the world's free trade lobby.

Four of these inflexion points suggest at least a retreat from the pace of globalization, and possibly a change in the direction of the globalization trend of the last decades of the twentieth century. But, of these four, the inflexion point linked to the tragedy on 11 September 2001 was heralded as most likely to mark a significant retreat from the pace and direction of market integration that the world had witnessed in the preceding two decades. The movement of capital across the globe was likely to be tempered by concerns about control of "terror-dollars". It was possible that further integration in the market for goods would be slowed out of a concern for the possibility of biological warfare. Also, of course, the least mobile factor of production – labour – was likely to become even less mobile in the context of concerns about the impact of uncontrolled levels of immigration.

Yet, even amidst the aftermath of September 11 and the concerns expressed by segments of the global community about the effects of globalization, it was still not clear how significant would be the process of retreat from the integration of global markets. For example, in the Doha inflexion point, which followed September 11, the world's developing countries appeared to accept the view that it was more appropriate to seek to be a party to trade liberalization discussions, and lobby for increased opening of markets in developed countries, rather than retreat to autarkic positions. This, even while they recognized the potential disruptive and risk-increasing effects of market opening.

In part, this perspective from the world's developing countries reflected the reality of the broad sweep of market integration processes. With the increased ability of capital to move around the world, the issue of the differential national returns to capital takes on greater prominence. Countries have been forced to recognize that they face global competition for capital, even that capital – and in some cases especially that capital – which belongs to their nationals and residents. Also, although labour markets around the world are not nearly as integrated as capital markets, and even with immigration concerns in most countries, many categories of skilled labour, and even some categories of relatively low-skilled labour, continue to compete on global labour markets.

Perhaps most importantly, the dramatic fall in barriers to communication and transportation has increased competition among countries in areas such as good governance and the role of civil society. To an extent that is unprecedented in the history of mankind, citizens and residents of nation states are made immediately aware of the improving or deteriorating circumstances of their counterparts in other nation states. This awareness explains why absolute standards of living in a country might improve yet the residents of that country experience relative deprivation, as they are made aware of far more rapid improvements in living standards of residents elsewhere.

Arising out of the general movement over the past several decades towards the integration of markets, small developing countries concerned about their ability to benefit from the process of market integration have two non-mutually-exclusive response options.[7] The first option is a defensive response. This response operates largely in the realm of politics and international relations. It might involve lobbying for an opt out of market-opening negotiations, for continued or new preferential arrangements, for lengthier adjustment windows, or for the inclusion of social clauses or "fair trade" considerations in regional and multilateral trade negotiations. It could also involve a decision to lobby for the abandonment of the market integration process, or a unilateral withdrawal from this process.

The second option is an attack response. This response operates principally in the realm of economics and international business, and it involves small developing countries seeking to position their economies and firms to be able to benefit from the integration of markets for products, labour, capital, technology, information and governance standards. This second option requires a focus on the competitiveness of countries and their resident institutions. While recognizing the possible need for, and the potential benefits of, the first option, it is the imperative of this second option that dominates the research on which this book reports. This imperative is likely to continue to occupy a prominent position on the agenda of small developing countries, whether or not the pace of globalization slows.

Competitiveness at the Level of National Economies

Although this book is about "national competitiveness", it is important to point out that there are competing perspectives on the usefulness of such a term. Management analysts, such as Michael Porter, are comfortable with an examination of national competitiveness,[8] while the economist Paul Krugman[9] queries whether the concept itself is meaningful. Indeed, Krugman suggests quite explicitly that "competitiveness is a meaningless word when applied to national economies. And the obsession with competitiveness is both wrong and dangerous."[10]

These positions are more reconcilable than is immediately apparent. Krugman's objection to the concept of national competitiveness is linked to his argument that nations do not compete with each other economically to any significant extent, despite the fact that this is what is suggested by the titles of the weighty tomes produced by other economists.[11] But Porter agrees with Krugman's general position. Both analysts are at one with respect to the notion that competition exists principally at the level of firms.

It is also clear that countries have access to internal markets and self-correcting mechanisms for recovery from economic downturns that are simply not available to firms. For example, Krugman makes much of the fact that in the economies of countries such as the United States and Japan, by far the majority of economic activity is directed at customers who are internal rather than external to the borders of the country.

Nevertheless, this book will present arguments suggesting that it is useful to view the challenges confronting small developing countries through the lens of competitiveness analysis. This is true for several reasons. One is that internal markets are less likely to be as powerful an engine for national development in small developing countries, because of the limited size of such markets. Krugman continues his argument by suggesting that "the idea that a country's economic fortunes are largely determined by its success on world markets is flatly wrong".[12] While Krugman's conclusion is certainly true in the context of economies such as the United States and Japan, in which activity directed towards domestic markets represents close to 90 per cent of total economic activity, in the context of small developing economies, the importance of success on world markets as a determinant of their economic fortunes represents a hypothesis to be tested. Krugman has not presented evidence in relation to this group of countries. Testing this hypothesis and presenting the resulting evidence is one of the tasks pursued in this volume.

Further, although it is companies rather than nations that compete, companies operate within national systems that provide incentives or disincentives for innovation, product development, human development and technological upgrading, the consensus factors that contribute to the long-term economic well-being of a country's citizens. National systems collectively representing this combination of incentives and disincentives that affect the performance of resident institutions can properly be examined under the rubric of national competitiveness.[13]

Finally, the supposedly comforting notion, and potentially complacency-inducing perspective, that a country is not a company because countries do not go bankrupt is far less persuasive from the perspective of a management analyst based in a developing country. Clearly, this characterization of nations is factually correct, but it is also not particularly meaningful in a world in which markets for information have converged. To be sure, countries whose national systems retard innovation, investment and human and technological development will not disappear from the face of the earth. This does not mean, however, that these countries cannot effectively become "failed economies" whose citizens, particularly those outside a privileged, often arrogant and paternalistic elite, might wish that their countries could undergo chapter 11–style reorganization (bankruptcy proceedings), preferably with new leaders at the helm of the reorganized economy. Were there true and complete integration of labour markets, the dynamics of restructuring failed economies would be very different, with far more shared international responsibility for national governance.

Indeed, by 2001 the economic crises of the late 1990s and early 2000s in Asia, Brazil, Russia and Argentina were leading to proposals for international involvement in country restructuring in a manner quite similar to the procedures available to firms. By December 2001, for example, Anne Krueger, the deputy managing director of the International Monetary Fund (IMF), had raised the possibility of sovereign bankruptcy procedures, suggesting that a country whose debts were "truly unsustainable" should have a mechanism for restructuring them, which was similar to the options available to companies under the bankruptcy laws of most countries.[14] Her proposal was that troubled countries would get legal protection from creditors when they suspended payments on their debts, in return for promising to negotiate with creditors in good faith and agreeing to follow sound economic policies.[15]

Identifying National Competitiveness and Its Underlying Derivatives

In differentiating among countries in terms of their overall competitiveness, this book will rely on income measures: both nominal and purchasing power parity (PPP) income, on a per capita basis, focusing on both static income and the growth of income over time. These measures are obviously incomplete and, indeed, flawed determinants of national well-being, but they are, nevertheless, useful in providing gross measures of economic performance, from which more fine-grained adjustments can be made for elements of national well-being not captured in income measures.

At the enterprise level, four indicators of competitiveness are used throughout this book:

- the ability of enterprises to export to an array of countries without special government support;
- the ability of enterprises to engage in foreign direct investment (FDI) based upon skills and assets developed at home;[16]
- the ability of enterprises to operate according to internationally accepted norms of cost, service, operational standards and quality;
- and the ability of enterprises to earn above-average returns in a market setting which includes domestic competitors and (relatively) unimpeded access for rival enterprises from other countries.

In examining the underlying factors that influence enterprise competitiveness, reference will be made to Porter's model of factors influencing competitive advantage at the national level, in the form of the diamond of national competitive advantage: factor conditions; demand conditions; firm strategy, structure and rivalry; and related and supporting industries.[17] One of the objectives of this book will be to examine the extent to which these variables apply to small developing countries. In so doing, this analysis will also draw from competing perspectives on factors influencing competitiveness, including double diamond[18] and virtual diamond perspectives.[19]

Examining Small Economies in the Caribbean

The subject matter of this book is the world's small developing economies. This is a grouping of economies that could be defined in different ways. In this volume, small economies are defined by their population, and comprise those with populations of fewer than five million persons. This group of economies includes as a subset economies that have been described as micro- or ministates in the small economy literature.[20] These minieconomies are an important focus of this study, to the extent that issues of competitiveness are likely to be of particular concern to them. Several of these economies are not nation states; this does not preclude their inclusion in the analyses that comprise this volume. Indeed, since the concept of sovereignty is such an important issue in the context of small economies, they represent an interesting comparative data set.

The Caribbean represents a region of the world that incorporates a number of small nations juxtaposed with micronations and economies. The divergence of economic performance within a relatively small geographical area makes the Caribbean an interesting region for a study of the effect of size on competitiveness. Most of the analyses presented in this volume seek to use the anglophone Caribbean region, in particular, to test hypotheses and garner insights about issues of competitiveness in the context of small developing economies. This is a well-studied region of the world in relation to culture, economy and governance structures. This volume will not seek to summarize these studies, while acknowledging their importance to an ultimate understanding of issues of competitiveness.[21]

Following this introduction, the book will include an analysis, in chapter 1, of competitive advantages in small economies, including those of the Caribbean region. Among other things, this chapter will test the Krugmanesque hypothesis of export orientation and national performance. Chapter 1 is the first of six chapters on the macrodimensions of competitiveness. The other chapters in this genre focus on exchange regime choice and competitiveness in the Caribbean (chapter 2), and in Barbados in particular (chapter 3); and on the role of government in enhancing competitiveness (chapter 4), focusing on the experiences of the so-called more developed countries (MDCs) of the Caribbean's principal integration area, the Caribbean Community (CARICOM). Finally, this section also incorporates a chapter on competitiveness and sovereignty (chapter 5), and one on the role of FDI in competitiveness enhancement in developing countries (chapter 6).

The remaining chapters bring more of a microperspective to the issue of investigating factors driving competitiveness, by examining the role of workplace transformation in enterprise competitiveness (chapter 7); by seeking to isolate factors determining enterprise competitiveness in the context of a growth-challenged national environment (chapter 8); by investigating competitiveness drivers in the context of non- or rarely traded products (chapter 9); and by assessing the role of microenterprise support and social policy in efforts to enhance national competitiveness (chapter 10).

The volume concludes by pulling together the strands from the various analyses presented throughout the chapters, in an attempt to identify the lessons that these analyses present for understanding competitiveness, at the macro and micro levels, in small developing economies.

Chapter 1

Competitiveness of Small Countries

The theme of this book is the competitiveness of small developing countries. These are small countries seeking to improve the overall productivity of their economies to match more closely productivity levels in developed countries. While small developing countries can make the transition to small, developed countries, they are far less likely to be able to become large. Consequently, the research study that begins the analyses reported on in this book focuses on the factors that differentiate economic performance between small and large countries, and within small countries of all income levels.

Indeed, one of the more popular areas of research on differences in economic performance across countries has been the stream of scholarship which focuses on whether "size matters" in this performance assessment. That is, do small countries systematically experience better or worse economic performance than their larger counterparts? In a recent study, which concluded that small countries have higher per capita incomes and show no significant difference in growth performance from other countries, Easterly and Kraay[1] suggest that these countries have received excessive attention from the literature "as special cases calling for special policy measures". The implication made by these authors is that further study of the relationship between country size and economic performance is unnecessary.

Yet there continues to be substantial debate about the challenges confronting small economies, especially among those operating within these economies. One such stream of research is well captured in an address by former

Commonwealth Secretary General Shridath Ramphal, himself a native of the small country of Guyana. At the first meeting of the Commonwealth Consultative Group on the Special Needs of Small States in July 1984, Ramphal captioned his address "small is beautiful but vulnerable".[2]

Since then various studies have focused on the extent to which small economies are highly vulnerable: economically, environmentally and in relation to matters of external security.[3] Other international organizations besides the Commonwealth Secretariat, notably the United Nations, have participated in such studies;[4] also, there have been several international fora, and special editions of scholarly journals, dedicated to the challenges confronting small countries.[5]

The study reported on in this chapter seeks to contribute to the debate about the impact of country size on economic performance, but to do so not only through the much-studied comparison between the economic performance of small and nonsmall countries, which is often conducted by comparing income levels and growth rates. Rather, this study also examines the factors that lead to differences in economic performance *among* small economies, in an attempt to elicit answers to the research question: what factors make small economies perform successfully relative to each other? In so doing, the study will also examine whether the factors that drive economic performance differ between small and large countries.

Competitive Disadvantages and Advantages of Small Countries

Much of the literature on small countries has focused on their disadvantages. Economic disadvantages identified in this regard include limited natural resource endowment and high import content, limitations on the extent to which they can diversify their economies, small domestic markets and dependence on export markets, dependence on a narrow range of products, limited ability to exploit economies of scale, limitations on domestic competition, and high per-unit transport costs.[6] Other economic disadvantages include their limitations in macroeconomic policy, exacerbated by the pressures on their administrators who are forced into inefficient multifunctionality.[7]

In addition to economic disadvantages, the literature on small economies has focused on their vulnerability in the area of external security[8] and in the area of the environment.[9] Arising out of these concerns, efforts have been made to develop vulnerability indices that attempt to identify in a single measure the challenges confronting small countries.[10]

Yet this literature also points to the fact that small countries are not necessarily outperformed by their larger counterparts.[11] Small countries that are also city states benefit from advantages such as the absence of a growth-braking rural hinterland. All small countries benefit from the relatively greater ability to adapt to change, and greater flexibility in administration.[12]

Research Methodology

The study reported on in this chapter began with the research question: what factors explain the divergence in economic performance across small nations? Analyses that helped to address this question would, it was felt, help to identify the factors that allow small nations to be competitive in a global economy. These analyses would help to delineate the "competitive advantages" of small nations. In an effort to respond to the driving question behind the research, the principal methodology employed was that of statistical analysis, in particular cross-sectional linear regression. It was felt that this was the most appropriate method to identify factors, in the aggregate, which differentiate economic performance among small nations.

The statistical analysis was informed by hypotheses about the factors likely to lead to differential performance. Also, in an effort to identify whether "size matters" in relation to these factors, the statistical analysis focused on both a set of small countries and a random sample of larger countries for which relevant data were available.

Defining Small Countries

One of the related debates in the "small country" literature is the appropriate measure for differentiating between small and larger countries. The most popular variable used has been population.[13] Yet the literature on this subject has also recognized that more composite measures may be appropriate, in particular a combination of population, gross national income and land area.[14]

In the absence of readily available composite measures, however, this study has followed the convention of using population as the measure for determining smallness. Even here, however, there is debate about the appropriate population cut-off point. This study follows scholars[15] who define small economies to be those with populations of less than five million. Those in the set examined were countries with populations between one and five million, for reasons of data availability. This group, however, excludes a particularly interesting group of small nations and territories. These are economies with populations of less than one million, which are often described as microstates, ministates, minieconomies or microeconomies.[16]

Economic data for these economies are notoriously unreliable and difficult to garner. Yet, understanding the dynamics of these economies is also important to the research question posed at the outset of this chapter. Consequently, a secondary component of the research reported on in this chapter involved an examination of several of these economies.

The World Bank reports on sixty of these economies, with populations as low as nineteen thousand (Palua), in a special section in the *World Development Report*. More than two-thirds of these territories are islands in the Mediterranean Sea, the Caribbean Sea, the Pacific Ocean, the Indian Ocean and the Atlantic Ocean, with the largest group of these economies (seventeen) being territories that lie in, or kiss, the Caribbean Sea. Indeed, although it has been argued that there is no conceptual difference between islands and small economies,[17] the island nature of these economies helps to explain the strong desire for independent economic governance, and why they have not been assimilated into larger territories.[18] This section of the study was particularly informed by the experiences of the Caribbean economies.

Importantly, this group of countries, on which the multilateral institutions report very little information, includes Luxembourg, the world's wealthiest economy in 2001, with a nominal per capita income of about US$45,000.

Research Hypotheses

The hypotheses that provided the platform for the statistical study are elaborated upon below.

Export Orientation

One of the most oft-quoted policy prescriptions to improve competitiveness is to increase exports. Indeed, the world has almost returned to a mercantilist perspective in such matters. In the context of this neomercantilist perspective, clearly countries with more export-oriented economies will perform at a higher level than their more domestic-oriented counterparts. This logic should apply with even greater effect in the context of small countries, which are likely to be more specialized, and therefore more dependent on international trade, than their larger siblings, although this dependence on trade is also one of the factors identified in the literature as creating economic vulnerability for small economies.[19]

The notion of a greater level of export orientation leading to improved national performance has been effectively and persuasively discredited in the context of large developed countries, in particular, in which trade constitutes a relatively small component of economic activity.[20] But even for small countries, anecdotal evidence suggests that one ought to be suspicious of the notion that countries more oriented towards exporting are likely to outperform their peers based primarily upon their greater export orientation.[21] There is no question that one of the world's richest small countries, and one most often featured in analyses of export orientation, Singapore, is extremely export oriented, with a ratio of exports of goods and services to gross domestic product (GDP) of about 200 per cent and a 2000 per capita income level of about US$25,000.

To take a counter example, however, the Republic of Congo, with a population of three million and a per capita income of $670 in 2000, has ratio of exports of goods and services to GDP of 79 per cent. On the other hand, Uruguay, a country of similar size (population also three million), had a per capita income of $5,900 and a ratio of exports of goods and services to GDP of 19 per cent in that year.

This study was agnostic with respect to the impact of export orientation, as defined by exports of goods and services as a proportion of GDP, on relative performance among small countries.

Service Orientation

One of the clear disadvantages of small countries is their inability to take advantage of economies of scale in the production process, in the context of research that suggests that taking advantage of increasing returns to scale is important for growth.[22] Against this background, it might seem reasonable to suggest that small countries are likely to be most successful if they shift economic activity away from industries for which economies of scale seem to be particularly important. Conventional wisdom suggests that economies of scale are more important in commodity-manufacturing and agriculture industries, and less important in service industries. It is this observation that leads to the conclusion that small countries are likely to achieve competitive advantage through the provision of services far more effectively than through the production of goods.

Thus hypothesis 1:

> **Hypothesis 1:** The service orientation of a small economy will be a significant factor in determining that economy's relative economic performance, with more service-oriented small economies outperforming their peers.

Political Risk

Small economies are likely to be either poor economies or vulnerable economies, or both. They are likely to be poor if they opt for autarky. Given the narrow resource base that typifies a small economy, autarky is likely to lead to low levels of output as resources cannot be directed to their optimal uses. But, because of the narrow range of resources, a small economy that opts for greater economic well-being by integrating into regional or world economies in order to be able to benefit from specialization will find that it is a highly vulnerable economy, subject to the vagaries of world markets.

In the context of a risk profile that is inherently high, it seems critical that a small economy offset international risk by minimizing the risks associated with the local economic environment. Otherwise, it is likely that the country will suffer from low levels of investment. In this respect, low levels of political and country risk are likely to be essential to prosperity among small economies.[23]

> **Hypothesis 2:** The level of country and political risk in a small economy will be a significant factor in determining that economy's relative economic performance, with lower-risk economies outperforming their peers.

Macroeconomic Risk

Concomitantly, small economies that have high country risk because of macroeconomic instability will find the international economy to be unforgiving. Indeed, residents of these economies are also likely to opt for investment instruments that lie outside of the territory. Macroeconomic stability is likely to be critical to the ability of small economies to perform well.[24]

> **Hypothesis 3:** The level of macroeconomic risk in a small economy will be a significant factor in determining its relative economic performance, with lower-risk economies outperforming their peers.

Quality of Infrastructure

The quality of infrastructure will have a significant impact on the ability of enterprises to operate successfully in a small economy. This element of national operations will also be important in efforts to entice beneficial FDI which, in turn, is likely to improve levels of per capita income. Foreign firms are particularly concerned about issues of infrastructure when contemplating investment in small economies.[25]

> **Hypothesis 4:** The quality of infrastructure in a small economy will be a significant factor in determining its relative economic performance, with economies with better infrastructure outperforming their peers.

Quality of Education

Related to the quality of physical infrastructure is the quality of human infrastructure, which is similarly likely to be important to the attractiveness of a small economy to foreign and local investment, and to its relative performance level.[26]

> **Hypothesis 5:** The quality of human infrastructure in a small economy will be a significant factor in determining its relative economic performance, with economies with better educational levels outperforming their peers.

Data Collection and Testing

The preceding hypotheses were tested, using a cross-sectional least squares regression, on a set of thirty nations with populations between one and five million. The countries included in the sample are listed in table 1.1

For these countries, relative economic performance was measured using the proxy of per capita income in 1999. For the statistical analysis, a semi-log model was used, and the actual measure used for the dependent variable of relative economic performance was the log of per capita income.

Table 1.1: Sample of Small Countries (populations between 1 and 5 million)

1. Albania	16. Lithuania
2. Armenia	17. Macedonia
3. Botswana	18. Mauritania
4. Central African Republic	19. Moldova
5. Republic of Congo	20. Mongolia
6. Costa Rica	21. Namibia
7. Croatia	22. New Zealand
8. Estonia	23. Nicaragua
9. Ireland	24. Norway
10. Jamaica	25. Panama
11. Jordan	26. Papua New Guinea
12. Kuwait	27. Singapore
13. Latvia	28. Slovenia
14. Lebanon	29. Togo
15. Lesotho	30. Uruguay

Although per capita income has been used as a measure of the performance of small economies in several studies,[27] there is debate about the utility of per capita income in this regard. An important element of the argument advanced by the school of thought focused on issues of vulnerability of small economies is that per capita income is a flawed measure of performance in relation to small economies because "in many cases relatively high per capita income occurs in association with a narrow and fragile economic structure".[28] This study accepts the overall concerns about issues of vulnerability of small countries, but does not accept that per capita income cannot be used as a proxy for the economic performance of small countries, particularly in an assessment of the intragroup performance of small countries. Although many small countries and territories clearly have highly specialized, and therefore risky, economic structures, some of these economies have sustained consistently high levels of per capita income for over twenty years.

To test the hypotheses outlined above, six variables were used as proxies. To test the impact of export orientation on relative economic performance, the variable used was exports of goods and services as a percentage of GDP. Information on this variable was taken from the *World Development Report* which, in turn, uses balance of payments data. Since tourism is an important element in the service exports of many countries, it is important to ensure that tourism flows are included in goods and service–export balances. They are. Central banks collect data on tourism flows for input into the current account of the balance of payments. The typical approach is to multiply tourist arrivals by a projection of the amount spent per visitor, which projection is based on survey information.

Hypothesis 1, on the effect of services, was tested using the variable of services produced as a percentage of GDP. The expected sign for this variable was positive. Hypothesis 2, on the effect of political and country risk, was tested using a composite International Country Risk Guide rating which is an overall index of investment risk in a country, ranging from zero to one hundred, with risks decreasing as the numerical assessment increases. The expected sign of this variable was also positive.

Hypothesis 3, on the effect of macroeconomic risk, was tested using the average inflation between 1995 and 1998 in the countries in the sample. The expected sign for the inflation variable was negative. Hypothesis 4, on the impact of infrastructure, was tested using the variable "paved roads as a percentage of total roads", and hypothesis 5, on the impact of education, was tested using the variable "per cent of relevant age group enrolled in secondary education". Both the infrastructure and education variables were expected to have positive signs.

Table 1.2 provides a summary of the variables used and their expected signs. Information on the inflation variable was obtained from the IMF's *International Financial Statistics* (December 2001). Information on all other variables was obtained from the World Bank's *World Development Report, 2000–2001*.

Statistical Results

Table 1.3 provides an indication of the results of the statistical least squares regression analysis on the set of data identified in tables 1.1 and 1.2.

The export variable had a negative sign, but was not statistically significant. All other variables had the hypothesized signs but, contrary to the expectations of hypotheses 1, 3 and 5, only the political/country risk (hypothesis 2) and the infrastructural (hypothesis 4) variables were statistically significant at the 5 per cent level.

Overall, the independent variables did explain much of the variation in relative economic performance among the countries in the sample, with the model generating an R squared level (adjusted for degrees of freedom) of 77 per cent.

Table 1.2: Variables for Regression Analysis on Sample of Small Countries

Variable	Proxy	Hypothesized Sign	Data Source
Economic performance	Log of per capita income (1999)	Dependent variable	World Bank, WDR[a]
Export orientation	Exports of G&S[b] as a % of GDP	Agnostic	World Bank, WDR
Service orientation	Services as a % of GDP	Positive	World Bank, WDR
Political/country risk	International Country Risk Guide (ICRG) rating	Positive	World Bank, WDR
Macroeconomic stability	Average inflation (1995–1998)	Negative	IMF, IFS[c]
Infrastructure	% Paved roads	Positive	World Bank, WDR
Education	% Age group enrolled in secondary education	Positive	World Bank, WDR

[a]WDR – *World Development Report*
[b]G&S – Goods and services
[c]IFS – *International Financial Statistics*

Table 1.3: Results of Regression Analysis on Sample of Small Countries

Variable	Beta Coefficient	Standard Error[a]	T Statistic
Constant	0.152953	1.031873	0.148228
Export	-0.001921	0.005444	-0.352865
Service	0.011414	0.009386	1.216066
Political/country risk	0.090460	0.020313	4.453305[b]
Inflation	-0.003930	0.019434	-0.202222
Infrastructure	0.009076	0.004541	1.998598[b]
Education	0.004803	0.009762	0.492009

Dependent variable: Log per capita income; R^2 (Adj.) = 0.772551, F = 17.4. DW – 2.071496

[a]Standard errors are White-corrected for heteroskedasticity
[b]Statistically significant

Correlation analysis of the independent variables suggested that there was no significant multicollinearity among the variables, and the standard errors shown in the table are all corrected for heteroskedasticity using White's test. The regression also showed no evidence of autocorrelation, as indicated by the

Table 1.4: Random Sample of Larger Countries (populations above 5 million)

1.	Algeria	16.	Indonesia
2.	Australia	17.	Italy
3.	Bangladesh	18.	Kazakhstan
4.	Benin	19.	Madagascar
5.	Brazil	20.	Mali
6.	Canada	21.	Morocco
7.	Chile	22.	Netherlands
8.	Colombia	23.	Nigeria
9.	Côte d'Ivoire	24.	Peru
10.	Dominican Republic	25.	Portugal
11.	El Salvador	26.	South Africa
12.	Ethiopia	27.	Sweden
13.	Guatemala	28.	Tanzania
14.	Germany	29.	Turkey
15.	Honduras	30.	Yemen

Durbin Watson (DW) statistic, and tests for bounded influence suggested no undue problems associated with outlying observations.

Another statistical analysis was conducted to test whether or not "size mattered"; that is, were small countries, in fact, different from larger countries in relation to the factors that explained variations in relative economic performance. This analysis was conducted on a random sample of thirty larger countries (that is, countries with populations in excess of five million). The countries included in the sample are identified in table 1.4.

The results of the least squares regression analysis, using the same set of variables used in the analysis of variation in relative economic performance among small countries, are portrayed in table 1.5.

This analysis was also corrected for heteroskedasticity through White corrections of the standard errors, and the analysis showed no evidence of multicollinearity, autocorrelation or problems of undue influence from outlying observations.

In this set of countries, the export variable has a negative sign, but is statistically insignificant. The service, political/country risk, infrastructure and education variables had the same signs as those hypothesized for small countries but, in the case of these larger countries, political/country risk and education were the statistically significant variables. Inflation had an unexpected positive sign, but was statistically insignificant.

Table 1.5: Results of Regression Analysis on Sample of Larger Countries

Variable	Beta Coefficient	Standard Error[a]	T Statistic
Constant	0.533147	0.861053	0.619180
Export	-0.002276	0.010462	-0.217549
Service	0.002152	0.009741	0.220901
Political/country risk	0.067189	0.017917	3.750014[b]
Inflation	0.017650	0.012333	1.431119
Infrastructure	0.003977	0.005080	0.782874
Education	0.033452	0.005034	6.645212[b]

Dependent variable: Log per capita income; R^2 (Adj.) = 0.882522, F = 37.3
DW – 1.982

[a]Standard errors are White-corrected for heteroskedasticity
[b]Statistically significant

Table 1.6: Results of Regression Analysis on Stacked Sample of Countries

Variable	Beta Coefficient	Standard Error[a]	T Statistic
Constant	0.048712	0.725122	0.067177
Export	-0.003704	0.004278	-0.865896
Service	0.012568	0.008496	1.479284
Political/country risk	0.067189	0.017917	5.034785[b]
Inflation	0.010113	0.009325	1.084504
Infrastructure	0.009039	0.003573	2.529807[b]
Education	0.020792	0.004672	4.450292[b]
Country size	0.134747	0.196226	0.686693

Dependent variable: Log per capita income; R^2 (Adj.) = 0.81877, F = 39.1
DW – 1.986

[a]Standard errors are White-corrected for heteroskedasticity
[b]Statistically significant

A final statistical test was conducted to assess the extent to which "size mattered" in relation to income differences across countries. This analysis was achieved by stacking the data on small and larger countries, and conducting an analysis on this combined sample of countries. One additional variable was included in the analysis: a dummy variable for size of country, with larger countries categorized as one and small countries categorized as zero. This test sought to identify whether or not country size helped to explain the variation in income levels across the combined sample of countries. The results of the least squares regression analysis on this combined set of countries is provided in table 1.6.

As in the other regressions, standard errors were White-corrected for heteroskedasticity, and there was no evidence in the regression of multicollinearity or autocorrelation.

Similarly to the other regressions conducted as a part of this study, the independent variables explained much of the variation in per capita income (Adjusted R squared of 82 per cent). The results of this analysis indicated three statistically significant variables: political/country risk, infrastructure and education. Among others, country size was a statistically insignificant variable.

Discussion of Findings

This study, like others before,[29] has found no systematic differences in economic performance between small and larger countries. This does not negate the argument of those who suggest that small economies are vulnerable. But it does suggest that their vulnerability is not adequately captured in per capita income data, which is a point readily accepted by those who suggest that small countries are highly vulnerable.

But the principal focus of this study was on the factors that influence differences in economic performance among small countries. In this regard, the results of this study indicate that small countries need to be cautious about conventional wisdom that suggests that the most important factor in improving relative economic performance in a small economy is the extent to which that economy's activities can be shifted towards export. An export orientation that does not increase an economy's average level of productivity is not likely to lead to increased economic welfare.

This is not to suggest that exporting is unimportant, but to recognize that it is the extent to which exporting adds, on a net basis, to national income that is critical, rather than the proportion of exports of goods and services in relation to total production of goods and services. This more nuanced view of export activity is captured in the work of Barro, who includes a terms of trade index as a factor affecting growth rates, rather than an export orientation variable.[30] Our analysis also suggests caution with respect to the importance of a service orientation. The service hypothesis elaborated upon at the outset of this chapter presumed that a greater service orientation would lead to improved national well-being in small economies because, since services are presumably less reliant on economies of scale, small economies would be in a position to produce services more effectively than physical goods.

Of course, it is quite possible that countries experience a shift towards services that is not representative of an overall increase in productivity within the economy. And, of course, it is also possible that certain categories of services are as reliant on economies of scale as is the production of goods. In such cases, an increased service orientation would have no causal impact on economic well-being. The positive, but statistically insignificant, service variable in the analysis suggests that caution needs to be expressed about the presumed link between service orientation and increased productivity in small countries.

For small countries, the most striking elements of the statistical analysis lie in the emphasis on the importance of reducing risk and improving infrastructure as mechanisms for improving relative economic performance. These were the statistically significant variables in the small-country regression analysis. The findings are in keeping with the hypotheses (2 and 4) suggesting that, given the vulnerability of small economies, it was critical that this vulnerability (that is, risk) associated with size-related factors outside of the country's control not be exacerbated by national-level, controllable risk factors. This latter observation is unsurprising and expected, but the result associated with the education variable is not as expected and is, indeed, counter-intuitive. There was no indication in the statistical analysis conducted on a sample of small countries that education played an important role in differentiating among high- and low-performing small countries.

The related analysis of a similarly sized sample of larger countries suggested that "size mattered" to some extent, in relation to an understanding of the factors that drive relative economic performance among nations. For these larger countries, the variables that were significant in explaining the variation in relative income levels were the level of country risk and the education level of the country's citizens. In the combined sample, inclusive of small and larger countries, the significant variables were country risk, education and infrastructure.

Understanding these differences, subtle as they are in cases, between the bases for relative economic performance in small versus larger countries is important in understanding the competitive advantages of small countries.

One potential explanation of the importance of risk reduction and infrastructure development to economic performance in small countries lies in an understanding of the type of sectors that have powered economic performance among small economies. If, for example, the sectors that have played the most important role in the success of small economies are sectors for which low country risk is very critical and infrastructure very important, this would certainly explain why these variables differentiate among small economies in relation to economic performance.

Such an analysis, however, is best conducted through a closer examination of the structure of these economies. The remainder of the empirical segment of this chapter will conduct such an analysis principally in the context of one group of small economies: those of the Caribbean region. In so doing, this analysis will also focus on really small, or micro-, economies, in addition to those (larger) small economies that were captured in the foregoing statistical analysis, and a few even larger Caribbean economies.

The Competitive Advantages of Small Caribbean Economies

The Caribbean is an intriguing location for examining the competitive advantage of small economies. The region comprises many small economies in close proximity to each other. The World Bank reports data on ninety-two small territories (for thirty-two it provides comprehensive data; for sixty microterritories with populations less than two million it provides a more parsimonious set of data). Of these ninety-two territories, eighteen are in the Caribbean, although only Jamaica falls within the category of the thirty-two countries on which there is full reporting, while seventeen of these territories are microeconomies. Another set of small economies that has elicited much scholarly interest lies in the South Pacific.[31]

Analysing the performance differences among these Caribbean countries is facilitated by the common heritage of many. Most of these countries are former, or current, colonies of the United Kingdom. In colonial days, when risk profiles and industries (primarily agriculture in the form of sugar and banana cultivation) were very similar across this set of countries, the most important influence on economic performance was country size. In this context, the largest English-speaking country, Jamaica, dominated the anglophone Caribbean and, indeed, sub-governed two of the territories – the Cayman Islands and the Turks and Caicos Islands – on behalf of the United Kingdom.

Since the widespread achievement of independence that began in the 1960s there has been a considerable divergence in economic performance across this group of countries. The economic performance of two of the larger (small) countries of the group, Jamaica and Guyana, which were first to gain independence, has stagnated and deteriorated significantly in relative terms. This deterioration has coincided with much higher levels of country risk in these countries relative to their neighbours.

Of the two other relatively large (small) countries, Trinidad and Tobago has performed reasonably well, largely on the strength of its oil and petrochemical industry, but linked to risk reduction efforts pursued during the 1980s (see chapter 4 in this volume), and Barbados has performed quite well. The economic performance of the smallest economies has been fair in the case of the Windward Islands, very good in the case of the Leeward Islands, and exceptional in the case of northern Caribbean islands such as the Bahamas, Bermuda, Cayman, Turks and Caicos, and the Virgin Islands.

Explaining Differential Economic Performance among Caribbean Economies

The significant variation in economic performance among Caribbean economies begs for explanation. An inspection of these economies suggests that they have very simple economic structures, and that these economies rely heavily on tourism and financial services to generate economic growth. The Caribbean small economies that have performed well, in per capita income terms, have been those that have developed successful tourism and international financial service industries, which is a pattern that is notable in high-performing small economies worldwide.[32]

This finding appears to conflict with the earlier finding of this study that an export orientation did not explain variations in economic performance across countries. But there may, in fact, be no conflict. Successful performance in tourism and international financial services does not mean that success is defined in terms of high ratios of exports of goods and services to GDP. A structured analysis of the impact of such ratios on the small economies of the

Caribbean, along the lines on which this analysis was conducted for "larger" small economies, is not possible because of problems of data availability. But a less structured analysis of these ratios in Caribbean economies suggests that it is difficult to identify a correlation between export-to-GDP ratios and per capita income levels, as noted in table 1.7.

Table 1.7: Relationship between Export-to-GDP Ratios and Per Capita Income Levels in Small Caribbean Countries

Country	Export of G&S[a] to GDP[b] (%)	Per Capita Income Level[c] (US$)
Antigua and Barbuda	70	8,300
Bahamas	55	(e)
Barbados	50	7,890
Grenada	61	3,450
Guyana	80	760
Jamaica	44	2,330
St Kitts and Nevis	43	6,420
St Lucia	55	3,770
St Vincent and Grenadines	52	2,700
Trinidad and Tobago	48	4,390

[a]G&S – Goods and services

[b]The most comprehensive comparative source of such data is the *International Financial Statistics* (IFS), although this publication provides data on only ten small Caribbean countries. The data used were the latest year available for each country, as recorded in the December 2001 IFS publication.

[c]Data used were from the World Bank's *World Development Reports* (1999/2000 and 2000/2001). For Barbados and Antigua and Barbuda the data are 1998 per capita income levels; for all other countries, 1999 per capita income levels. The per capita income figure for the Bahamas (e) is estimated by the World Bank to be high income (that is, US$9,266 in 1999).

To take but two examples from this table, the Bahamas and Barbados, two of the relatively high-income Caribbean small countries, have ratios of exports of goods and services to GDP that are not dissimilar from those of much lower-income countries in the Caribbean. As in other economies, one might well conclude, it is the value added in the export activity that matters, rather than the extent to which these economies are engaged in export activity.

Based upon the information from the foregoing analyses, we can draw inferences about the factors that have been important in the differential economic performance across this group of countries. The first, and overriding, factor has been differential levels of macrostability, in the form of economic, political and social stability. On the economic side, many small economies in the Caribbean have maintained macroeconomic stability anchored around fixed exchange regimes (see chapters 2 and 3) with open foreign exchange windows.

Political and social stability have also been far more evident in the economies that have performed at higher relative levels. The macrostability has been essential to the growth of the two industries that have dominated economic activity in these more economically successful countries: tourism and international financial services. The striking element of economic success in these Caribbean economies has been the extent to which they have been able to play host to foreign residents (through their tourism industries) or disembodied foreign capital (through their offshore financial service industries).

To provide some examples of the differential level of success in these industries, consider that in the late 1990s the US Virgin Islands attracted close to twenty-one tourists per person, and the Cayman Islands and the Bahamas each attracted thirteen tourists per person. Jamaica, on the other hand, attracted fewer than one tourist per person. In relation to international financial services, in the late 1990s the Bahamas was the largest euro-lending centre outside of London and Zurich, and was responsible for 10 per cent of the global euro market.

Bermuda, with its ten tourists per capita, and a world leader in offshore insurance, boasted one of the world's highest per capita incomes. Cayman's very high per capita income level resulted from an active programme of international company registration, which saw the economy registering over forty thousand international companies per year in the late 1990s, in addition to its thirteen tourists per capita. To be sure, many of these economies have been listed as tax havens by the Organisation for Economic Cooperation and Development (OECD). They have been so described because the OECD argues that they are engaging in harmful tax competition, and thereby diverting taxable income away from OECD member countries.[33] Several of the Caribbean economies were, at the turn of the millennium, involved in efforts to upgrade their international financial service policies and laws to seek conformance with OECD guidelines.

It is, of course, noteworthy, that other successful small economies have used a similar formula of hospitality to the world, either through similar success in playing host to tourists (Hawaii is a striking example), or through similarly playing host to disembodied foreign capital through successful financial services industries (Luxembourg and the Isle of Man are examples), or by playing host to embodied foreign capital in the form of FDI (for which the striking examples over the last several decades have been Singapore and Ireland, with Costa Rica executing a well-documented coup in this regard in recent years).[34]

In summary, it is reasonable to conclude that income levels across these economies vary based upon their level of integration into the world economy. Based upon the analyses reported on in this chapter and elsewhere, the extent to which these economies can benefit through integration into the world economy can be defined through their attractiveness to tourists; their attractiveness to disembodied international capital; their attractiveness to FDI, particularly the export-oriented variety that is easily transferable into prowess in producing goods and services for export; their ability to export natural resources; their ability to export workers and benefit from worker remittances and eventual brain circulation;[35] and their ability to access international aid, directly or through trade preferences.

Conclusion

The analyses conducted in the research study reported on in this chapter suggest that certain factors are critical in explaining differential performance across economies. The factor that plays the most significant role in explaining performance variation across countries is risk. Those countries with higher risk levels underperform their counterparts that offer lower levels of risk.

Stability has been particularly important in small economies in the context of the industries that have been important in their efforts to improve levels of economic performance. An examination of small economies in the Caribbean suggests that two industries have been particularly critical in this region of the world: tourism and international financial services. Both of these industries place a significant premium on macrostability – economic, political and social – and on infrastructure development.

Indeed, the fundamental competitive advantage of a small economy is the ability to be hospitable to the world, but simultaneously to take advantage of its small size by being nimble. Small economies do not have to integrate with the world. They can choose a path of autarky. But this is likely to lead to self-sufficient impoverishment, albeit with attendant low levels of risk in the sense that the impoverishment will be stable and not subject to variation based on the vagaries of the world economy.

But if a small economy, desirous of higher standards of living, chooses the more risky path of integrating with the world, it has to integrate properly by carefully identifying its niche market. Even with the successful identification of a niche market, the specialization associated with this approach will leave risks that are difficult to mitigate. The events of September 11 illustrate this point. The risks of tourist-linked specialization were evident not only in the small economies of the Caribbean, but even more dramatically in Hawaii, where a government spokesperson suggested that the aftermath of September 11 had created the most significant crisis in the state's history.

Small economies cannot reduce all these risks. They can seek some diversification across industries, which was the driving force behind the movement to international financial services within the Caribbean, or within industries but across customers, as has been evident in the efforts of Caribbean economies to diversify their tourism offerings away from their traditional reliance on the US market. But even with these efforts there will be risks that lie outside of the control of the authorities that govern small economies, as illustrated by the OECD assault on risk havens in primarily small economies. But, in the face of the inevitable vulnerability and risk resulting from specialization, it is critical that these authorities reduce the risks that are within their control.

Identifying the macroelements of stability and local risk reduction, and infrastructure development, as the foundation upon which small economies generate competitive advantage is not to downplay the microeconomic elements of competitiveness.[36] Similarly, this identification is not to downplay the importance of other factors examined in the analyses that did not produce statistically significant results in relation to the differential economic performance of small countries. A notable example in this regard is education, with its counter-intuitive, statistically insignificant result in explaining the differential performance of small countries.

Education plays a fundamental and multifaceted role in a developing economy, including increasing the prospects for social, economic and political stability, which this study has suggested is critical to economic performance in small countries. It is also noteworthy that education is one of the statistically important variables in explaining variation in income levels among larger countries, and small and larger countries combined. Yet there is a very important implication arising from the analysis reported on in this chapter. It is that governments of small countries that seek to expand educational opportunity by trading off macrostability do so with potential risk to the economy's level of performance.

In conclusion, the research documented in this chapter suggests that small economies do have the potential to operate successfully in the context of a global economy. But they are only likely to so do to the extent that they face squarely their areas of competitive advantage and carefully leverage these advantages for the benefit of their residents and citizens.

Chapter 2

Exchange Regime Choice: Caribbean Experiences

The preceding chapter emphasized the importance of stability in an analysis of competitive advantage in small economies. One element of a country's economic environment that is often examined in the context of stabilization policy is the country's exchange rate. The exchange regime is also one of the factors that is typically raised in discussions in small developing countries about the need to generate higher levels of internationally competitive economic activity among the nations' firms.

The exchange regime's impact on the international competitiveness of firms in small developing countries is usually considered from two perspectives. Fixed exchange regimes create a greater likelihood of real exchange rate overvaluation, with the obvious negative impact on the export prospects of the nations' firms. Flexible exchange regimes, on the other hand, could quite easily be a disincentive to the investment that is necessary to create and nurture internationally competitive firms. This is because flexible exchange regimes create a greater likelihood of macroeconomic instability.

This chapter examines the issue of exchange regime choice in small developing countries. The analysis is anchored in empiricism through an examination of the exchange rate policies of the small developing countries of the Caribbean. For purposes of this analysis, the Caribbean region includes all countries and territories that occupy islands in the Caribbean Sea, plus the three mainland territories (Guyana, Suriname and Belize) that are members of

CARICOM. Most of these territories are microstates, based on the size of their populations. Others, such as Cuba and the Dominican Republic, have populations that would lie outside most definitions of small countries, but they share many of the issues of vulnerability that characterize small economies, and so are also included in the study reported on in this chapter.

In examining the exchange rate systems adopted by these economies, exchange rate policies are linked to other economic and political characteristics in these territories. The chapter concludes with a discussion of the implications of the study's findings for exchange regime choice in small developing countries.

Types of Exchange Policy Regimes

In descending order of exchange rate flexibility, the options available to countries for the prudent management of exchange rate regimes include flexible exchange regimes (fully flexible or managed floats), and fixed exchange regimes. Fixed exchange regimes, again in descending order of flexibility, include pegged rates, currency boards and dollarization. The range of options is captured in table 2.1.

Table 2.1: Types of Exchange Rate Regimes Globally

Note: All above regimes assume open foreign exchange windows.

It should be noted that the assumption in the exchange-rate regime management options identified above is that the market for foreign exchange lies within official banking channels. That is, both the flexible and fixed exchange regime options imply "open windows" for foreign exchange, in which the formal banking system will supply the foreign exchange demanded. In situations where fixed exchange regimes are adopted with closed windows for foreign exchange, these regimes take on some of the characteristics of a flexible regime. This is because a fixed regime, with a closed window, does not place the same constraint on the monetary policy options of governments.

In general, the advantage of flexible regimes is that they make it easier for a country to avoid exchange rate misalignments. In so doing, they also allow a country to maintain the flexibility to respond to exogenous shocks, and they give governments and central banks the use of the full set of monetary policy options.[1] The advantage of fixed exchange regimes, on the other hand, tends to be the financial discipline they impose on governments.[2]

Exchange Regimes and Territorial Clusters

The exchange rate regimes and other pertinent characteristics of these Caribbean territories are identified in tables 2.2 and 2.3. Note in table 2.2 that within the Caribbean region there are examples of three of the five possible types of exchange regimes.

Table 2.2: Types of Exchange Rate Regimes in the Caribbean

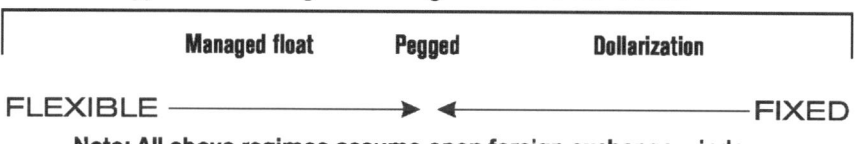

Note: All above regimes assume open foreign exchange windows.

Table 2.3 indicates the population size, sovereign status and income category of territories, in addition to identifying the nature of the exchange regime in use.

Based upon these data, figure 2.1 indicates that the Caribbean territories coalesce into four territorial clusters.

Cluster One is comprised of dependent territories using fixed exchange regimes, and therein lie the smallest and highest-income territories in the region. Several of these territories have the most fixed form of exchange regime, since they have adopted the currency of another country. In some cases, this is the country to which they owe political allegiance, but this is not the case in all instances. Thus, for example, the British dependencies, the British Virgin Islands and Turks and Caicos, have adopted the US dollar rather than sterling as their currency of choice.

In relation to the income levels of these economies, the World Bank reports that Anguilla, Bermuda, the Cayman Islands, Netherlands Antilles, Martinique

Table 2.3: Context of Caribbean Exchange Regime Choice

Territory	Population	Sovereign Status	Income Category	Exchange Regime
Anguilla	9,000	British dependency	High income	EC$: Pegged to US$
Antigua and Barbuda	66,000	Independent within OECS	Upper middle income	EC$: Pegged to US$
Aruba	84,000	Partner territory within Kingdom of Netherlands	High income	Pegged to US$
Bahamas	278,000	Independent since 1973	High income	Pegged to US$
Barbados	260,000	Independent since 1966	Upper middle income	Pegged to US$
Belize	210,000	Independent since 1981	Lower middle income	Pegged to US$
Bermuda	60,000	Oldest British colony	High income	Pegged to US$
British Virgin Islands	16,000	British dependency	High income	Dollarized
Cayman Islands	32,800	British dependency (formerly via Jamaica)	High income	Pegged to US$
Cuba	11m	Independent	Low income	Fixed regime with closed window; Floating market rate
Dominica	71,000	Independent within OECS	Lower middle income	Pegged to US$
Dominican Republic	7.7m	Independent since 1924	Lower middle income	Managed float
French Guiana	146,000	Overseas Department of France	High income	Pegged to currency of France
French West Indies (Guadeloupe, Martinique, St Martin, St Barthélémy)	519,000	Overseas Departments of France	Upper middle income/ high income	Use currency of France
Grenada	91,000	Independent within OECS	Lower middle income	Pegged to US$
Guyana	758,000	Independent since 1966	Low income	Managed float
Haiti	6.5m	Independent since 1804	Low income	Managed float
Jamaica	2.5m	Independent since 1962	Lower middle income	Managed float
Montserrat	11,000	British dependency	Upper middle income	EC$: Pegged to US$
Netherlands Antilles (Curaçao, Bonaire, Saba, St Maarten, St Eustatius)	190,000	Partner territory within Kingdom of Netherlands	High income	Pegged to US$
Puerto Rico	3.5m	Commonwealth of US	Upper middle income	Dollarized
St Kitts and Nevis	42,000	Independent within OECS	Upper middle income	EC$: Pegged to US$
St Lucia	138,000	Independent within OECS	Upper middle income	EC$: Pegged to US$
St Vincent and Grenadines	108,000	Independent within OECS	Lower middle income	EC$: Pegged to US$
Suriname	425,000	Independent since 1974	Lower middle income	Managed float
Trinidad and Tobago	1.3m	Independent since 1962	Upper middle income	Managed float
Turks and Caicos Islands	15,000	British dependency (formerly via Jamaica)	High income	Dollarized
US Virgin Islands	102,000	US unincorporated territory since 1954	High income	Dollarized

Figure 2.1: Exchange Regime and Territorial Clusters in the Caribbean

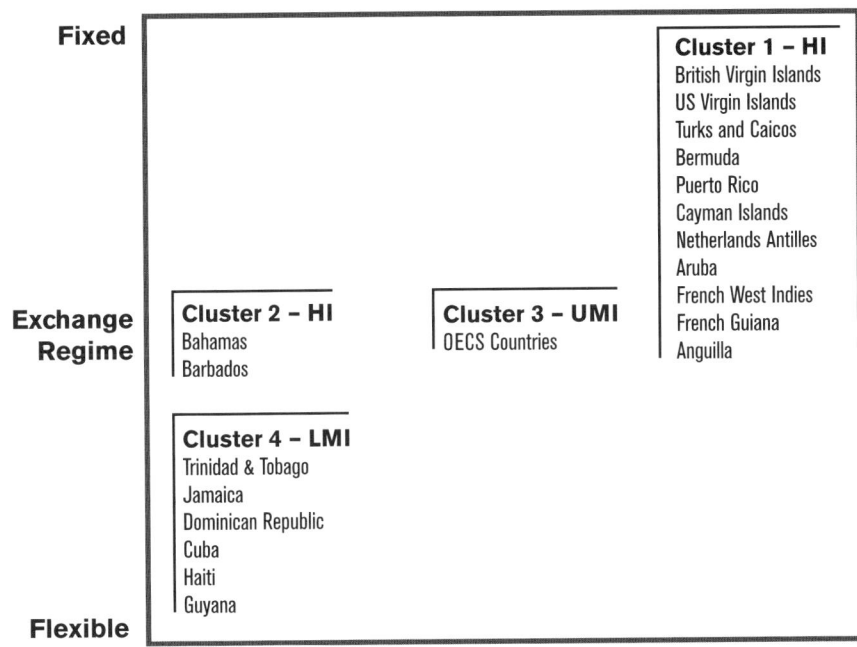

LMI: lower-middle income (US$756–$2,995); **UMI**: upper-middle income (US$2,996–$9,265); **HI**: high income (>US$9,266).

Note: Belize is the lone Caribbean territory that does not fit into one of the above four clusters.

Source: World Development Report 2000/2001.

and Guadeloupe (of the French West Indies), French Guiana, Turks and Caicos, the US and British Virgin Islands, and Aruba are high-income economies, defined to include economies with a 1999 per capita income in excess of US$9,266. In fact, the per capita income of some of the territories in this group far exceeds that level. The Cayman Islands, for example, had a per capita income in the mid-1990s of US$27,480. Bermuda was reported during the same period to have one of the world's highest per capita incomes.[3]

This group of territories is of the view that their nonindependent status enhances the perception of political and economic stability that is critical to their principal forms of economic livelihood: offshore financial services and tourism. As recently as 1995, the citizenry of Bermuda overwhelmingly rejected independence from the United Kingdom in a vote of 74 per cent against, and 26 per cent in favour of, independence.[4] Following the outcome of this referendum,

Bermuda continued to be Britain's oldest crown colony, with internal self-government since 1620, and host of the oldest parliament in the Commonwealth after Westminster. Because of the nature of their sovereign status and the exchange regime that restricts their monetary policy options, these territories are categorized as having low political and economic policy independence.

Cluster Two comprises a group of countries and territories that joined to create the Organisation of Eastern Caribbean States. The members of the Organisation of Eastern Caribbean States are largely independent Eastern Caribbean countries, with the exception of Montserrat, which is a British dependency. But while these countries are politically independent, their monetary policy independence is constrained by their membership in this regional economic union. It is for this reason that they are characterized in figure 2.1 as having intermediate political and monetary policy independence. The unifying characteristic of these countries has been economic stability. The regional union has forced on all the countries a degree of macroeconomic discipline, leading to little deficit spending and low inflation rates.

The countries share a common currency, the Eastern Caribbean dollar (EC$), which has been pegged to the US dollar since the formation of the economic union. The average 1999 per capita income of the seven independent countries in this eight-territory grouping was US$5,100. As a group this cluster is, therefore, characterized as upper-middle income (US$3,031–US$9,360). Individually, six of the seven countries are upper-middle income.

Cluster Three consists of two countries, the Bahamas and Barbados. These two countries are independent in both political and economic policy terms, but both have held to a fixed exchange regime since independence. The fixed exchange regime is viewed as a critical part of economic governance in these countries. Indeed, Barbados indicated an intention to maintain its exchange peg in the face of opposition from the multilateral financial institutions in the early 1990s (see chapter 3 in this volume). Both countries are of the view that their choice of exchange arrangements has assisted in the stabilization necessary for the success of their principal industries of tourism and financial services, which, in turn, have contributed to their relative prosperity. The average per capita income of these two countries, approximately US$10,000, places them in the high-income group of countries.

Cluster Four comprises the seven largest economies in the Caribbean. All are independent countries, with Haiti having achieved independence in 1804.

With the exception of Cuba, these countries all officially have managed exchange rate floats. Cuba's official exchange rate is fixed, but in the presence of a closed foreign exchange window, it essentially has a flexible exchange regime, with the market rate becoming the *de facto* exchange rate in Cuba, given the marked divergence between the official and market rates.

In terms of economic performance, these countries constitute the least successful group of Caribbean economies. The average per capita income of the six market economies in this group was US$1,900 in 1999. This places this group in the lower-middle-income category. The World Bank also estimates that Cuba is a lower-middle-income country. But not all countries are lower-middle income. Trinidad and Tobago is an upper-middle-income economy, and Haiti and Guyana are low-income economies.

As a group, these countries have experienced decades of macroeconomic instability fuelled by an unhealthy coalition of deficit fiscal spending, internal and external government borrowing, high levels of money supply growth and a constantly depreciating currency. The governments of these countries, as a general rule, have not been restrained in their fiscal excesses by independent central banks, nor did they have other mechanisms in place that could exert financial discipline.

This group of countries has seen improvements in macroeconomic management in recent years. The Dominican Republic has grown very rapidly during the 1990s, after stabilizing its economy at the beginning of the decade, and in the context of significant levels of direct investment. Trinidad and Tobago has been the most stable and best-performing economy of the group, and showed particular resolve in stabilizing its macroeconomy in the wake of a halving of its per capita income after the precipitous drop in oil prices in the early 1980s. Both Jamaica and Guyana have also seen improvements in macroeconomic management in recent years (see chapter 4 of this volume).

In examining these four clusters of Caribbean territories, we are particularly mindful of the caution from the exchange rate policy literature about drawing causal links between exchange rate regimes and levels of economic performance in cross-sectional comparisons across countries.[5] Yet it is not easy to embrace this call for caution in the context of the small territories of the Caribbean. Indeed, the data presented make it difficult to disagree with the position that the more prosperous countries of the Caribbean all utilize fixed exchange rate regimes.[6]

In fact, it has long been observed, in the literature on optimal currency areas, that small, open economies adjacent to dominant currency areas have difficulty wielding an independent exchange rate policy. That is, according to Mundell, who first spawned this literature, the smaller the currency area and the higher the proportion of imports to total consumption, the more appropriate are fixed exchange regimes.[7]

In the above analysis of the clusters of territories in the Caribbean, we note the context in which exchange regimes have been chosen. Smaller countries with less political independence have tended to use fixed exchange regimes, which in turn has constrained their monetary policy independence. The larger countries with greater levels of independence have tended to utilize flexible exchange regimes. Yet the countries in this latter group have not used their monetary policy independence well.

In the experience of the Caribbean, the disadvantage of exchange rate misalignment that characterizes fixed exchange rate regimes has been overwhelmed by the disadvantage of the temptation towards fiscal indiscipline that arises when governments, through their flexible exchange regimes, have access to the full set of monetary policy options. This element in the differentiation of economic performance among Caribbean economies is tested in a regression model that examines the extent of variation in per capita income levels of Caribbean economies based upon the single factor of whether or not these economies have adopted a fixed exchange rate regime. This single variable explains almost 45 per cent of the variation in income among Caribbean economies. See table 2.4 for the results of this regression analysis.

Table 2.4: Results of Regression Analysis on Sample of Twenty-five Caribbean Economies

Variable	Beta Coefficient	Standard Error	T Statistic
Fixed vs. flexible exchange regime[a]	1.593609	0.345171	4.61687[b]

Dependent variable: Log per capita income; R2 (Adj.) = 0.448312, F = 21.31

[a]This variable was proxied through a dummy, with countries with fixed exchange regimes (1) and those with flexible regimes (0).

[b]Statistically significant

It should be noted that the Caribbean experience is driven by the fact that the Caribbean territories that have adopted fixed exchange regimes have avoided the types of inconsistent exchange rate–based stabilization policies in which exchange rates are fixed without the underlying fiscal adjustments (see chapter 3 in this volume). It is inconsistency in exchange rate–based stabilization policy that leads to the balance of payments crises modelled by Krugman.[8]

The Continued Debate on Exchange Regime Choice

But the debate on exchange regime choice lives on within and outside the Caribbean. In particular, since the "Tequila Crisis" of 1994–1995, involving Latin American countries, and the Asian/Russian/Brazilian crises of 1997–1999, the received wisdom has been that developing countries, in the current global environment of freely mobile capital, should adopt exchange regimes "at the corners". That is, they should adopt flexible regimes, or, if fixed, firmly fixed regimes, such as currency boards or dollarization.[9] In the late 1990s, the contrasting cases of Mexico, which was unable to maintain its peg, and Argentina, which had, to that point, maintained its more rigid currency board arrangement, were used to illustrate the vulnerability of exchange rate pegs to speculative attack.[10]

But by 2002 Argentina had defaulted on its debts and abandoned its fixed exchange regime that most analysts had identified as a currency board arrangement.[11] Some analysts pointed to the fixed exchange regime as the precipitate cause of the country's default. They suggested that it had contributed to a multiyear recession, with exporters unable to compete as the Argentine peso appreciated in line with the appreciation of the US dollar, especially in the context of the depreciation of the currency of neighbouring Brazil.[12]

Others indicated that the problem was the fiscal challenges faced by Argentine central and provincial governments, exacerbated by the difficulty associated with continued access to external finance in the aftermath of September 11.[13] Irrespective of the ultimate outcome of this debate on causality, given the Argentine experience and those of the Asian countries that maintained pegs, flexible exchange regimes seemed even more attractive to the international community by 2002.

Proponents of flexible exchange rate regimes argued that they could be managed because if inflation is carefully controlled, there should be little exchange rate change. Yet, to the extent that the country does experience greater inflation than its trading partners, the flexible regime will allow for exchange rate adjustment to offset any appreciation of the real exchange rate. This will allow for firms to maintain their levels of price competitiveness on world markets.

Central to this position is the PPP model of exchange rate determination, which argues that inflation is the causal factor driving exchange rate change. Despite the orthodox views on PPP, however, there continues to be debate about the direction of causality between exchange rate change and inflation. But recent research on the economy of Jamaica has suggested that the orthodox model of PPP may not always apply in the context of small developing countries.

Using an error-correction model, Emmanuel and Wint[14] suggest that the celebrated PPP relation did hold for Jamaica and the United States between 1966 and 1999. However, the data did not support the usefulness of PPP as an empirical model of exchange rate determination. Movements in exchange rates were not significantly explained by the differential inflation between the two countries. Instead, exchange rate changes had a significant impact on the inflation differential.[15] This finding allowed the authors to concur with Frankel in deriving a "price equation".[16]

Conclusion

The study reported on in this chapter provides evidence suggesting that the more prosperous economies of the Caribbean have had a relatively long experience of utilizing fixed exchange rate regimes (with open foreign exchange windows). On the other hand, some of the poorer economic performers in the region, with a history of macroeconomic instability spanning several decades, have featured flexible exchange regimes that include managed floats and fixed exchange regimes with closed foreign exchange windows.

The chapter has also supplied some contextual information, which suggests that the association between economic performance and exchange regime choice is not coincidental. The economies that have relied on fixed exchange regimes have been the smaller, more dependent economies within the region, in which governments have been forced into fiscal and financial discipline because of a limited set of monetary policy options. The larger, more independent economies have not been similarly constrained, but have been less successful in imposing upon themselves a similar level of discipline.

The data provide enough evidence to question, in the context of the small economies of this region, the presumed superiority of flexible exchange regimes relative to fixed exchange regimes. Further, while countries in Latin America and the Caribbean, generally speaking, may be shifting towards flexible exchange regimes,[17] this shift is not apparent in the small countries of the Caribbean. Indeed, many of these countries have expressed a very strong desire to maintain their fixed exchange rate systems (see chapter 3).

In essence, these small Caribbean countries argue that their exchange rate pegs represent an anchor for their programmes of macroeconomic stabilization, and that the low inflation levels generated through these pegs avoid severe problems of overvaluation. At the same time, the fixed exchange rates create an environment of stability that is conducive to investment and trade, particularly in the areas of financial services and tourism that dominate economic activity in this region. This does not represent an "orthodox" economic position, since the dominant view on exchange rate determination, operating through the PPP principle, is that inflation differentials determine exchange rate movements, rather than exchange rate movements determining inflation.

The causality between exchange rate movement and inflation is not necessarily as unidirectional, however, as is suggested in conventional perspectives on PPP; this is suggested by the Emmanuel and Wint study, which used thirty-three years of inflation and exchange rate data in Jamaica to test the existence of correlation between exchange rate change and inflation, and to investigate the issue of causality. While, as expected, there was correlation, the principal causal relationship was from exchange rate change to inflation, rather than the other way around.[18]

There are two possibilities that could account for this somewhat unexpected finding. The first relates to the thin and relatively uncompetitive markets that have characterized developing countries for many years. In the context of such markets, and a history of exchange rate instability, firms are likely to overcompensate for past exchange rate changes in their pricing mechanisms, in an effort to provide insulation against exchange rate changes they expect in the future. These responses represent potentially self-fulfilling exchange rate change expectations. These responses will be inflationary, and thereby become self-fulfilling, if they are monetized, which may well occur in the absence of careful money supply management.

A second possibility exists from the wage side of the economy. Employees in the public and private sectors are also likely to seek insulation from their expectation of future exchange rate change, based on a history of exchange rate movement. As they negotiate wage increases beyond productivity levels in response to past exchange rate change, their actions are likely to be inflationary. Again, these inflationary impulses will require monetization, but such monetization is likely, in response to the demands placed by governments and in the absence of strongly independent central banks. Governments, in turn, are often reacting in response to the pressures of strong unions. Both of these factors are likely to have occurred in Jamaica, the country that was used to test the PPP theory. In the context of the probability of exchange rate changes leading to inflation, it is clear why fixed exchange rates have contributed to more stable macroeconomies.

Although this chapter concludes that the small countries of the Caribbean have benefited from their pegged exchange rate systems, it does not advocate a universal movement among developing countries, even small ones, to exchange rate pegs or other types of fixed exchange regimes. There is enough empirical evidence pointing to the potential inflexibility of fixed exchange regimes, which suggests that such regimes can also present significant problems to countries. Instead, the chapter advocates, with respect both to countries and to multilateral institutions, an analytical and flexible approach to prescriptions on economic policy, as opposed to an approach of restricted options, such as the notion that countries should occupy positions at the "corners" of the exchange regime continuum.

Indeed, by 2000 the IMF was articulating a position in support of an analytical and contextual approach to advice on the choice of exchange regime.[19] Other analysts, notably John Williamson, also continued to articulate the need to consider all exchange regime options, including those options that are between the "corners", or intermediate between firmly fixed and floating regimes.[20]

Small developing countries in search of an economic environment that is likely to provide the optimal platform for spawning internationally competitive firms need to consider carefully the advantages and disadvantages of various exchange rate systems. If governments can demonstrate the ability to be responsible with respect to their fiscal operations and the management of their monetary operations, ideally through the co-ordinated efforts of ministry officials and central banks whose unequivocal mission is price stability, then a flexible exchange regime is consistent with macroeconomic stability, and may well be the more appropriate exchange regime option.

If these conditions do not apply, however, then the problems of macroeconomic instability are likely to outweigh those of real exchange rate overvaluation, and a fixed exchange rate regime is more suited to such a country. This is because the fixed exchange regime has the ability to impose a level of discipline on government's fiscal operations that can be understood by the various interest groups within the country. In sum, this chapter argues in support of an analytical approach to the management of small developing economies, as these countries seek to improve their levels of international competitiveness.

Chapter 3

Exchange Regime Choice: The Case of Barbados

The previous two chapters have pointed to the importance of stability in enhancing competitiveness in small economies. The experience of Caribbean economies suggests that fixed exchange rates, despite their disadvantages, have been more conducive to maintaining economic stability and growth in small countries than have flexible rates. This chapter turns to the experience of a single economy – Barbados – to examine the implications of maintaining a fixed exchange rate. Focus on a single country enables us to look at experience over a number of years and in a greater level of detail. This adds to the understanding that the previous chapter provided based on a cross-sectional, more cursory, examination of a number of countries and territories.

For over twenty years Barbados has used a fixed exchange rate as an anchor in its attempt to maintain stability within its economy. This chapter traces those efforts and seeks to identify whether there are any lessons for macroeconomic stabilization programmes in other small countries.

The Antecedents of the Barbadian Experience

The origins of the Barbados experience can be traced to the early 1970s. Under the fixed exchange rate regime of the time, the Barbadian currency, like those of other Caribbean countries which were former British colonies, was pegged to the UK pound. After the move to floating exchange rate regimes, the fact that much of Barbadian trade was dollar denominated meant that the country experienced some instability with respect to fluctuations between the UK pound and the US dollar. Accordingly, in 1975, Barbados decided to peg its currency to that of its dominant trading partner, the United States. It chose to do so at an exchange rate of B$2 : US$1, even though this exchange rate represented a slight revaluation of the Barbadian currency against the US dollar, since the prevailing rate was B$2.07 : US$1.

There was important symbolism associated with establishing such an exchange rate, even though it required a slight revaluation. First, it suggested the beginning of the Barbadian experiment, in that the prevailing wisdom for developing countries eager to promote their export sectors is that currency revaluation or appreciation should be avoided because such action reduces the competitiveness of export industries. The adoption of a 2-to-1 exchange rate, however, indicated the policy intention of establishing an exchange rate around which national support could be galvanized, and about which a sense of permanence could quickly be established. This would have been more difficult to achieve with an exchange rate of B$2.07 : US$1.

At the outset, also, Barbadian policy makers illustrated that the macroeconomic stability of which the exchange rate was a symbol would be supported by prudent economic policy and fiscal conservatism. The first illustration of this economic strategy can be traced to the 1970s during the period of the oil crisis. Most non-oil-producing developing countries experienced significant budgetary imbalances as a result of the quadrupling of oil prices in 1973. But at around the same time, there was an increase in the revenues many developing countries received from their commodity exports.

Most countries were not able to offset the increased oil import bill with improved commodity earnings. Barbados, however, was able to achieve such an offset to the extent that a surplus fund was created from increased sugar earnings. The fund was earmarked for housing, but was actually not spent due to the fiscal conservatism that was employed within the country.[1] This focus on conservative fiscal policy that emerged at the start of Barbadian efforts to create a stable macroeconomy was also in evidence during the country's efforts to respond to attacks on the stability regime.

The first assault on the regime came during the early 1980s. In the run-up to the 1981 general election, the public sector deficit grew quite dramatically. This deficit, which was 1.5 per cent of GDP in 1979, increased to 3.5 per cent of GDP in 1980 and increased again to 6.8 per cent of GDP in 1981, the election year. The response to this problem was immediate and comprehensive. After the election, the newly elected government embarked upon a deficit correction programme that involved the imposition of new taxes and reduced expenditure. The fiscal correction was so comprehensive that it allowed Barbados to negotiate a standby agreement with the IMF without requiring any discussion on exchange rate adjustments. Any such adjustment was anathema to Barbadian policy makers. This issue was to reappear a decade later, however, in the context of the 1991 crisis.

The 1991 Crisis

The seeds of the 1991 crisis were sown, it might be argued, in the fiscal relaxation of 1986. In the context of the election of that year, a tax reform programme was implemented that significantly undermined the revenues collected by the government. The programme involved a significant reduction in the number of individual taxpayers (estimates suggest a reduction from sixty or seventy thousand to about twenty thousand) because of a notable increase in the tax threshold such that the threshold was equivalent to the average wage earned. In tandem with this increase, there was an expansion in the number of allowable deductions.

This reduction in the government's revenue base had the effect of leading to a gradual deterioration in the fiscal position. The government's fiscal deficit, already high in 1986 at 5.3 per cent of GDP, deteriorated to the level of 8.8 per cent of GDP in the aftermath of this tax-restructuring programme. The initial response was to offset declining revenues with foreign borrowing. This borrowing, in turn, served to increase the foreign debt service ratio, which went up to 21.3 per cent in 1987 from 10.4 per cent in 1985. The fiscal changes also led to a worsening of the country's external balance position; the current account position as a percentage of GDP declined from a 5.5 per cent surplus position in 1985 to a 1.3 per cent deficit position in 1987.

These problems were exacerbated by reductions in export earnings associated with the collapse of the Trinidad domestic market, which in turn was a result of Trinidad's deflationary efforts. This combination of events led to an economic crisis in Barbados. By 1991, Barbados was truly in the throes of this crisis, with available foreign exchange reserves that could cover less than three weeks of imports. Further, the government and central bank were in breach of regulations with respect to the extent of advances that the Central Bank of Barbados could provide to the government. In the face of internal and external financial imbalances, discussions with the IMF were held beginning in 1990, but no programme was put in place until after the 1991 general election, which was held several months before it was constitutionally due.

Responses to the 1991 Crisis

The negotiations surrounding the financial arrangements with the IMF were arduous. The Barbadian negotiating team followed the policy articulated by previous administrations; that is, they indicated that the issue of devaluing the currency was not open to negotiation. The value of the Barbadian dollar was sacrosanct. This position led to problems with the multilateral institutions. A consortium that included the IMF, the Inter-American Development Bank and the World Bank had been discussing a stabilization package for Barbados. The World Bank, however, indicated that it would participate in a stabilization agreement only if a devaluation of the Barbadian currency was one of the components of the agreement.

Interestingly, there was greater ambivalence on the part of the IMF negotiating team with respect to the desirability of a devaluation as a part of a stabilization programme. There was, at the time, an intense debate within the IMF on the desirability of a fixed exchange rate as an anchor for a stabilization programme. Fortunately for the Barbadian negotiators, the leader of the IMF team was a believer in the use of a fixed exchange rate, with stabilization adjustments executed through the use of fiscal contraction rather than through an excessive reliance on exchange rate movement. Ultimately, the willingness of the IMF to provide financial assistance was to rest on the team's view of the credibility of the fiscal adjustments proposed by the Barbadian negotiators.

Fiscal Adjustment via Wage and Salary Reductions

The principal fiscal adjustment was to be an effort to reduce the amount of recurrent government expenditure. As in most developing countries, the principal controllable element of this expenditure was wages and salaries. Against the backdrop of the need for external financial assistance, the government began discussions with the Barbados trade union movement and public sector workers with respect to the need to reduce wage and salary expenditure if the economy were to be rescued. Explicit in the government's position was that a devaluation of the Barbadian currency should be avoided, and that the only way such a devaluation would be avoided was to accomplish the necessary reduction in expenditure.

The Barbados government began negotiations with the trade union movement in the country in an effort to arrive at a formula for the reduction of the public sector wage and salary bill. On 31 July 1991 Prime Minister Erskine Sandiford called together a group of trade union leaders to inform them that the Barbados economy was in crisis, and to solicit their support for the imposition of measures to stabilize the economy. Under the leadership of the only umbrella trade union in the country, the Barbados Workers Union, this group of union leaders formed the Coalition of Trade Unions and Staff Associations of Barbados (CTUSAB). The CTUSAB was to continue a process of dialogue with the government over the next several months.

The government's principal proposal for dealing with the significant budget deficit, which in 1991 had climbed to a level of 8.4 per cent of GDP, was for an 8 per cent across-the-board cut in wages and salaries (that was to be in place for eighteen months) and a 10 per cent cut in the size of the public sector. The CTUSAB, which was also committed to a policy of no change in the value of the Barbadian currency, countered with a proposal to release pressure on the public finances by providing government workers with bonds in lieu of salary until stability had been reattained within the country. Indeed, union leaders in Barbados claim that an understanding was reached with the government that bonds, rather than pay cuts, would be the principal mechanism used.

But discussions between the CTUSAB and the government broke off in September 1991 when the government decided to take the issue of wage and salary reductions directly to public sector workers. The workers received forms from the government requesting them to sign – without the benefit of anonymity – if they were willing to accept an 8 per cent cut in wages in order to restore stability to the Barbadian economy. Government-led discussions indicated that, were these cuts not made, the government would be forced by the IMF to devalue the Barbadian currency. The negative experiences of Barbados's CARICOM colleagues, Jamaica and Guyana in particular, with currency devaluations over many years figured prominently in these discussions.

The Barbadian government was able, in this context, to gain an agreement to cut salaries from a majority (about 75 per cent) of public servants. Effective 1 October 1991 the government took a series of actions, including: reducing public servants' pay by 8 per cent, severing over two thousand casual and temporary workers, introducing short weeks, reducing unemployment and severance benefits, passing legislation to compel workers to contribute to their own severance packages, and refusing to pay monies in lieu of notice, which had been the norm under the existing severance payments legislation.

The CTUSAB was of the view that, with the unilateral implementation of these actions, the government had reneged on a commitment to negotiate in good faith. Accordingly, it pursued two approaches to the government's actions. The first was to organize a series of national marches in protest. These marches were held on 24 October and 4–5 November 1991, and involved all the unions in the country. Other groups joined the workers in their protest action, including employers, representatives from church groups and from nongovernmental organizations. The political opposition, in the form of the Barbados Labour Party, was also involved and, indeed, called for the resignation of Prime Minister Sandiford. The second action was to take the government to court on the grounds that its unilateral reduction of public servants' pay was in violation of the Barbadian constitution.

The marches were followed by meetings with government officials. This combination of marches and dialogue had the effect of forcing the government to amend some of the employment policies that had been implemented. Thus, eventually workers did receive payment in lieu of notice, the work week was restored, severance payments were increased (relative to the government's proposal but still far less than pre-existing severance payments) and there was an understanding that the government would seek to ensure that there were no increases in basic costs over the near term. The CTUSAB was not successful, however, in overturning the decision on the 8 per cent pay cut. The case was taken as far as the privy court in the United Kingdom, where that final court of appeal concluded that the action did, in fact, conform to the principles of the Barbadian constitution.

Other Fiscal Adjustments

Although the principal mechanism for adjusting fiscal policy was the reduction in the government wage bill, other efforts were also made to reduce significantly the growing fiscal deficit. Chief among these were privatizations and a revisiting of the tax reform programme that had been instituted in 1986. With respect to privatizations, a number of entities were returned to the private sector. These included the national telecommunications network, in which Cable and Wireless purchased a majority ownership stake, and the local flour-milling company, among others. In relation to the tax programme, many of the deductions (such as those for mortgage interest and house repair expenses) that had been granted under the 1986 tax reform programme were eliminated. The fiscal adjustment also involved reducing capital expenditures. Indeed, at least one large construction project was halted in mid-stream, providing visible evidence of the national austerity programme that had been implemented.

The fiscal adjustments introduced by the government were to be linked to a series of complementary adjustments introduced by the private sector. Both sets of adjustments were pursued in the context of the efforts, activities and concerns of the trade union movement. These all took place under the umbrella of a tripartite social partnership which negotiated the "Protocol for the Implementation of a Prices and Incomes Policy".

The Protocol for the Implementation of a Prices and Incomes Policy

Tripartite discussions among the government, the trade union movement and the Barbadian private sector began in 1991 with the government's initiation of discussions with the trade union movement. This movement coalesced into the CTUSAB, while at the same time the private sector groupings came together under the umbrella organization, Barbados Private Sector Agency, whose founding president was noted Barbadian industrialist Sir John Goddard, chairman and chief executive officer (CEO) of Goddard Enterprises.

These discussions began in 1991. The impasse between the government and the union movement, symbolized by the marches held in October and November 1991, stalled these discussions for some time, but they were restarted in 1992. The first protocol was eventually signed in August 1993, with its arrangements set to apply retroactively to April 1993.

The protocol called for responsible action by all three social partners. It was built on the principles of the importance of peaceful, harmonious and mature labour-management relations, the effectiveness of tripartism in national development, the importance of just and equitable development of labour and capital, the freedom of association, and the realization that the competitiveness of Barbados had been eroded. Built on these principles were the protocol's objectives of safeguarding the existing rate of exchange between the Barbadian and American currencies, the need to expand the economy, the need to improve the competitiveness of Barbadian goods and services, the need to restrain wages, the restructuring of the economy, and the promotion of a national commitment to improved productivity and increased efficiency.

Against the backdrop of these principles and objectives, the protocol represented an agreement to freeze increases in wages and salaries (on all pay including payments in kind, fringe benefits and lump sums) in both the public and private sectors. The only exception was for increases that arose from profit-sharing arrangements or productivity bonuses. Implicitly, the protocol also anticipated minimal inflation and, by extension, an understanding that the government and the private sector would ensure that the prices of goods and services would also remain stable.

The most important institutional vehicle established by the protocol was the National Productivity Board, a tripartite advisory and educational body that would be involved in alerting the nation to the importance of increased productivity and in initiating a process of productivity measurement for organizations in the public and private sector. The initial protocol was negotiated for a period extending from 1 April 1993 to 31 March 1995. Importantly, it was negotiated as an agreement among the social partners but was not a legally binding document (in a manner similar to collective labour agreements in Barbados, which are also not legally binding).

All three social partners were of the view that the first protocol worked reasonably well. Accordingly, prior to its expiration, negotiations commenced for a successor protocol. This second protocol was signed on 30 August 1995 but would apply retroactively to 1 April 1995, for a two-year term that was to expire on 31 March 1997. The principal distinction between the two protocols was that the second substituted wage restraint (in both the public and private sectors) for the wage freeze that had been an important element of the first protocol. This second protocol also established a subcommittee of the social partners as the first line of consultation regarding all aspects of the protocol's implementation, and put in place arrangements for quarterly meetings among the social partners, under the chairmanship of the prime minister.

From the government's side, the signatory to the second protocol was the Barbados Labour Party–led government headed by Owen Arthur, which successfully contested the 1994 elections. The other signatories remained the same: the Barbados Private Sector Agency and the CTUSAB (which was renamed in 1995 to become the Congress of Trade Unions and Staff Associations of Barbados).

Monetary Policy Adjustments

Among the mix of policy instruments for achieving stabilization, policy makers in Barbados focused their efforts largely on fiscal policy. This is because Barbadian policy makers, particularly officials of the Central Bank of Barbados, have long held the view that monetary policy plays a limited role in the context of an open economy such as the Barbadian economy. In particular, analysts in Barbados suggest that open market operations have been quite ineffective in economic stabilization efforts.[2] The stabilization programme did incorporate other monetary policy tools. Interest rates were raised by several percentage points. Also, the central bank introduced a global credit ceiling for a period of six months, in an attempt to restrain the expansion of credit and, by extension, the growth of money supply.

The final element in the stabilization programme was exchange policy. The commitment to maintaining the value of the Barbadian currency underpinned all other elements of the programme. It was a commitment shared by the government, workers and their unions, and the private sector, even though it was also quite widely held that the Barbadian currency was overvalued.

The other element of exchange policy, however, was the continued reliance on some exchange controls. Barbados had long had exchange controls on capital account transactions, but it had never enforced controls on current account transactions in the manner that had characterized exchange control regimes in other Caribbean countries. Thus, there was little in the way of rationing of foreign exchange, and the requirements for gaining access to foreign exchange had never been onerous.

The first governor of the Central Bank of Barbados, in an autobiographical account of his years in office, pointed out that the purpose of exchange control was to monitor payment flows and gather qualitative information about such flows. Outflows of foreign exchange were to be restricted, not at the water's edge, but at the fountainhead – through the tightening of monetary and fiscal policy . . . . I warned the Exchange Control Department against challenging the public to a game of foreign exchange hide and seek: there were 250,000 of them working day and night and only 20 exchange control officers working forty hours per week! We simply could not win.[3]

The approach to exchange control did not change during the stabilization programme. Unlike all three of the other "More Developed Countries" (MDCs) in CARICOM, which eliminated exchange controls in the liberalization of their exchange regimes in the early 1990s, Barbados continued to maintain these controls. Foreign residents were not allowed to hold foreign exchange accounts unless they could demonstrate a need due to exporting or other related requirements. Also, capital account transactions that involved the export or import of foreign exchange required governmental approval. These controls were maintained as a part of the stabilization programme because Barbadian policy makers were of the view that they would assist in deterring the speculative inflows and outflows of capital that have a potentially destabilizing effect.

The Impact of the Stabilization Programme

The stabilization programme in Barbados can be evaluated at two levels. The first is the extent to which it did, in fact, assist in stabilizing the economy, defined in terms of low inflation, low interest rates and sustainable fiscal and external balance positions. The second is the effect on growth, since economic stability is not an end in itself, and is routinely viewed as a necessary platform for generating economic growth.

On the first count, the Barbadian stabilization programme was very successful. As indicated in the table below, for the period 1990 to 1992 inclusive, inflation averaged 5.2 per cent, decelerating to an average rate of 2.3 per cent between 1993 and 1999. Interest rates declined, on average, between 1992 and 1999. The fiscal deficit declined from 7.2 per cent of GDP during the crisis year to 1.6 per cent after the structural adjustments, and stabilized thereafter. Similarly, the external debt position and the foreign exchange cover both improved substantially after the policy corrections of 1991.

On the second count, there was also evidence that the stabilization policies provided a platform that contributed to economic growth.[4] Over the 1993–1999 period, the unemployment rate declined substantially and consistently from its peak of 24.3 per cent in 1993 to 10.4 per cent in 1999. This was due in no small part to the fact that the Barbadian economy began to experience consistent real growth rates between 1993 and 1999, with annual GDP growth rates climbing to a peak of 4.4 per cent in 1998, representing the highest annual growth rate since the 5.1 per cent growth recorded in 1986.

Table 3.1: Barbados Selected Economic Indicators 1990–1999

Economic indicator	1990	1991	1992	1993	1994	1995	1996	1997	1998	1999
Consumer inflation (%)	3.1	6.3	6.1	1.1	0.1	1.9	2.4	7.7	1.3	1.6
Treasury bill rate (%)	8.1	11.3	6.6	7.2	7.8	8.3	5.6	4.9	5.7	6.1
Fiscal deficit as % of GDP	7.2	1.6	1.6	2.1	1.0	0.8	3.2	1.4	0.9	1.8
Foreign exchange reserves (weeks of retained imports)	3.7	2.9	10.1	7.4	11.5	11.7	15.2	13.6	12.9	14.3
External debt/GDP (%)	31.4	33.0	35.6	31.7	29.2	25.6	23.2	19.4	19.1	19.7
External debt service ratio (%)	18.0	19.5	19.0	12.8	12.9	12.0	11.6	9.7	7.1	7.7
Unemployment rate (%)	NA	17.3	23.0	24.3	21.8	19.6	15.8	14.5	12.3	10.4
Real GDP growth (%)	-3.3	-3.9	-7.2	0.8	4.3	2.3	2.5	2.9	4.4	2.5

Source: Central Bank of Barbados, *Annual Statistical Digest*, October 2000.

Lessons from the Barbadian Experience

The central feature of the Barbadian experience is the effort to use a nominal exchange rate as the visible and enduring plank of a macroeconomic stabilization programme. The other feature of the experience, aligned to this central feature, is the role of fiscal policy.

Exchange Rate Policy

The movement away from fixed exchange rates in the 1970s gave developing countries the opportunity to adopt independent exchange rates for the first time since many of these countries had attained independence. Even though most developing countries continued to peg their exchange rates to an internationally convertible currency, the incidence of exchange rate changes was much higher in the post-1973 period.

Barbados eschewed the approach of exchange rate changes. This strategy rested on the view of Barbadian policy makers that a small country like Barbados, which was so integrated into the US currency area, could not operate with an independent currency. Indeed, various analysts have supported the view that small, open economies, adjacent to dominant currency areas, will have difficulty operating an independent exchange rate policy.[5] Barbadian policy makers took as a vindication of this position the fact that the more prosperous countries of the Caribbean region all (with the lone exception of Trinidad and Tobago) have exchange rates that are fixed in relation to the US dollar (see chapter 2).[6]

Over a long period of time, this policy was communicated to the public under the principle of the critical importance of maintaining a stable exchange rate in order for Barbados to avoid the problems of inflation, social instability and other ills that seemed so evident in those Caribbean countries that had not adopted a fixed exchange rate as the anchor for their stabilization efforts.[7] The Barbadian authorities were convinced that the preservation of the fixed exchange rate parity of the Barbadian dollar to the US dollar was vital to the maintenance of investor confidence, macroeconomic stability and a healthy industrial relations climate.

The principal problem, however, associated with the use of a nominal exchange rate as an anchor is that such an exchange rate easily becomes overvalued, and the Barbadian experience illustrated this problem. In the context of Barbadian inflation that is higher than US inflation, there will be increases in the real effective exchange rate of the Barbadian currency. This increase in the real effective exchange rate, other things being equal, reduces the level of export competitiveness of Barbados.

The possibility of an appreciation in the real effective exchange rate is particularly high where a government maintains policy control over the growth of money supply, as opposed to having money supply growth determined endogenously in order to maintain the fixed exchange rate. The use of a currency board, the movement to a policy of dollarization, or even the existence of a highly independent central bank outside of political control, are all institutional options that would help to ensure that money supply was endogenously determined and thus reduce the possibility of a currency misalignment due to local price increases triggered by the relatively higher growth of money supply.[8] Of course, the lesson from fixed exchange rate management, as demonstrated in chapter 2, is that complementary fiscal policies are important even where there is endogenous growth of domestic money supply.

Barbados also sought to avoid a significant misalignment of its currency through the implementation of complementary fiscal policies.

Fiscal Policy

Indeed, the Barbadian experience speaks quite eloquently to the role of fiscal policy in stabilization efforts, particularly a stabilization effort that relies on the use of a nominal exchange rate anchor, which takes away degrees of policy freedom with respect to money supply policy, for example. The pursuit of stabilization through such a route forces a level of money supply growth that would be compatible with the viability of the nominal exchange rate. If money supply growth, and by extension inflation, deviates too far from that of trading partners, it will force a significant appreciation in the real exchange rate. This is likely to lead to a deterioration in the country's external accounts, which, ultimately, will make the nominal exchange rate unsustainable.

Money supply growth could be contained, in the short run, through monetary or fiscal policy. Barbadian policy makers, however, placed most emphasis on the use of fiscal policy in this regard because of an assessment that monetary policy instruments, particularly in the form of open-market operations, were both relatively ineffective and ultimately unsustainable because of the small, open nature of the country's economy.[9] It was this perspective that provided the impetus for a focus on fiscal policy as the main weapon of money supply control in the context of the fixed nominal exchange rate regime. In particular, the stabilization programmes implemented in 1981 and again in 1991 were both heavily slanted towards the use of fiscal policy.

The Barbadian experience also illustrates the temptation towards fiscal profligacy during election seasons. It suggests that the use of a fixed exchange rate as a nominal anchor does not necessarily reduce the temptation to resort to fiscal imprudence and a corresponding inflation tax, but it does induce a rapid return to fiscal propriety if the anchor is not to be lost.

The Juxtaposition of Fiscal and Exchange Policies

The Barbadian and international experience suggests, therefore, that there is a rather tight linkage between the use of the nominal exchange rate as an anchor and the need for fiscal discipline to underpin the nominal exchange rate. In effect, the true anchor is fiscal discipline, and the nominal exchange rate is simply the visible manifestation of that discipline that serves to provide immediate and ongoing information about the low-inflation stance of government policy.

With the use of a nominal exchange rate anchor, however, there is the problem of the elimination of money illusion. Money illusion refers to the idea that individuals react differently to a 3 per cent increase in wages coupled with a 5 per cent increase in inflation on the one hand, and a two-percentage-point reduction in their salaries, on the other, even though these two states of affairs both correspond to a two-percentage-point reduction in their purchasing power. It is one of the arguments put forward by those who argue that while low inflation levels have a positive impact on growth, zero inflation ought not to be the policy target.[10]

Fixed nominal exchange rates create, one might argue, a similar effect. An increase in differential inflation or reduction in relative productivity in the country that is using the exchange rate as an anchor cannot be accommodated through relative price changes. These real changes in relative costs, therefore, have to be dealt with through wage or expenditure reductions throughout the society.

Efforts to postpone the adjustment process, through borrowing funds externally or internally, for example, only put off the day of reckoning when there will be either compensating price changes through increased productivity or reduced differential inflation. Otherwise wage and expenditure reductions will once again become necessary. The fact that prices are "sticky downwards" makes such adjustments difficult. What also makes the adjustments difficult is the fact that they may well need to be ongoing. As long as differential inflation or differential productivity levels exist, there will be a need for offsetting shifts in real local cost structures if a fixed nominal exchange rate is to be maintained. In the context of such a system, therefore, fiscal probity is an ongoing requirement for competitive success.

Yet prudent fiscal policy is also important to the country that is seeking to manage a flexible exchange rate regime well.[11] The trade-off between fixed and flexible regimes effectively becomes one of potential overvaluation associated with a fixed exchange rate regime, versus the higher cost and reduced effectiveness of stabilization with a flexible exchange regime, because such a regime creates a more nurturing arena for gaming, by both the government and private agents, which results in increased inflation.

But in important respects, the debate between fixed and flexible exchange regimes in developing countries, or about the choice of a nominal anchor, should be recognized as important only to the extent that there is a commitment on the part of government to the appropriate fiscal path, or to the extent that a particular regime choice forces upon the government greater fiscal probity. In the absence of prudent fiscal policy there will be no successful stabilization, regardless of the exchange rate regime that is adopted.

An additional perspective arising from the Barbadian experience relates to controls on capital. Barbadian policy makers were of the view that not only should the nominal exchange rate remain fixed, but full liberalization of the foreign exchange system was not appropriate. The argument proposed was that while current account transactions should face the minimal possible bureaucracy, there should be some controls on capital account transactions to prevent the destabilizing impact of speculative capital flows. These speculative flows would also be minimized by a stabilization process that concentrated on fiscal policy, because they would not be lured by the high real exchange rates that are used in a stabilization programme with a monetary policy focus. In such a programme, capital flows induced by high real interest rates represent the force that offsets the high differential inflation levels (induced at least in part by fiscal profligacy) within the country seeking macroeconomic stability.

Finally, a significant issue brought out in the Barbadian experiment was the role of public education, dialogue, interest and commitment in the process of stabilization. For over twenty years the Barbadian people had grown to view the parity value of their currency as a mark of national pride. While economically irrational on the face of it, this perspective has to be understood in the context of rapidly depreciating currencies elsewhere in the Caribbean and Latin

American region, and the instability that such exchange rate changes both represented and caused. In that context, the Barbadian view was a rational reflection of the importance of stability for investment and growth. It was hard to identify a voice in Barbados, whether in government, the opposition, unions, exporters, other private sector firms, and the citizenry at large, that was critical of the country's exchange policy.

The national consensus on the issue of exchange policy provided the platform, in 1991, upon which was built widespread agreement on the need for fiscal discipline and general wage and price containment. Building this consensus was not easy, as was readily demonstrated by the 1991 marches and the testing of the government's wage reduction action in court. Nevertheless, the tripartite discussions between the government, labour unions and private sector firms that culminated in the two protocols on the implementation of a prices and income policy have become models for tripartism, national consensus and dialogue in support of national efforts at macroeconomic stabilization. The building of this consensus in Barbados must also be seen in the framework of the generally high level of social capital in this country, which has one of the highest literacy levels in the world (98 per cent), and has one of the highest human development ranking among developing countries.[12]

In conclusion, the Barbadian case provides several possible lessons for macroeconomic stabilization efforts in small developing countries, and, indeed, some lessons for these efforts in all countries:

- Small open economies adjacent to dominant currency areas are likely to experience difficulties establishing an independent currency. The smaller the economy, the more difficult the establishment of an independent currency.
- Small open economies are also likely to experience difficulty using monetary policy effectively.
- Economies that opt to use a nominal exchange rate as an anchor for their stabilization efforts must recognize the need for complementary fiscal policies to avoid the problems of real exchange rate appreciation that can so easily occur with fixed nominal exchange rates. For small economies, with limited effective monetary policy options, complementary fiscal policy becomes particularly important. Conservatism in fiscal policy is also critical because fixed exchange rates eliminate the

possibility of "money illusion", requiring that adjustments take place on the "real" side of the economy.

- Small open economies may need to consider some controls on capital account transactions, in addition to the avoidance of high interest rates induced by an inappropriate focus on monetary policy, to deter the potentially destabilizing effects of short-term capital flows.
- There is a critical role for public education, social capital development and trust in the implementation of a fixed exchange rate policy in a small open economy.

Chapter 4

Risk Reduction Efforts in CARICOM's MDCs

The preceding chapters have examined important elements of the role of government in enhancing competitiveness in small developing countries. This chapter continues this process and uses the experiences of the four more populous countries[1] in the anglophone Caribbean – Jamaica, Trinidad and Tobago, Guyana, and Barbados – to identify lessons for the role of government in small developing countries and, indeed, developing countries of any size.

In the introduction to this volume, the case was made that it was becoming more important for enterprises in small developing countries to operate at internationally competitive levels. The introduction also indicated the criteria that could be used in judging the extent to which enterprises operated at such levels. But governments of developing countries often have to make special efforts, and engage in policy adjustments, in order to enhance the levels of international competitiveness of the institutions that reside in the countries they manage. This chapter focuses on the policy adjustments often required by governments seeking to enhance international competitiveness in small developing economies.

Enhancing International Competitiveness in Developing Economies

The fundamental policy problem facing the governments of such countries is the fact that an inadequate number of their resident institutions operate at internationally competitive levels.

In developed countries, international competitiveness, to a large extent, is synonymous with entrepreneurship, or the organization, management and assumption of the risks of a business. Most new enterprises are immediately confronted with the imperatives of international competition, either in the form of imported goods or in the form of existing competitors within the relevant industry that are themselves operating at internationally competitive levels. It is for this reason that studies seeking to understand the incidence of export activity from firms, even small firms, in developed countries, have concentrated principally on attitudinal issues: that is, on the need for managers to change their attitudes to embrace an export focus.[2]

In developing countries, however, the objective circumstances have been very different in the past. For many enterprises in these countries, entrepreneurship has not been synonymous with international competitiveness. Enterprises have been organized in markets sheltered from international competition. Indeed, many have been established in monopolistic market settings in which there has been neither foreign nor domestic competition. For these countries, attaining international competitiveness requires a revisiting of entrepreneurship. Indeed, international competitiveness is conditional upon international entrepreneurship, that is, the assumption of the risks of operating an enterprise exposed to international competition. Shifting to a focus on international competitiveness has implications for all phases of the management of operations, from operations to marketing, to human resource management, to financing.

I suggest four non-mutually exclusive categories of solutions to the problem of inadequate internationally competitive entrepreneurial activity, which might be pursued through the public policy initiatives of national governments in developing countries. These are:

- the attraction of firms capable of internationally competitive operations;
- engagement in a process of socialization, training and education to spawn new internationally oriented entrepreneurs;
- engagement in state entrepreneurship;
- engagement in a process of reducing the risks associated with internationally competitive entrepreneurship.

These policy initiatives have been pursued with different degrees of success by governments of developing countries. The attraction of firms capable of internationally competitive operations is one of the most popular public policy initiatives among developing countries eager to improve their international competitiveness. This attraction effort is concentrated, today, on inducing export-oriented foreign direct investors to invest in developing countries. Developing countries around the world have promotional organizations whose fundamental reason for existence is the attraction of FDI.

Much research has been conducted on the role of government in attracting export-oriented FDI.[3] In the mid-1990s Costa Rica's promotional organization, CINDE, attracted a major investment from Intel Corporation, providing additional evidence that such initiatives can generate results.[4] Nevertheless, it is also clear that the market for attracting export-oriented investors is highly competitive. These issues are examined in greater detail in chapter 6 of this volume.

Nearly all developing countries now have programmes in place aimed at socializing and training a new breed of internationally oriented entrepreneur. Training programmes in business management and entrepreneurship used to be rare in developing countries; they are now often the most popular courses of study. In many countries, there was typically a stigma associated with business activity, particularly in contrast to traditional professions such as law, medicine and engineering. This may well have been related to the level of rent-seeking and government patronage often linked with business activity in highly regulated economies.

With the reform and liberalization efforts that have taken hold throughout the developing world, and with firms now involved in competition across borders, successful business executives are now viewed in a far more positive light. But, even with these changes, new programmes to train and orient individuals towards internationally competitive entrepreneurial activity are still likely to have long gestation periods before results will be visible.

Many frustrated national governments have resorted to attempts by the state to engage in the entrepreneurship that the private sector either will not, or apparently cannot, do. These efforts at state entrepreneurship, however, have generally been met with very high levels of failure. Such an outcome is not surprising because of the inappropriate incentive structure, and the poor levels of market discipline, typically associated with entrepreneurial activity by the state.

This takes us to the fourth category: the involvement of the state in reducing the risks associated with internationally competitive activity. The rationale for the support of the state in reducing these risks is linked to the problem of market failure. Internationally competitive entrepreneurship creates positive externalities that make it highly beneficial from the perspective of a developing economy. In essence, the internationally competitive elements of an economy subsidize those elements of the economy that are not operating at international standards.

But while beneficial to the society, internationally competitive activity can also be quite risky. In developing countries these risks can be particularly high because of unstable macroeconomic climates, poor investment climates, and inadequate infrastructure, skill levels and market information. Consequently, in the absence of a comprehensive programme for reducing risks, internationally competitive entrepreneurship is likely to be undergenerated in developing countries. The risk faced by small developing countries, with their limited opportunities for scale economies in the domestic market, suggests that in these countries there is particularly likely to be undergeneration of internationally competitive entrepreneurship in the absence of dedicated efforts in this direction.

It is against this background that one of the most important public policy initiatives in small developing countries geared towards enhancing development prospects has been the effort of national governments to reduce the risks associated with internationally competitive entrepreneurship.

Risk Reduction Approaches among CARICOM's MDCs

Each of CARICOM's MDCs, Trinidad and Tobago, Barbados, Jamaica, and Guyana, has sought to develop policies aimed at reducing the risks associated with internationally competitive activity, in an effort to nurture an increased incidence of this activity.

Risk Reduction Efforts in Trinidad and Tobago

An early explicit effort by a group of Caribbean policy makers to reduce the risks associated with internationally competitive activity is reflected in the experience of Trinidad and Tobago, the largest economy in the anglophone

Caribbean. The origins of the Trinidadian effort can be traced to 1982 when oil prices fell precipitously, to about one-third of their 1981 levels. The result was that Trinidad's highly oil-dependent economy contracted almost commensurately. The economic crisis led the government to appoint two high-level commissions, the recommendations from which were eventually to correspond to the two-part programme of risk reduction implemented by the Trinidadian government.

The first commission, under the chairmanship of noted Caribbean economist, William Demas, proposed that the Trinidad and Tobago government reduce risks through a process of macroeconomic stabilization in the wake of economic contraction. The report of the commission recommended that stabilization be sought through a significant adjustment to the fiscal accounts, achieved through a freeze on wages and salaries, a reduction in transfers to state enterprises, an increase in tariffs by state utilities, a reduction in subsidies, a review of the role of the state and rationalization of the portfolio of state enterprises, and reform of the public and private sectors. The report also recommended appropriate monetary policy adjustments to assist in the stabilization process. Finally, the Demas Report went beyond issues of stabilization to economic growth and adjustment, and advocated the importance of reorienting production to serve extraregional markets and of expanding the non-oil sectors of the economy. The focus of the report was on mechanisms to increase investment levels in the Trinidad economy.

Following receipt of the Demas Report in 1983, successive governments of Trinidad and Tobago implemented many of its recommendations with respect to both fiscal and monetary policy. The net result of these policies was that the economy of Trinidad and Tobago was able to adjust to a 50 per cent reduction in per capita income levels while controlling money supply and inflation. This ensured that Trinidadian firms did not encounter the risks associated with macroeconomic instability. These policies were not easily achieved, however, and Demas himself was, at one point, hung in effigy as Trinidadians protested against the short-term impact of the stabilization programme.

At the same time as the macroeconomic stabilization programme was initiated, the government began efforts to diversify the country's export base, as the second prong of its programme of risk reduction. In so doing, it drew on the recommendations of another high-level commission, the Non-Oil Committee. This committee recommended the establishment of an export development organization and the implementation of a programme of incentives designed to reduce the risks faced by Trinidadian manufacturing firms.

The incentives recommended and adopted included a programme of accelerated depreciation of capital equipment. This process involved firms being able to add additional investment allowances to the normal provisions for accelerated depreciation, which allowed them to depreciate capital equipment fully in the year of acquisition.

Other incentives that were introduced included a programme of flexible export allowances, in which firms received tax relief in direct proportion to their exports; a grant scheme for marketing related expenses, in which firms received 50 per cent of the cost of marketing expenses incurred in penetrating new extraregional export markets, but only up to the point of the first commercial shipment; tax deductions on promotional expenses, up to the amount of 150 per cent of approved expenses; and attempts to ensure that input costs were at international levels.[5]

Additionally, trade policy played a critical risk reduction role in the ultimate development of export competitiveness on the part of several Trinidadian firms, beginning with protection and extending to trade liberalization and the development of free trade agreements with neighbouring countries.

Beyond liberalization of trade, the Trinidadian government also engaged in a process of liberalizing other elements of its economy by the early 1990s. In particular, the foreign exchange system was liberalized in order to provide greater incentives for exporters and to eliminate this remaining distortion within the economy. Importantly, however, the liberalization process was managed very carefully. Trinidad's CARICOM neighbour, Jamaica, had liberalized shortly before Trinidad. Trinidadian policy makers sought to ensure that the Trinidad process would be conducted more smoothly than that of Jamaica, and, in particular, without the macroeconomic instability that had accompanied foreign exchange liberalization in Jamaica.

It was the combination of these mechanisms that had a powerful effect on the development of competitive export firms. To take but one example of their combined effect, the accelerated depreciation programme worked particularly well in the Trinidadian case because the firms had been profitable previously as a result of monopoly rents gained through a protectionist trade policy. Facing the choice of paying taxes or buying new equipment, these firms retooled. This retooling process, in large part, was what allowed many Trinidadian companies to take advantage of the export-oriented marketing and fiscal incentives when the country's trade policy shifted in the late 1980s. Confronted with excess capacity and increased competition in their domestic market, these firms could maintain their historical profit levels only through export-oriented production.

As a result of their successful efforts, Trinidad's nontraditional exports, particularly to the Jamaican market, to other countries in CARICOM and to Latin America increased substantially between the early 1980s and the mid-1990s.

Risk Reduction Efforts in Barbados

The principal risk reduction approach in Barbados was the stabilization policy pursued by the country in the wake of the 1991 fiscal crisis. This effort is comprehensively reviewed in chapter 3 of this volume.

Risk Reduction Efforts in Jamaica

The third illustration of a programme of reducing the risks associated with internationally competitive entrepreneurship comes from Jamaica, CARICOM's largest country and second largest economy. The Jamaican effort was captured in an industrial policy document that the Jamaican government unveiled in 1996.[6] The policy document represented a comprehensive effort to reduce the risks faced by Jamaican firms. It clearly articulated the government's intention to restore macroeconomic stability after some two decades of economic instability. The problem of macroeconomic instability in Jamaica had become particularly acute in the period immediately preceding the development of the industrial policy. The Jamaican government had liberalized its foreign exchange system in early 1991, amid increasing rates of money supply growth. Monetary expansion continued immediately after the liberalization, as the central bank engaged in a process of unsterilized acquisition of foreign exchange reserves.[7] The result of these actions was an inflation rate of over 80 per cent in fiscal year 1991–1992.

In light of the fiscal imbalances that had characterized the Jamaican economy for years, the industrial policy enunciated a process of focusing greater attention on fiscal policy than in the past, in order to achieve the hitherto elusive macroeconomic stability. It also focused on a social partnership among the key actors in the Jamaican economy: governments, unions and firms. Other risk reduction measures beyond stabilization of the macroeconomy included the development of infrastructure and the provision of performance-based incentives to which all exporters would be eligible, dedicated to assisting these exporters overcome the market access, financing and production risks to which they were subject.

Given constrained resources, the policy called for the targeting of infrastructure (though not of incentives to which all exporters would be eligible) to particular categories of firms. In so doing, the policy, based upon a detailed assessment of Jamaican industries and world market conditions, developed clusters of economic activity in which the country might be expected to have a competitive advantage. The targeted clusters included a tourism-based cluster which would be linked to entertainment, sports and crafts; an agro-processing cluster, linked to agriculture and marine products; a shipping-based cluster, linked to air-cargo; a mining-based cluster, driven by bauxite and alumina but linked to limestone, lime and industrial minerals; and an assembly-based cluster, driven by garment assembly but linked to the machine tool industry, textiles, footwear and assorted sewn products.

After the introduction of this policy, the Jamaican economy experienced three consecutive years of negative growth, the destruction of its indigenous financial sector, continued disinvestment in manufacturing, increasing levels of unemployment and a reduction in export activity. Clearly, the government's effort to reduce the risks associated with internationally competitive operations bore little, if any, dividend in the immediate aftermath of the policy's promulgation.

There are a number of factors that explain this failure, but chief among these was the fact that the most critical risk reduction element of the industrial policy was never effectively and comprehensively implemented. The policy was predicated upon the rapid (that is, within eighteen months) achievement of economic stability in Jamaica.[8] There were significant efforts to stabilize the Jamaican macroeconomy, with success in the reduction of money supply growth and its corollary, inflation. Unfortunately, however, against the explicit prescription of the industrial policy, this was not achieved through a focus on fiscal policy, but rather with a very heavy bias in the use of monetary policy. This policy mix kept real interest rates in Jamaica extremely high, and acted as a severe disincentive to internationally competitive economic activity. The fact that the proposed social partnership among the key actors in the economy was never implemented on an economy-wide basis also contributed to slowing the process of attaining macrostability.

The impact of high real interest rates and other outcomes of the disinflation strategy, as well as imprudent management by leaders in the financial sector, contributed to a severe crisis in the financial sector, which added significantly to the debt burden of the Jamaican government (see chapter 7).

As the Jamaican government's efforts to reduce risks generally were stymied, however, there was an important positive development in Jamaica that should assist in reducing the risk of establishing a certain type of investment, particularly in relation to addressing the challenges of globalization. This was the government's successful negotiation of liberalization in the telecommunications sector in 1999. This liberalization was achieved without having to resort to the politically risky approach of unilateral changes in the government's agreement with the monopoly telecommunications operator, Cable and Wireless, and without the country incurring the costs of providing monetary compensation to Cable and Wireless.

Much earlier, in 1988, as a part of its privatization programme, the Jamaican government had granted five telecommunications operating licences to Cable and Wireless, the new majority owner of the nation's telecommunications system. But, unlike in other countries in Latin America that were privatizing telecommunications at that time, the Jamaican government granted Cable and Wireless a monopoly over both local and long-distance traffic. This monopoly was granted for a twenty-five-year period, with an option to renew for another twenty-five years, up until 2038. The negotiations associated with this privatization showed little evidence of careful preparation on the part of the government; for example, there was no bidding process, and negotiations were conducted only with Cable and Wireless.[9]

Eventually, the Jamaican government came to realize that it had negotiated an inappropriate agreement. The agreement did create an incentive for capital expansion, leading to the installation of critically needed telephone lines. But the absence of competition was a disincentive to investments in the type of technology that were critical to the country's effort to keep pace with the technological changes that are a central element of the process of globalization.

Consequently, in 1999, the Jamaican government negotiated a new agreement with Cable and Wireless.[10] This agreement established the basis for an orderly transition to open competition in the Jamaican telecommunications sector, and a process for revoking Cable and Wireless's existing licence, and establishing a new regulatory regime.[11] The "Heads of Agreement" negotiated between the Government of Jamaica and Cable and Wireless called for continued expansion in the telecommunications network, the phased introduction of competition over three years, and full liberalization of the Jamaican telecommunications industry by the third anniversary of the agreement. This process of liberalization was expected to contribute to increases in investment, jobs and exports.[12]

By 2002, despite the continued problems associated with the country's policy reform efforts,[13] the economy was more stable, interest rates were declining and economic growth had returned. Still, two critical risk indicators had the potential of thwarting hopes of long-term economic recovery: continued high levels of debt and intolerable levels of violent crime.

Risk Reduction Efforts in Guyana

The process of liberalization has also been at the forefront of risk reduction efforts in Guyana, our final case of risk reduction efforts in a CARICOM MDC. Between independence in 1966, and 1988, Guyana pursued an economic policy of co-operative socialism. The state played a very significant role in productive activities within the economy, including intervening through price, credit and foreign exchange controls, and restricting foreign and domestic private investment. In particular, the two most significant components of the economy, the sugar and bauxite industries, were nationalized.

The result was slow growth in income. Economic growth averaged an anaemic 0.4 per cent per year between 1966 and 1988. In the period after nationalization of the bauxite and sugar industries, the production of sugar fell from 350,000 tons per year to 130,000 tons, and that of calcined bauxite from over 800,000 tons per year to less than 200,000 tons. The period saw a steady emigration of skilled personnel. The private sector responded to the strict controls imposed upon their activities by transacting business outside the official economy, leading to the development of a strong underground economy. Further, the reduced revenue and the emigration of skills during this period led to a breakdown in the provision of infrastructure and to reduced quality in social services such as health and education. The situation steadily worsened, and during the period 1980–1988, GDP declined by 2.8 per cent per year, while external debt increased significantly to a level of US$2.4 billion, or some six times the country's GDP.

It was against this backdrop that the government began in 1988 a process of changing its economic policy. The new policy had two objectives. The first was the encouragement of private investment that would improve the economy's growth prospects. The second was a focus on reducing the risks associated with the introduction of the type of private investment likely to be most effective at improving prospects for economic growth. The government embarked upon an "Economic Recovery Programme" designed to shift the country towards a market economy. This programme included enhanced fiscal performance through expenditure restraint and tax reform, the abolition of price controls, and the liberalization of the financial and foreign exchange systems. It also included the liberalization of trade through tariff reductions and the elimination of import restrictions, the implementation of a programme of privatization, and the liberalization of the country's foreign investment regime.

Growth in Guyana increased significantly after the introduction of the economic recovery programme. The economy grew by an average of 5 per cent per year between 1989 and 1997, for example. Linked to this, the country maintained relative macroeconomic stability. Inflation declined from 83 per cent in 1991 to 10 per cent in 1993 and 4 per cent by 1997. Between 1990 and 1996, the overall public sector deficit declined from 65 per cent to 11 per cent of GDP. External debt declined from US$2.5 billion to US$1.4 billion, albeit largely due to a significant debt write-off from Guyana's Paris Club of creditors.

Although the Guyanese economy has grown since liberalization, this growth has been in the traditional, commodity-driven sectors of the economy: forestry, gold and sugar, for example. The programme of risk reduction has yet to lead to movement towards international competitiveness more broadly throughout the economy. Indeed, also troubling is the fact that the 1998–1999 period saw an increase in another form of risk, political risk, which will need to be resolved before one can anticipate significant new private-sector investment, or the return of scarce technical skills to the country. In the late 1990s per capita incomes in Guyana were increasing, and exports comprised a significant component of GDP (as much as 80 per cent, as shown in chapter 1). Yet, at the same time, Guyana continued to rank as one of the poorest economies in the Western Hemisphere.

Lessons from the Risk Reduction Efforts of CARICOM MDCs

The experiences of these four CARICOM MDCs provide lessons for developing economies, with respect to efforts to increase levels of international competitiveness amid the challenges of globalization.

The Importance of Fiscal Responsibility in Liberalization and Stabilization Efforts

The experiences of these four economies point to the positive impact that liberalization and stabilization policies can have on economic growth. In the case of Trinidad and Tobago, the stabilization process sought to induce private-sector investment, while the incentive and liberalization processes tried to improve the international competitiveness of that investment, with positive consequences on growth. Liberalization and stabilization were also critical in contributing to growth in the Guyanese economy, and stabilization efforts in Barbados were instrumental in maintaining and enhancing the competitiveness of that economy, particularly in the context of its fixed exchange rate regime.

But these experiences, and that of Jamaica, also illustrate how important fiscal responsibility is in stabilization and liberalization efforts. In Jamaica, liberalization and the subsequent efforts at stabilization did not immediately lead to growth in the Jamaican economy. This was largely because the stabilization process relied disproportionately on the use of monetary policy. Recall that an important part of the stabilization process in Jamaica related to the need to redress the problems of monetary creation that resulted from unsterilized acquisition of foreign exchange reserves in the immediate post-liberalization period. The heavy use of monetary policy, in the face of lax fiscal policy, led to extremely high nominal and real interest rates.[14] These did nothing to reduce either the absolute or the relative risks associated with internationally competitive activity.

In contrast to the Jamaican experience, the liberalization and stabilization policies in Trinidad and Tobago, Barbados, and Guyana all placed a premium on fiscal responsibility. The lessons on this point seem particularly clear.

The Risks Associated with Targeted Risk Reduction Measures

Governments in small developing economies ought to seek to reduce the risks associated with internationally competitive activity. And macroeconomic instability is certainly a highly visible risk that ought to be reduced. Macroeconomic stabilization is also, however, one of the risk reduction activities that is most general in scope: that is, it does not involve much in the way of selectivity. But in their efforts to reduce risks, policy makers encounter a strong temptation to engage in a process of selective risk reduction.[15] This typically involves identifying sectors or firms likely to be of most national benefit and focusing the risk reduction process on these firms and industries. Such an approach, while tempting, is also difficult to implement in an effective manner.

The difficulty, of course, lies in the choice of the appropriate industries or firms on which to focus risk reduction efforts. Historically, different industries have found favour. Agriculture was the favoured industry at one point. Then there was the move to manufacturing, operating on the premise that developing countries had to "industrialize". As more and more economies have shifted towards services, these have been viewed as the economic sectors of the future and have represented the "flavour of the day".

But more recently, analysts have pointed out that the appropriate focus should not be by industry, but rather by the orientation of industry. Thus, governments should not "pick winners" but rather allow the winners to pick themselves, by focusing on existing exporters, for example. Governments, according to this view, should seek to reduce the risks faced by existing exporters whether they are involved in agriculture, manufacturing or services. Of course, this takes us to the observations about the broad scope of internationally competitive activity which were developed in the first chapter of this volume.

It would seem obvious that exporters should be the favoured progeny of the national economy. After all, they generate the foreign exchange that pays for imports. Is it not they, therefore, who should have their risks reduced preferentially because of the positive externalities they generate for the economy as a whole? But if exporting is all that matters, why is it that Guyana, where exports are a far greater proportion of the national economy than in Barbados, is so poor relative to Barbados? Why is it that Trinidad, routinely viewed as the export powerhouse of the Caribbean, exports less as a proportion of its national production base than a poorer CARICOM MDC, Jamaica?

The answer, as pointed out in chapter 1, is that exporting is not "all that matters". Effective state intervention that seeks to reduce risks preferentially should be targeting industries or sectors where a given risk reduction intervention should lead to the highest improvement in productivity. In some cases, this is easy to measure or to estimate. Most cases of risk reduction, however, are not easily tied to productivity enhancement and, therefore, require careful analysis.

This is not to suggest that there is no case for targeted risk reduction measures, for example in the form of infrastructural enhancement, but rather that the process of choosing the appropriate intervention target is not simple, and can easily result in a misallocation of resources. If the appropriate target were all exporters, as is the current fashion in many countries, the analysis would be relatively simple. But, in the context of this volume's broader perspective on international competitiveness, the optimal target is a recipient that is likely to benefit most in enhanced international competitiveness (or relative productivity) from the intervention. Here, a measurement problem arises; this problem can lead to a misallocation of resources. The probability of misallocation increases as the risk reduction effort is more narrowly targeted.

The Importance of International Benchmarking for All Sectors

The final lesson of this chapter, particularly in the context of the challenge of globalization, is the importance of benchmarking against international competition in all sectors of the national economy. This is, in essence, the burden of the more expansive definition of international competitiveness, and the challenge of an increasingly borderless world.

Even in small economies, such as those of the Caribbean, almost half of all economic activity is not involved in direct exports. Some component of the remainder of the economy will encounter international competition directly in the form of imports. If globalization and trade liberalization continue their march forward, overcoming the opposition to the process pointed out in the introduction to this volume, this competition is likely to become even more direct. Both of these groups will, therefore, inevitably be confronted with the need to assess the capabilities of international competitors and measure these capabilities against their own.

This process must also operate in other segments of the economy in the context of a national competitive strategy, particularly for small economies.

International benchmarking has to be extended to the government bureaucratic apparatus, health sector,[16] education sector, energy sector, financial sector and distributive trade, to name a few examples. In part this is because many of these sectors are also increasingly likely to encounter competitive threats as services, for example, are more easily purchased and sold across borders. But it is also important because the productivity of export sectors is directly affected by the level of international competitiveness of other sectors of the economy.

This chapter's proposal for a comprehensive examination of the international competitiveness challenge is not to suggest that all sectors of an economy will move with equal alacrity to international standards. What this approach does suggest, however, is that, in a globalizing world, the effort to enhance the level of national competitiveness should be broadly defined and inclusionary, and be pragmatic and as nondiscriminatory in its orientation as possible. Ideally, it should discriminate, where necessary, only in favour of optimizing the process of relative productivity enhancement. This is the complex, process-oriented arena in which governments will be faced with the challenge of enhancing the international competitiveness of their nation states, in a world marked by increasingly more integrated markets.

Chapter 5

Growth, Public Policy and Sovereignty

As discussed in previous chapters, the efforts to enhance the competitiveness of a country's institutions are designed to accelerate economic development and improve national welfare. Since governments in many countries have accepted the doctrine that "the private sector is the engine of economic growth", however, there is dispute as to whether the challenge of accelerating levels of economic development is one that is to be overcome via public policy or through private entrepreneurial activity.

One immediately recognizes that the appropriate response is neither public policy nor private entrepreneurship, but rather both. But it is important to express with some greater degree of detail the nature of the respective roles of these actors. This chapter focuses on the role of public policy in driving economic growth, assesses the extent to which these policies vary between small and larger countries, and evaluates the linkages between growth-oriented public policies and sovereignty. Subsequent chapters will focus on the particular role of private sector institutions in generating economic growth through a process of enhanced firm-level competitiveness.

Growth and Development

Since improving the level of development in a country requires increasing rates of economic growth, this chapter, beyond the next few paragraphs, will not make distinctions between growth and development. This is not to suggest that economic growth and development are completely synonymous. Clearly it is possible for countries to experience increased income levels and not to have those levels translated into improved development, particularly for the majority of the population. Increased income could be channelled into the pockets of a minority of a country's population and thereby result in worsening inequality. Indeed, it is possible that worsening inequality resulting from unequally distributed economic growth could lower the average development level for the population.

The proceeds from economic growth could be used to acquire weapons that are used to intimidate neighbouring populations and even the citizens of the country who produced the growth. Economic growth could come at the expense of environmental degradation that discounts the development prospects of future generations. There are many possibilities, each of which could justify its own separate and exhaustive discussion. But, having dealt with all these possibilities, there still remains the conceptual and empirical reality: it is extraordinarily difficult for countries to accelerate levels of development without increasing levels of economic growth. Consequently, the role of public policy in accelerating development is first one of managing a process of economic growth.

Public Policy and Economic Growth

Can countries manage their way towards economic growth, or is economic growth an elusive variable that is associated more with chance than with purposive action? Clearly, the answer to this question will identify the nature and extent of public policy's potential role in generating economic growth. There are, indeed, a number of perspectives on the factors that drive economic growth, and each of these suggests that economic growth occurs not by happenstance, but is more likely under particular circumstances. Public policy is one of the most important influences on these circumstances that make growth more or less likely.

For several years the multilateral institutions, notably the World Bank and the IMF, have advocated a perspective that they argue creates the conditions for economic growth. This so-called Washington Consensus suggests that economic growth is more likely in situations where countries adopt the following policy prescriptions: fiscal discipline; public expenditure priorities in education and health; tax reform; positive but moderate market-determined interest rates; competitive exchange rates; liberal trade policies; openness to FDI; privatization; deregulation; and protection of property rights.[1] Note that this Washington Consensus represents a menu of policy instruments lying solely within the ambit of public policy.

The Washington Consensus has been criticized from both within and outside of Washington. Scholars whose work focuses on the dilemma characterizing developing countries have been most scathing in their criticisms of the notion of a universalistic policy prescription to the development problem that is anchored primarily in the notion of economic liberalization.[2] From inside Washington, the principal criticism of the Washington Consensus in recent years has not been to suggest that the policy prescriptions are incorrect, but rather that the Washington institutions have been naïve in their de-emphasis of the importance of institutions in the implementation of policy.[3] Indeed, this recent recognition of the importance of institutions is captured in a new school of economic thought: the new institutional economics (NIE).

The NIE does not reject the importance of the principles espoused by the Washington Consensus but, instead, it seeks to provide explanations for the lack of success of these principles in generating the level of economic growth and development expected by adherents to the Washington Consensus. Note, for example, the response of a leading advocate of the NIE:

> An aspect of economic development that has been relatively neglected by economists is the administrative capacity of government. Development practitioners have long been acutely aware of the enormous gap between policy pronouncements and implementation on the ground, but this recognition has often been missing from accounts by economists of the determinants of prosperity. The NIE has called attention to the vital role of government administrative capacity in shaping the institutional environment of business. Moreover the NIE – and in particular the new economics of organization – may help to explain why bureaucracies perform well or badly and how the inefficient and corrupt ones might be reformed.[4]

With this focus on the importance of the institutional environment surrounding economic policy, the views of the NIE intersect, at one level, with those of developing country scholars who have long argued for a perspective on the economic reform process that was less universalistic in its prescriptions, and that recognized the importance of incorporating political and social variables into the economic reform equation.

Empirical work on the factors affecting economic growth has tended to incorporate elements both of the Washington Consensus and the NIE. This work has also implied that public policy is the most critical variable in determining growth trajectories in countries. Barro,[5] for example, points to several factors as determinants of economic growth. He identifies initial levels of GDP having a negative relationship with growth. This negative relationship provides some evidence of the potential convergence effect in inter-country income levels anticipated in neoclassical growth theory. This relationship, however, is not consistent with endogenous growth theories, which tend to resonate more closely with current thinking on growth patterns.

Other variables with a negative relationship to growth in the empirical analyses conducted by Barro include the fertility rate, government consumption ratio, and inflation. Variables with a positive relationship to rates of per capita economic growth include male secondary and higher schooling, life expectancy levels, the rule of law index, the terms of trade change, and democracy levels.

Yet another stream of research on economic growth focuses exclusively on the appropriate nature of government intervention within economies, as elaborated on in the previous chapter in the area of governmental targeting of candidates for risk reduction. Debate on the nature of government intervention was crystallized in attempts to identify the parenthood of the East Asian "Growth Miracle" during the period from the late 1960s to the late 1990s. Analysts on both sides of the debate found fodder for their arguments in the successes of East Asian economies.

The approach of the Washington Consensus to government intervention, which focused on macroeconomic stability and economic liberalization, in the context of broad-based, functional interventions of government, found support in the policies of East Asian countries. But so too did those advocates of more targeted selective government intervention.

Research on Caribbean economies has suggested that the functional versus selective intervention divide in relation to the role of government may be overstated, since the fundamental policy challenge of governments in developing countries is to reduce the risks associated with the nurturing of internationally competitive entrepreneurial activity. Such a process will require functional interventions, but may well also require selective interventions (see chapter 4 in this volume).

Another perspective on the determinants of economic growth examines this issue in the context of the competitiveness of nations.[6] Porter's well-known typology of the conditions that nurture competitive industries and firms in countries focuses on the importance of competitive domestic markets, interindustry linkages and the development of natural and human resources and high standards. Porter views the role of public policy as ensuring competitive markets, aiding in the development of natural and human resources, and enforcing high product standards.

Thus, in all the varied discussions on facilitating economic growth, there is no debate about whether there is an important role for public policy. The debate lies only in the precise configuration of that role. Pulling the various policy prescriptions together, important growth-inducing policy variables appear to be macroeconomic stability, anchored by fiscal discipline and relatively low levels of government consumption, but with public expenditure priorities that include health, education and physical infrastructure.

Three other variables present themselves: ongoing efforts to improve the country's terms of trade; the protection of property rights and a dedication to the rule of law, both of which are most likely to be implemented through democratic systems of governance; and the development of competitive, but appropriately regulated, domestic markets. These policies also need to be implemented through institutions dedicated to sound governance and in recognition of the particular social and political realities of the country in question.

Although the above focus is on public policy, the role of government in accelerating rates of economic growth needs to also reflect an enterprise focus: that is, a principal objective of government ought to be to create an environment conducive to investment by private capital since, as pointed out in chapter 4, a key development challenge confronting developing countries is an inadequacy of internationally competitive entrepreneurial activity.

Public policy can address this challenge by seeking to attract internationally competitive firms from abroad, and by reducing the risks associated with internationally competitive activity by indigenous firms. Risk-reducing activity includes several of the policy goals identified heretofore: macroeconomic stability, macropolicy stability, enforcement of the rule of law and appropriate levels of publicly organized infrastructure. But risk-reducing activity also includes appropriate management of trade and economic liberalization, and governmental assistance in reducing the production, marketing and finance risks confronting enterprises seeking to move towards international standards of performance. Table 5.1 summarizes the elements of a growth-inducing public policy agenda, based upon the literature on economic growth.

Table 5.1: Elements of a Growth-Inducing Public Policy Agenda

Macroeconomic stability (defined by low inflation, low interest rates, sustainable fiscal and external positions).

Macropolitical stability (observed through consistency of public policy, maintenance of rule of law, belief in integrity of contracts, protection of property rights).

Government consumption (expenditure) priorities (focused on health, education, physical and intellectual infrastructure).

Competitive but appropriately regulated domestic markets.

Improvement in terms of trade (through encouragement of higher local value-added, productivity improvement, innovation).

Enterprise focus on enhancement of internationally competitive activity (through attraction of internationally competitive enterprise and by reducing the risks, such as macroinstability, poor infrastructure, production, finance, marketing, inappropriate government regulations and avoidable costs, facing indigenous enterprises seeking to become internationally competitive).

Institutional focus on sound governance.

Orientation to, and embrace of, environmental, social and cultural realities of country.

Public Policy and Economic Growth in Small Countries

This chapter has yet to address the issue of whether the role of public policy in addressing the challenge of advancing rates of economic growth differs between small and large countries. The literature on the determinants of growth in small countries is not nearly as rich as the literature on the determinants of growth across all types of countries. Indeed, the literature is virtually silent on the notion that country size matters, conceptually, in relation to economic growth.

In this chapter I submit the proposition that the variables affecting economic growth do not vary significantly between small and large countries, but that attention to many of the growth-inducing variables recorded in table 5.1, from a public policy perspective, is even more significant in small countries than in large countries. In essence, the proposition is that small countries have fewer degrees of freedom, that is, fewer opportunities for correcting policy errors, in relation to the linkage between public policy and economic growth. I elaborate upon these issues in the following sections.

The Challenge of Stabilizing Macroeconomies in Small Countries

In all countries, the achievement of macroeconomic stability is evidenced by low relative inflation, low relative interest rates and sustainable fiscal and external positions. There are two sets of related activities that drive a process of macroeconomic stability: government monetary and fiscal policy, on the one hand, and balance of payments management on the other. Small countries face similar challenges to large countries in the area of government monetary and fiscal policy management. For all countries, an important mechanism for monetary policy management has involved insulating monetary authorities from direct and ongoing political influence.

In some countries this insulation is achieved through the independence of a national monetary authority; in others, through the ceding of national monetary authority to regional institutions;[7] and in yet others, by the coupling of pegged currencies to open foreign exchange windows, thereby effectively restricting the national monetary authority's ability to change money supply conditions.[8] Small countries that have insulated their monetary authorities from direct and ongoing political influence through one of the above mechanisms have tended to enjoy higher income levels than their counterparts that have not implemented such insulation measures, as shown in the context of the Caribbean (see table 5.2). (Note also the discussion on this point in chapter 2 of this volume.)

The insulation of monetary authorities from political influence is only one leg of the macroeconomic stability challenge facing small countries. Another is the peculiar challenge such countries face relating to maintaining sustainable external positions. Small countries are much more heavily reliant on external trade than larger countries, simply based upon their greater need to specialize because they have a narrower set of factor endowments than larger countries.

With this production specialization comes the likelihood of greater variability in export earnings. A dip in world markets associated with one or two

Table 5.2: Relationship between Per-Capita Income Levels and National Political Control of Money Authorities in the Caribbean

Territory	Population	National Political Control over Monetary Authority	Income Category
Anguilla	9,000	No: Member of OECS	Upper middle income
Antigua and Barbuda	66,000	No: Member of OECS	Upper middle income
Aruba	84,000	No: Partner territory within Kingdom of Netherlands	High income
Bahamas	278,000	No: Pegged currency with open forex window	High income
Barbados	260,000	No: Pegged currency with open forex window	Upper middle income
Belize	210,000	No: Pegged currency with open forex window	Lower middle income
Bermuda	60,000	No: Pegged currency with open forex window	High Income
British Virgin Islands	16,000	No: Dollarized	High income
Cayman Islands	32,800	No: Pegged currency with open forex window	High income
Cuba	**11m**	**Yes**	**Lower middle income**
Dominica	71,000	No: Member of OECS	Lower middle income
Dominican Republic	**7.7m**	**Yes**	**Lower middle income**
French Guiana	146,000	No: Pegged currency with open forex window	High income
French West Indies (Guadeloupe, Martinique, St Martin, St Barthélémy)	519,000	No: currency of France is legal tender	Upper middle income
Grenada	91,000	No: Member of OECS	Lower middle income
Guyana	**758,000**	**Yes**	**Low income**
Haiti	**6.5m**	**Yes**	**Low income**
Jamaica	**2.5m**	**Yes**	**Lower middle income**
Montserrat	11,000	No: Member of OECS	Upper middle income
Netherlands Antilles (Curaçao, Bonaire, Saba, St Maarten, St Eustatius)	190,000	No: Pegged currency with open forex window	High income
Puerto Rico	3.5m	No: Dollarized	Upper middle income
St Kitts and Nevis	42,000	No: Member of OECS	Upper middle income
St Lucia	138,000	No: Member of OECS	Upper middle income
St Vincent and Grenadines	108,000	No: Member of OECS	Lower middle income
Suriname	**425,000**	**Yes**	**Lower middle income**
Trinidad and Tobago	**1.3m**	**Yes**	**Upper middle income**
Turks and Caicos Islands	15,000	No: Dollarized	High income
US Virgin Islands	102,000	No: Dollarized	High income

industries can have a devastating impact on export earnings for small economies. In order to maintain consumption levels in the face of reductions in export earnings, such countries often feel the need to borrow on external markets, with the hope of repaying such loans from increased future earnings. If therefore, instead of variability, there is actually a secular decline in world market prices for the exports of these countries, then their balance of payments accounts (external accounts) are likely to be shifted into an unsustainable position.

The Challenge of Macropolitical Stability in Small Countries

An important growth-inducing policy variable for all countries is macropolitical stability. Macropolitical stability relates to the consistency of public policy, the maintenance of the rule of law, the protection of property rights, and the government's role in protecting the integrity of contracts through the judiciary and by government example. Such stability is necessary to facilitate private investment activity.

While macropolitical stability is an important growth-inducing variable in all countries, it is particularly important in small countries because the citizens of small countries tend to emigrate to a greater extent than those of larger countries. It is not unusual for small countries to be able to report that as many of their citizens live abroad as at home. Such a statistic is far less likely to emanate from a large country, where there are greater possibilities for internal migration.

But even when citizens of small countries do not emigrate, they often ensure that their capital resides in other places. This strategy is largely one of risk diversification. Although this problem affects small countries differentially, it is not unique to small countries. Developing countries, as a group, have experienced capital flight and diversification activities over many years. And it is a problem that is very amenable to policy solutions. Thus, in many developing countries, the action taken by governments to liberalize foreign exchange regimes has resulted in massive reflows of capital to the country. But, nevertheless, the particular risk factors inherent, by definition, in small countries ensure that issues of macropolitical stability are even more critical for these countries than they are for larger countries.

The Challenge of Government Consumption
Levels and Expenditure Priorities

Another policy variable that is particularly important in the context of small countries is the extent to which government consumption comprises a reasonable proportion of national GDP. The empirical reality is that government consumption levels at high proportions of GDP have not been associated with rapid levels of economic growth.

Yet this does not suggest that certain types of government consumption and expenditure are not important for growth. Expenditure on particular public goods is quite important. The most critical public goods in this regard are education, health and infrastructure. None of these can be completely characterized as public goods. In all cases, there is the possibility and, indeed, the desirability of some component of private financing. But no country has been able to leave all expenditure in these areas up to the vicissitudes of the private marketplace.

For small countries, there is both an opportunity and a need to focus even more narrowly on expenditure priorities than is true in larger countries. The opportunity arises from the fact that small countries can, reasonably, dispense with one of the public expenditure items regarded as critical in larger countries: external defence.

A small country cannot mount a reasonable physical defence of its territory from any much larger country interested in territorial acquisition. The options for such a country, therefore, become alignment with a regional defence programme, or reliance on the acquisitive intentions of a potential marauding territory being held at bay by the opprobrium of the international community. In neither case does maintaining a standing army to protect the territory against external attack appear to be a reasonable government expenditure priority.[9] Costa Rica, for example, has long and famously adopted a policy of no standing army.

While the expenditure priority of external security ought to be of less importance to a small country, that of infrastructure development typically takes on even greater urgency. This relates to the importance of infrastructure to small countries, as pointed out in chapter 1.

The Challenge of Creating Competitive, Appropriately Regulated Domestic Markets

The scale of small countries creates a peculiar challenge in nurturing competitive domestic markets. Several generations of economists have spoken to the importance of competition in spurring innovation and growth, yet for several decades domestic competition in many developing and developed countries was stifled in favour of nurturing national champion firms.

It is easy to understand why governments in small developing countries have accepted the argument of national champions. Whereas the logic for national champion protection in a continental-sized country such as India is hard to discern, one can more readily understand why governments of small developing countries would posit that the small scale of their country can only accommodate a single firm. And, further, that this firm would need to have exclusive access to the local market in order to gain the dynamic scale and learning efficiencies implicit in endogenous growth theories. Only then, goes the argument, could the national champion firm compete with its international counterparts.

But governments of small countries need to resist this argument. Some of these national champions have matured into world-class companies,[10] but by far the majority of companies sheltered from both domestic and international competition have not performed well.[11] It is this empirical reality that has reinvigorated an emphasis on the importance of competitive domestic markets, both for goods and in areas such as foreign exchange systems and financial markets.

For many countries, however, the movement to liberalize domestic markets in goods, services and finance has created additional problems because of the approach to liberalization. Financial markets represent the most striking example of liberalization gone awry in many developing countries. Many countries liberalized financial markets by allowing many additional players to enter their financial markets without improving their regulatory systems and procedures.

This poor regulation of financial institutions was later to be evidenced in financial crises associated with undercapitalized financial institutions engaged in imprudent lending practices, often in the form of lending to connected parties.[12] Further, liberalization of foreign exchange markets has to be appropriately managed because of the potential challenges of speculative foreign exchange activity. It is for this reason that an emphasis on competitive markets must be linked to the importance of regulation, particularly in areas such as finance and infrastructure.

The Challenge of Improving Terms of Trade

The ultimate path to improving economic growth and development lies in productivity improvements across the economy. For all countries, one indication of improved productivity relative to comparator countries lies in improvements in the ratio of prices of exports to prices of imports, or improvement in the country's terms of trade. This improvement is critical in small countries also, but for such countries the terms of trade variable is likely to loom even larger as a predictor of economic growth because of the extent to which small countries rely on trade compared to larger countries.

Improvement in the terms of trade is also important for small countries because these countries are less likely to have the diversification effect of producing many different products for world markets. Countries with a diversified production base are more likely to find that their export revenues are stable because the products they produce benefit from market cycles that move in offsetting directions.

The Challenge of Assisting Enterprises Enhance Internationally Competitive Activity

In many respects, creating an environment in which enterprises can operate at an internationally competitive level is one of the most significant challenges facing public policy in developing countries. There are two related mechanisms available for responding to the challenge of enhancing levels of internationally competitive activity by resident firms. The first mechanism is that of attracting to the country firms that have demonstrated their internationally competitive credentials in other sovereign jurisdictions.

This strategy differs from the industrialization-by-invitation strategies applied by developing countries during the era of import-substitution industrialization. In that former era, many of the foreign companies invited to enter did not take with them internationally competitive business operations. These companies were attracted by the competition restrictions they were offered as an investment incentive, and many of these operations never achieved world-class operating levels. As developing countries have liberalized trade, many such investments have disappeared as foreign investors have shifted from multi-domestic to global investment strategies in response to the trade liberalization activities of developing country governments.

For small developing countries the challenge of attracting internationally competitive FDI is twofold. First, such countries have to be willing to accommodate such investment and to implement policies that will make their territories conducive to investment, following on some key examples of success stories of investment attraction in developing countries.[13] In some cases these policies run afoul of concerns relating to sovereignty. Issues, for example, such as allowing foreigners to own land in the quantities necessary for investment in tourism or agriculture, liberal approaches to expatriate employment and equity involvement, and simplified business regulatory processes have been troubling for governments in many small countries.

But even governments that have dealt with these issues find that they continue to face a significant problem when seeking to attract internationally competitive FDI. Small developing countries have relatively weak bargaining power when seeking to attract FDI. Thus, even those small developing countries eager to attract investment find it very difficult to attract significant amounts of export-oriented FDI, despite all the advice about how to attract such investment,[14] in an environment where the competition from all countries for attracting such investment is extremely intense, as discussed in greater detail in chapter 6 of this volume.

FDI attracted to small developing countries is particularly beneficial, because these enterprises are much more likely than domestic firms to build internationally competitive production facilities. But, in the absence of the panacea of investment attraction,[15] governments of small developing countries are likely to have to improve levels of international competitiveness among resident firms the hard, slow way. They are going to have to systematically reduce the risks associated with developing internationally competitive enterprises, as noted in chapter 4.

This risk-reducing activity involves several of the policy planks already discussed: macroeconomic stability, macropolitical stability, development of physical and intellectual infrastructure. But it also involves assisting resident enterprises, through training and other programmes, with the production, financing and marketing risks they face in seeking to improve their perform-ance to world-class levels of operation. That is, the process of explicitly focus-ing on enhancing enterprise performance involves more than the ideology that unfettered markets alone will lead to high-performing enterprises.

This risk-reducing activity, focused at the level of enterprises, is likely to be particularly important to the enterprises in small developing countries, which will experience scale and associated self-confidence problems that militate against effectively competing on an international basis. In all of these efforts, governments in small developing countries will need to emphasize the impor-tance of sound institutions in responding to the various policy challenges, be alert to the peculiar realities of their national settings, and wrestle with the implications of policy on national sovereignty.

The Challenge of Governance and National Realities

Institutions matter for economic growth, but they probably matter even more for small countries than for large ones. The importance of institutions and sound governance in the context of small countries relates to the fact that these countries are unlikely to be able to experiment simultaneously with different policy approaches. This is in contrast, for example, to a country like China, with defined regions that allow for multiple policy approaches to take place simultaneously.

In small countries, national policy is all policy, and mistakes made at the level of national policy and governance are likely to reverberate throughout the entire economy. On the positive side, successful national policy is likely to have an immediate effect on the entire country. This is yet another manifestation of the risky nature of small countries, which have few opportunities for diversifi-cation, even at the level of policy.

Small countries are not unique in the need to incorporate national realities, whether social, environmental or cultural, into the process of developing an agenda for growth. For many small countries, however, these realities are par-ticularly pressing. Environmental issues, for example, are often far more urgent in the context of small economies because of limited land space, and because many small countries are islands, whose competitive advantages are tied closely to the quality of their natural environments. Further, the fact of small size also places a premium on the importance of maintaining a distinctive culture, since the culture of a small country is easily overwhelmed by the dominant cultures of neighbouring large countries.

Indeed, for small countries there is often an ongoing focus on the need to establish a rationale for the existence of the territory as a nation state. It is for this reason that issues of sovereignty are of so much concern in the context of small countries. Indeed, it is possible that concerns surrounding sovereignty can have an impact on factors linked to growth and development.

The Challenge of Coupling Growth with Sovereignty

One of the overarching challenges facing small countries is that of whether their desire for sovereignty could impede their ability to grow and develop. In essence, the question is linked to that of whether or not there is a minimum efficient scale (MES) for a country. Does a territory require a certain population level or size before it can operate as an economically viable country, able to take onto itself all the trappings of statehood? A related question is whether or not territories can operate at levels below the MES if they are willing to give up some of the normal symbols attributable to a sovereign nation.

There are at least four public policy variables in which there seems to be potential tension between sovereignty and economic growth in the context of small economies. These are: macroeconomic stability, investment attraction, the nurturing of national champions, and public expenditure on an externally focused military.

The discussion of macroeconomic stability pointed out that, generally, countries seem much better positioned to maintain a level of macroeconomic stability if they insulate their monetary authorities from direct and ongoing political influence. Improper management of a country's supply of domestic currency is the primary cause of macroeconomic instability. Pressures to increase the stock of domestic currency for political reasons are so strong that it is difficult for political authorities to resist such pressures unless there is an institutional mechanism that impedes their ability to act impulsively and unilaterally in this regard.

Although political authorities of all countries face such pressures, those in small countries are particularly vulnerable, because in small territories governments often operate paternalistically, and the public perceives the government as the solution to economic problems. High-income small countries have, generally, insulated their monetary authorities from political influence. In so doing, they have given up one of the institutions that has historically been viewed as a trapping of sovereignty: a fully functioning central bank under the political control of the nation state.

Another area of potential tension is that of investment attraction. Many developing countries have been concerned about the effects of significant inflows of FDI, but small countries have seemed particularly concerned. Many such countries are ex-colonies in which foreign capital was linked to foreign political control, which together are believed to have conspired to ensure that local peoples had no form of self-determination. It is in this context that suspicions abound about the impact of FDI on the viability of local businesses, on the country's nonrenewable resources, on the access of local interests to the land of the small country,[16] and on the ability of locals to obtain reasonable positions in foreign-controlled companies.

On the other hand, small countries are recognizing that this tension is least gripping in the context of the type of FDI likely to be attracted to small countries in the current era of liberal trade: internationally competitive export-oriented FDI. Small countries have been at the forefront in developing linkages between this type of FDI and indigenous firms, for example.[17]

Indeed, the process of developing linkages with foreign direct investors and of exposing local companies to competition from home and abroad is proving to be more effective in improving the competitiveness of local firms, even in small developing countries, than was the strategy of nurturing national champions via protection from foreign and local competition. On the other hand, in this new approach to developing competitive enterprises, it is more difficult for governments to dictate which firms and industries will be targeted for champion status. As a consequence, countries may find that some of the industries that seemed to be synonymous with sovereign status are not viable, whether these are airlines, financial institutions or other flag-flying entities.

A final area of potential tension between growth-inducing variables and sovereignty is national security. Historically, the *sine qua non* of sovereign status has been the ability to mount a military force that can defend the country from external attack. Yet it seems quite clear that small countries that focus government expenditure on the development of a military defence capability are likely to have to trade off their supposedly enhanced security against economic growth. Since, regardless of the amount spent on augmenting such a security presence, such countries will have no forces capable of deterring attacks by the many larger countries that surround them, this raises the question of the utility of such a force.

De-emphasis of forces for external security does not have to be viewed as a sacrifice of sovereignty, but instead a focus on economic rather than military sovereignty. In this area, like that of macroeconomic policy, the seeming decline in national sovereignty can be made more palatable by ceding power to regional authorities. By coupling regional action in some areas with national action in others, small countries can effectively reduce the MES of a country, while continuing to grow and develop.

Indeed, examples of tiny countries suggest that the MES for a country is very low. The independent country with the lowest population is probably St Kitts and Nevis in the Caribbean, with a population of forty-one thousand and a 1998 per capita income of US$6,130. But this country has joined with others in the Organisation of Eastern Caribbean States and ceded responsibility for monetary affairs and security to the regional organization. In fact, throughout the many small countries and territories in the Caribbean region there is an inverse relationship between the extent of national political control over monetary affairs and per capita income levels, as shown earlier in table 5.2.

The data on the Caribbean reflect a broader tendency. While the average income levels of (larger) small countries (that is, those with populations between one and five million) vary little from those of all countries, the microterritories of the world have a per capita income profile that is much higher than world averages.[18] Some of these microterritories are independent countries, while others are not. But those territories that are politically independent, like St Kitts and Nevis, have found mechanisms that allow them to cede some of the typical costs and burdens of traditional national sovereignty in order to concentrate on self-determination through economic growth.

In conclusion, I suggest that while small countries face pressing public policy challenges in the context of economic growth and development, there need be no fundamental trade-off between economic growth on the one hand and sovereignty on the other, as long as sovereignty is viewed not as symbols and trappings, but in its purest form as national self-determination.

Chapter 6

FDI-Driven Competitiveness: The Locational Challenge

I n 1966 Raymond Vernon, one of the few individuals who could have claimed the scholarly field of international business as his progeny, had a seminal international business article published.[1] It put forth the idea of a pattern by which firms from innovating countries shifted their production activities to developing countries in the mature phase of a product's life cycle.

In 1968 Lee Kuan Yew, the father of modern Singapore, took a short sabbatical from his position as head of state. He journeyed to Harvard University where he met with faculty, in particular, with Professor Raymond Vernon of Harvard Business School. Lee Kuan Yew indicates that "Vernon dispelled my previous belief that industries changed gradually and seldom moved from an advanced country to a less-developed one".[2]

Acting on Vernon's advice, Lee Kuan Yew accelerated efforts to attract US multinationals to Singapore and, through the country's Economic Development Board, initiated, over the next several decades, an aggressive campaign of investment promotion. This successful campaign has been the most important element of a carefully orchestrated development strategy that has led to Singapore's experiencing what is probably the most dramatic single-generation improvement in comparative living standards in the history of mankind.

The successful Singapore experience, and that of other countries such as Ireland that have successfully attracted significant flows of foreign direct investment, has been an important catalyst for a drive among many developing countries over the last two decades to engage in activities aimed at attracting increasing flows of FDI. By the turn of this century, there was virtually no developing country that did not sing the mantra of attracting FDI as an important component in a programme of enhancing the competitiveness of its resident firms, in an effort to achieve a "Singapore-like" competitiveness enhancement miracle.

During the 1980s and 1990s these songs were accompanied by efforts to liberalize national investment environments, as many governments engaged in regulatory changes in the direction of making their investment environments more liberal. Even though regulatory changes, by themselves, do not provide compelling evidence that national investment environments have become more welcoming to FDI,[3] national governments have complemented new, more liberal investment legislation with efforts to court investors. But after almost two decades of experience with this shift towards more liberal and heavily promoted investment environments, it is appropriate to revisit the question of the impact of investment liberalization and promotion on inflows of FDI.

To the comfort of developing countries, there are clear examples of causal links between liberal investment environments and promotional efforts on the one hand and inflows of investment on the other. Further, there are strong indicators suggesting that, on a worldwide basis, investment inflows to developing countries have increased in concert with the movement to more investor-friendly economic environments.

To the discomfort of many of these countries that have implemented reforms, however, investment inflows to developing countries are not nearly as ubiquitous as are the reforms designed to attract them. Instead, there appears to be a trend towards the concentration of FDI inflows in a few developing countries. This trend raises the question of the options available to developing countries, particularly those countries that face locational disadvantages in their efforts to attract FDI. This chapter seeks to examine the reality and the prospects for FDI to developing countries. In particular, it builds on FDI theory to assess the prospects for FDI in countries that face locational disadvantages.

It does so by examining a conceptual model of investment attraction effectiveness, and by assessing the experiences of FDI attraction efforts in four small developing countries in the Caribbean region: Jamaica, Guyana, Trinidad and Tobago, and Panama. I studied investment attraction efforts in these countries during the late 1990s through a process of structured interviews with executives from agencies responsible for attracting investment. In addition, I interviewed foreign investors, indigenous investors and government policy makers in all four countries.

This chapter seeks to unearth lessons from the experiences of these Caribbean economies for the management of FDI attraction efforts by other developing economies facing locational challenges with respect to the attraction of FDI.

The Importance of Location in Foreign Direct Investment Theory

Foreign direct investment theory focuses on two interrelated sets of questions. One stream of research examines why firms invest overseas. The consensus response to this question from researchers has been that firms invest overseas either to take advantage of certain ownership advantages they possess or to acquire intermediate products that they need. Because of problems of market failure, these firms choose to internalize the market for their intangible assets or the intermediate products they require.[4]

Answering this first question still leaves unanswered an important question with respect to FDI: what factors determine which countries receive the investments generated from these firms eager to operate through international but intrafirm mechanisms? The answer to this question has been sought principally through statistical analyses of those economic, political and institutional factors that seem to be causally linked to FDI flows. The two factors that dominate in most such studies are market size and income levels.[5] Other factors identified in statistical and other studies seeking to isolate the influence of locational variables on FDI flows include market growth rates,[6] political stability,[7] inflation rates and current account positions,[8] quality of infrastructure,[9] fiscal incentives,[10] "good events",[11] government policy,[12] and investment promotion efforts.[13]

In an attempt to draw together both the factors that lead to investment and those that identify which countries are likely to be the recipients of FDI flows, researchers have developed integrative or "eclectic" theories of FDI. The most popular such theory[14] develops the OLI eclectic paradigm, in which foreign investment occurs because firms have certain ownership (O) advantages, which they exploit in countries that offer the requisite locational (L) advantages, through a process of internalization (I).

This perspective not only places the issue of location squarely within FDI theory, but it builds on the school of thought in which FDI has been viewed through the lens of a bargaining power framework. According to this framework, foreign investors bring to the bargaining table their ownership advantages, while countries bring to the bargaining table their locational advantages. The incidence of foreign investment in a country and the terms under which investments will enter countries become a function of the relative bargaining power of firms and national governments.[15]

Much of the research that is focused on the issue of the factors affecting the location of investment, however, has neglected to differentiate according to different types of FDI. FDI can be classified into the following principal forms: extractive or resource-seeking investment that involves investment to extract natural resources; market-seeking or domestic-oriented investment that is targeted towards the domestic market of a foreign country; and export-oriented FDI that seeks to use a foreign country as a platform in which the firm produces for export to regional or global markets.

When researchers do make this distinction, particularly between export-oriented and market-seeking FDI, there are some changes in the critical factors determining location decisions. For market-seeking investment, the critical factors continue to be market size, income levels and growth rates. With respect to export-oriented investment, market growth rates and income rates continue to be important, possibly as proxies for other factors such as quality of infrastructure, but fiscal incentives and investment promotion take on a more prominent role than the negligible one these factors play in market-seeking investment. Additionally, other factors such as infrastructure quality and the ease by which profits can be repatriated also take on a role of significance in the context of export-oriented FDI.

The Locational Challenge in Investment Attraction Efforts

Based upon the theoretical and empirical analyses of investment flows, the characteristics required of countries seeking to attract FDI are clear. For FDI, in general, the importance of market size, growth rate and income levels suggests that most FDI will flow to developed countries, with a minority of such flows directed towards developing countries. Those flows that are directed to developing countries will flow to the developing countries with the largest markets, the most rapidly growing economies and the highest income levels. But when flows are disaggregated into the categories of extractive, market-seeking and export-oriented investment, the locational predictions are slightly more nuanced.

For extractive FDI, the locational advantages of countries that are host to the requisite resources are high relative to the ownership advantages of firms seeking to extract these resources. Such countries can attract these types of investment, with the ease of the attraction effort dependent upon the uniqueness of the resource in question. Such countries are also in a strong bargaining position with respect to the nature of the terms of the investment, and, indeed, will find that their bargaining power is strengthened once fixed investments are in place, causing the initial bargain to obsolesce and leading to changes in the terms of the investment.[16]

For market-seeking investment, the critical variables are market size, income levels and growth rates. The extent of a country's locational advantage in the context of attracting market-seeking FDI depends not only on these factors, however, but also on the other options available to firms for exploiting their ownership advantages in these markets.

Market imperfections induced by government policy have the potential to increase the bargaining power and locational advantage of the host nation, relative to the ownership advantage and bargaining power of the foreign firm. Trade barriers, for example, that restrict access to a host market by a foreign firm increase the locational advantage of the nation and tend to induce market-seeking FDI. It was the existence of these barriers that created the impetus for market-seeking FDI in a range of developing countries, including small developing countries, during the period of import-substitution industrialization.

Such market imperfections, however, are rapidly disappearing in the context of the trend towards trade liberalization that has swept the world over the last two decades. Given the existing degree of trade liberalization, and expectations among foreign investors that this trend will continue and intensify during the foreseeable future, market size, growth and income levels would be expected to be particularly important in determining the location of market-oriented FDI. According to this reasoning, countries with small markets which are growing slowly, and in which income levels are low, would face locational disadvantages in the context of their ability to attract such forms of investment. Most small developing countries face locational disadvantages in attracting market-seeking FDI.

To the extent that export-oriented FDI is also induced by factors such as market size, growth rates and income levels, these countries would find little respite from their investment-attraction problems in the context of export-oriented investment. Yet there are other factors that researchers have suggested might influence export-oriented FDI that could provide hope for such countries.

In particular, since such flows are found to be influenced by government policies with respect to incentives and promotional efforts, then countries that are otherwise locationally challenged might be able to offset their locational disadvantages through government policies. It is this premise that is examined throughout the remainder of this chapter, through an analysis of the investment attraction efforts of four small developing countries in the Caribbean that face locational challenges in their efforts to attract FDI, and by an examination of trends in investment flows to developing countries in the aftermath of the liberalization and promotion efforts that have dominated investment policy in recent years.

Investment Attraction Experiences in the Caribbean

During the 1950s through 1970s, in all four countries included in this study there were inflows of market-seeking FDI to take advantage of national markets. Although these markets were small, they were attractive because of the high import barriers that accompanied the import-substitution industrialization development model which all of these countries pursued.

Since the 1980s these four Caribbean countries have also adopted common approaches in their efforts to attract FDI. They have developed more liberal investment policies, shifted the orientation of their management efforts *vis-à-vis* foreign investors by replacing foreign investment screening institutions with foreign investment promotion institutions, and targeted in their promotional efforts specific categories of export-oriented foreign investors, whose activities would build upon advantages unique or nearly unique to the country in question.

Policy Changes

The most significant changes in policy that affected the environment for FDI in these Caribbean countries were, ironically, more general policy changes whose impact would be felt by foreign and local investors alike. Panama had long used the US dollar as its currency of legal tender, and so had no exchange controls. But during the early 1990s, Guyana, Jamaica and Trinidad and Tobago all engaged in a process of exchange liberalization in which exchange controls were eliminated or ignored. The exchange liberalization process also involved the three anglophone Caribbean countries moving to market-determined exchange rates.

This policy change eliminated the requirement that foreign investors gain approval from the central bank prior to investing. Investors would also no longer need to seek permission from the central bank in order to repatriate capital or remit dividends. During the period of exchange controls, foreign exchange tended to be scarce. Therefore, it was likely that investors would have to join lines in order to gain permission to repatriate capital or remit dividends. Consequently, exchange controls had often been an impediment to FDI, particularly export-oriented investment, which was less tolerant of restrictive government practices.

In all four countries, another form of liberalization that influenced FDI was the widespread movement to trade liberalization. Panama engaged in a process of trade liberalization throughout the 1980s. Jamaica, Trinidad and Tobago and Guyana are all members of CARICOM, which opted during the late 1980s to embark upon an ambitious programme of trade liberalization. It allowed countries within the integrated area two options for participating in the trade liberalization programme. The first was a fast-track option in which countries would commit to regular reductions in tariffs on all imported goods, except agricultural imports, between 1992 and 1997. The goal was that applicable tariff rates should fall within a band of 0–20 per cent by January 1997. The alternative was a non-fast-track option in which tariff reductions would be implemented more gradually. All three of the CARICOM countries studied adopted the fast-track option.

Liberalization of trade in these countries was likely to have a two-pronged effect on FDI. Trade liberalization would make market-seeking investment in these countries less attractive, as foreign firms could gain access to these small markets through exports rather than by having to invest. Ideally, on the other hand, it would make export-oriented investment more attractive as these investors could more easily import raw materials, intermediate goods and capital equipment at world market prices, improving their ability to produce goods at internationally competitive prices.

Other policy changes were more specific to the various countries. Guyana eliminated visa requirements for individuals from key capital-exporting countries such as the United States, Canada, Japan and the countries of the European Union. Trinidad and Tobago repealed the Alien Landholdings Act, which had made it difficult for foreigners to own land in the twin-island republic. In concert with this repeal, restrictions were removed on foreign investors acquiring shares in local companies. Finally, the Panamanian government engaged in a number of labour market reforms designed to reduce labour market rigidities in that country.

Institutional Changes

In all four countries, these policy changes were complemented by the building of new institutions to court export-oriented FDI. Among this sample of Caribbean countries, Jamaica led in implementing the institutional changes. In 1981, shortly after a change in government to an administration more welcoming of FDI, the Jamaica Industrial Development Corporation (a screening and land development agency) was replaced by the Jamaica National Investment Promotion Agency (JNIP), whose mandate was to attract export-oriented FDI to Jamaica.

In 1989 this agency was merged with the Jamaica National Export Corporation, an export promotion agency, to become Jamaica Promotion Company (JAMPRO), with a mandate to promote investment and exports. JAMPRO was established as a quasi-government agency, with significant private sector representation on its board of directors. It reported to the government through the Ministry of Industry, Investments and Commerce. In the 1990s JAMPRO operated several overseas offices. In support of its export promotion activity, it also operated a productivity centre (which later became a separate government agency, the Jamaica Business Development Centre) geared to assisting in the enhancement of the productive capability of indigenous firms.

In Trinidad and Tobago the investment-screening agency, the Industrial Development Corporation, was merged with the Tourism Development

Association and the Export Development Corporation in 1994 to become the promotion-oriented Tourism and Industrial Development Company of Trinidad and Tobago. The new company was charged with promoting investment, exports and tourism. Most of the members of the board of directors of the Tourism and Industrial Development Company, including the chairman, were from the private sector. The institution was formed with a small, highly professional operating staff.

In Guyana, also in 1994, the screening institution, the Guyana Manufacturing and Industrial Development Agency, was replaced by the Guyana Office for Investment (GoInvest). GoInvest's mandate was to promote Guyana as a site for FDI. It was established as a "lean" organization, comprised of only four professional staff: a director and three investment service officers. The director of GoInvest reported to cabinet through the minister of trade.

In Panama, the institutional changes in the direction of promoting FDI were initiated in 1988. In that year, an investment promotion department was created in the Panamanian Foreign Trade Institute (IPCE), which had, in turn, been created in 1984. In 1995 there were further institutional developments in Panama's effort to court FDI; the National Commission for the Promotion of Foreign Investments (Pro Panama) was formed by executive decree.

Pro Panama comprised three structural elements: a governing board of senior government officials presided over by the president of the republic, with the minister of foreign relations responsible for its overall operations and functioning as its vice-chairman; a commission of fifteen Panamanian businessmen; and a secretariat that operated as a department within the foreign relations ministry and that had responsibility for developing and executing a national programme of foreign investment promotion.

In addition to Pro Panama, a variety of other institutions engaged in promoting Panama as a site for export-oriented FDI. Aside from the investment promotion department in the Foreign Trade Institute (IPCE), investment promotion was conducted by IPAT (the Institute of Tourism of Panama), ARI (the Regional Oceanic Authority, responsible for promoting the areas that reverted to Panamanian control following the withdrawal of the US military command which had managed the Panama Canal from its construction), the Export Processing Zone Authority (responsible for promoting investment in these zones), and the Colón Free Zone (responsible for promoting investment in the oldest free zone in the Americas, established in 1948).

Targeting Export-Oriented Foreign Direct Investment

In all four Caribbean countries, these newly created organizations focused on the targeting of export-oriented FDI. Guyana's GoInvest, up to the time of this study, had not yet developed a track record in the targeting of export-oriented FDI. In Jamaica, Trinidad and Tobago, and Panama, however, there were notable examples of the efforts of these countries to target export-oriented FDI.

Jamaica

Jamaica, with the oldest effort to attract FDI, saw the first success story of this group of countries under the aegis of JNIP, the predecessor of JAMPRO. JNIP was involved in enticing Asian investors to Jamaica during the 1980s. These investors were searching for access to country quotas that would allow them to export to the US market under the terms of the Multilateral Fibre Arrangement (MFA). At the time, Jamaica had negotiated generous quotas for garment exports to the United States, which were underutilized. The JNIP's strategy involved direct marketing efforts in Asia through an Asian overseas marketing presence and investment missions throughout the region. Mr Chang, general manager of Seban Industries Limited, a major Korean garment manufacturer, later declared that his company was "so impressed by the JNIP presentation in Korea that we decided to choose Jamaica over other locations in the Caribbean".[17]

The JNIP's effort to establish an export garment industry was complemented by other government interventions that focused specifically on the needs of this industry. These included a technical consultancy in garments with the international garment consultancy, Kurt Salmon and Associates; negotiated access to the US market culminating in the 1986 United States-Jamaica bilateral trade agreement in textiles and apparel; and the building of factory shells, including shells in a free zone dedicated to the garment industry, by Factories Corporation of Jamaica, a Jamaican government agency.

JNIP was also the co-ordinating agency for the distribution of fiscal incentives to the industry through the Export Industry Encouragement Act, for those garment manufacturers that did not establish their facilities in one of the country's three free zones. As a result of this combination of efforts garment exports from Jamaica, which valued less than US$16 million in 1983, had increased to over US$500 million by 1995, becoming Jamaica's third largest export, behind tourism and bauxite/alumina.

But the garment industry suffered tremendously during the late 1990s, due principally to the loss of Jamaica's relative advantages following from Mexico's accession to NAFTA. Thereafter, the garment industry declined precipitously and was quite vulnerable to additional decline. The Doha trade negotiations that were initiated in 2001 were likely to include a review of the MFA, which review promised further uncertainty in this industry.

In the late 1990s JAMPRO, supported actively by the Jamaican Ministry of Investment, Commerce and Technology, was seeking to target information technology investors, and had a goal of creating forty thousand jobs (or about 4 per cent of the labour force) in this industry within five years. In 2001 one of the firms which had promised to create substantial jobs in this sector, and which had benefited from government loans from a fund created with the proceeds from the sale of cellular licences, went bankrupt. This event precipitated much discussion in the country about the role of financial incentives in the attraction of FDI. Also during this period, Jamaica was successful in attracting FDI to purchase government interests in the financial sector. (The government had acquired an ownership interest in several financial institutions after a financial crisis had devastated the indigenous financial sector.)

Trinidad and Tobago

Another example of targeting export-oriented FDI comes from Trinidad and Tobago, but it predates the formation of the Tourism and Industrial Development Company, which had the responsibility to promote non-oil-related FDI. With the mandate to attract investment in the oil and gas sector, Trinidad and Tobago's National Gas Company embarked upon a highly targeted effort to attract export-oriented FDI into this sector of the Trinidadian economy. The chairman of the company and his team were instrumental in targeting and personally courting North American interests in an effort to attract investment that would develop the country's considerable gas reserves. The energy industry is relatively small and closely knit. The chairman, who had worked in the industry, used the network that he had established to contact key decision makers in specific firms that would be likely to have an interest in the competitive advantages offered by Trinidad and Tobago in areas such as natural gas.

In this process, the team from National Gas also engaged in systematic research into the operations of specific North American–based energy companies. The goal was to refine their attempts at strategic intervention into the locational decisions of these companies. As a result of such intervention, Trinidad and Tobago was able to attract at least two very large investments. One investment was projected at US$300 million and involved the production of iron for export to the United States, using natural gas as the principal material for processing the iron. Another investment project, proposed during the late 1990s, was a US$1-billion project for the export of liquefied natural gas.

I interviewed senior executives associated with the first of these investment projects shortly after the start of project implementation. The company they represented had an interest in investing within the hemisphere to produce iron for export. This was to be the company's first overseas investment project, and decision makers were trying to identify a location in the hemisphere with supplies of natural gas.

I was told that the key factors in the decision to invest in Trinidad were the direct marketing activities of the team from National Gas. Indeed, the company's first reaction when visited by this team and encouraged to invest in Trinidad and Tobago was, "Where's Trinidad?" Other elements of the Trinidadian environment that ultimately proved to be influential in the company's decision to establish in that country were a very welcoming orientation on the part of the government, fiscal incentives, and the very high quality of the Trinidadian workforce, from secondary school graduates to university-trained engineers. In the decision to locate in Trinidad and Tobago, the company opted for a more expensive source of natural gas than would have been available elsewhere in the hemisphere.

Panama

Panama provides a third example of the manner in which these Caribbean countries have sought to target export-oriented FDI. This country is one of only eight countries in the world that has formed diplomatic relations with Taiwan. In the mid-1990s Panama was particularly eager to attract export-oriented FDI in light of the imminent departure of US military forces with the expiration of US control of the Panama Canal. Consequently, the CEO of Panama's newly formed Pro Panama spearheaded negotiations with the Taiwanese in an effort to encourage business executives from that country to establish export operations in Panama.

In the mid-1990s the Evergreen Shipping line, a large Taiwanese company, established operations in Panama's world-renowned shipping industry. Also at that time, Pro Panama announced that fifteen hundred Taiwanese investors would be coming to Panama over the next several months to investigate the possibility of investing in a free zone to be established within the reverted areas (that is, the regions to be returned by the United States to Panama). The free zone would be run by Taiwanese businessmen and would be dedicated to export-oriented assembly-type manufacturing operations. The Panamanian government offered the facilities, including existing buildings, to the Taiwanese under a fifty-year lease, after which all facilities would revert to the government. The quid pro quo was that the Taiwanese were asked to commit to the creation of twenty thousand jobs.

But, despite the efforts of all of the Caribbean countries that I studied, their FDI inflows continued to fall short of creating a significant and long-lived impact on total investment flows, employment and overall national competitiveness. This is because these countries suffer locational disadvantages when it comes to attracting FDI, as do many other small developing countries.

Trends in Foreign Direct Investment Flows

The countries of the Caribbean are not atypical among developing countries in their efforts to attract FDI. Each year during the 1990s the United Nations reported that an overwhelming majority of changes to FDI regimes were in the direction of investment liberality. In 1998, for example, out of 145 regulatory changes made in that year by 60 countries, 94 per cent created more favourable conditions for the entry of foreign firms.[18] Nor are the countries in the Caribbean unusual in the methods they are using in the execution of those efforts. And these efforts among developing countries are bearing fruit.

During 1984 to 1989, for example, while the liberalization and promotion efforts of developing countries were just gathering steam, developing countries obtained, on average, 19 per cent of all FDI inflows. By 1990 to 1995, however, when the liberalization and promotion efforts had been institutionalized for several years, the annual average had increased to 30 per cent of total flows. This trend of increasing FDI flows to developing countries continued through the 1995–1997 period, when the annual average level of FDI flowing to developing countries was 37 per cent. But the late 1990s showed a relatively sharp reversal. Between 1998 and 1999, FDI flows to developing countries, on average, were 25 per cent of total flows.[19]

But even before the late 1990s reversal, there was a disconcerting pattern in the FDI flows to developing countries. This was the extent to which FDI flows were concentrated in but a few developing countries. During 1984–1989, for example, the top ten recipients of FDI among developing countries received 64 per cent of the total flows directed to developing countries. By 1995, the top ten recipients of FDI among developing countries received 78 per cent of total flows to the developing world. At the other end of the spectrum, the one hundred countries receiving the smallest amounts of FDI, cumulatively, received 1 per cent of global FDI inflows. By 1999, the level of concentration had increased further, and the top ten recipients of FDI among developing countries received 80 per cent of the total flows directed to developing countries.

Life Cycle Issues in Investment Promotion Effectiveness

In spite of the correlation between policy changes, promotional activities and FDI flows, it is not obvious that the changes actually lead to the growth of FDI. The extent to which the effectiveness of promotional activity influences flows of FDI to developing countries was tested by Wells and Wint in a study published in 1990.[20] This study indicated that promotion had a statistically significant positive impact on investment flows to developed and developing countries. This research suggesting that promotion can help to influence inflows of FDI has been particularly encouraging to developing countries eager to attract such investment.

Since 1990, most developing countries have shifted towards more liberal attitudes regarding FDI. The increasing similarity in national policies towards FDI and the wide dissemination of best-practice in investment promotion raise anew the question about the continued differential effectiveness of promotion. Have promotional activities and liberal investment policies begun to lose their ability to influence FDI flows, now that most countries have similar policies? Is there, in fact, a life cycle to the differential effectiveness of special programmes that seek to attract investment? (See figure 6.1.)

Of course, first mover countries which come up with new and innovative policies or new types of programmes might, by so doing, establish the growth stage of a new effectiveness life cycle that would lead to a new best-practice

Figure 6.1: Life Cycle Issues in Differential Effectiveness of Special FDI Attraction Programmes

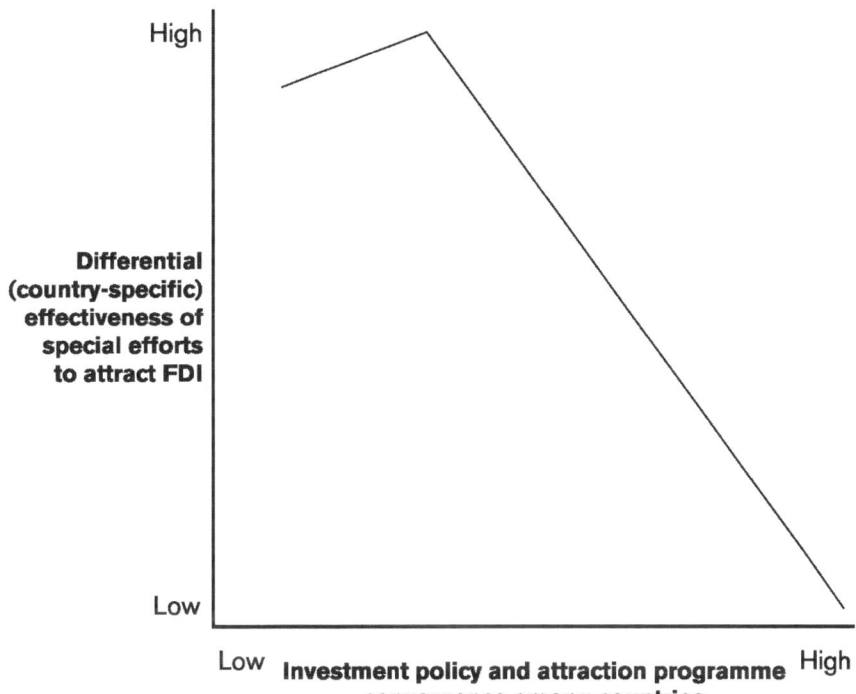

[a]Assuming that policy convergence is in the direction of investment liberality and programme convergence is toward best promotional practice for attracting investment.

standard and imitation by other countries. Furthermore, one can conceive of a separation of investment policy regimes and investment promotion programmes. Thus, where there is convergence among countries with respect to investment policies, differentiated or divergent promotional programmes might still be effective in distinguishing one country as a site for investment relative to another (see figure 6.2).

But even if policies and promotional activities converge among developing countries, this would not lead to the policy conclusion that these countries could prudently abort their special efforts to attract FDI. Obviously, the country that stopped such efforts would stand out in a negative way from the crowd of developing countries. The distribution of investment would be unchanged only if all countries simultaneously aborted their efforts.

Figure 6.2: Implications of Investment Policy/Programme Convergence for Effectiveness of FDI Attraction/Repulsion Efforts

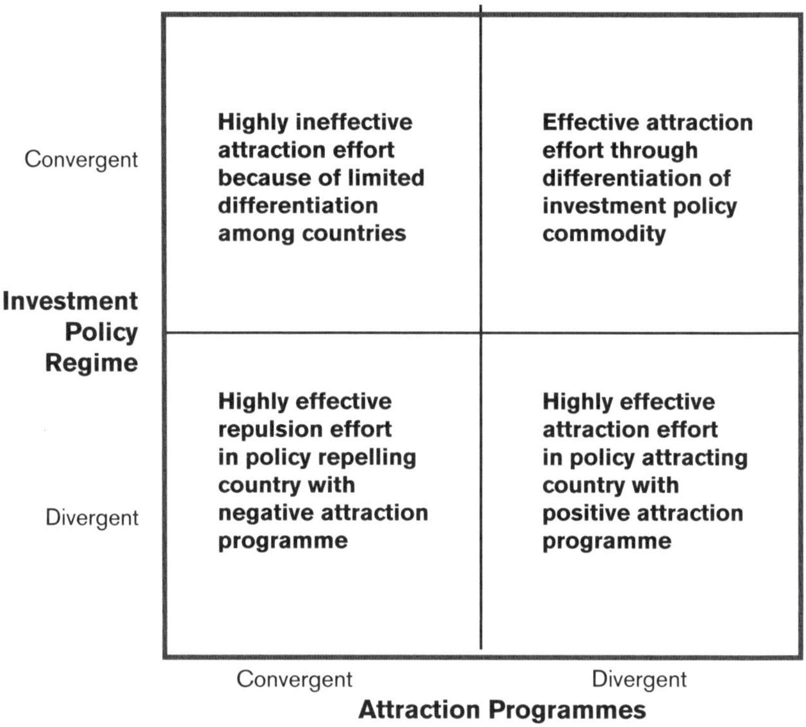

Even if countries could co-ordinate simultaneous reductions in expenditure on promoting investment, this apparently cost-saving response may not be appropriate, to the extent that promotional efforts increase aggregate flows of FDI. With policy and promotional congruence, and after non-policy/promotional variables important in locational decisions have already been accounted for, these increased aggregates would flow to developing countries as a group. Therefore, developing countries would gain additional investment, even if no particular country's policy and promotional effort could lead to a differential increase in FDI inflows.

The issue of whether such a conceptual life cycle would ever be translated into reality would also rest on the likelihood of policy and promotional best-practice convergence among developing countries. Because of the disjuncture between concept and implementation, the process of best-practice convergence might be a very long one. Developing countries seeking to adapt best practices are likely to encounter a series of political leadership and institutional design challenges along the way. This is what occurred with investment screens: these screens remained, in practice, as vestiges of a prior era even when investment policies and government rhetoric were in the direction of investment liberality.[21]

Indeed, practitioners involved in providing advice on foreign investment policy matters suggest that despite the view that developing countries, as a group, are liberalizing policies towards FDI and creating investment-friendly promotional structures, there continue to be significant differences between investment-reforming countries and their recalcitrant counterparts.

One approach to assessing life cycle issues in the effectiveness of investment attraction efforts is to re-examine the role of investment promotion in a statistical study of factors influencing FDI flows. The goal of such an assessment is to examine the role of investment promotion and other determinants of FDI flows in the post-reform period, which appears to be characterized by much greater convergence among developing countries with respect to investment policy and promotional programmes.

Determinants of Foreign Direct Investment in Developing Countries in Post-Reform Period

In an attempt to test the factors that determine the flow of FDI to developing countries in the post-reform period, a recent study developed a statistical model of explanatory factors affecting FDI flows.[22] Following other researchers, this study tested, in a sample of thirty countries, the following factors deemed to affect inflows of FDI: interest rates, per capita income, growth rates, current account position, literacy rates and promotion.

In generating the promotion variable, this study departed from the existing research. In their 1990 study, Wells and Wint had used as a proxy for the effectiveness of investment promotion a dichotomous (dummy) variable based upon whether or not the country had overseas promotional representation in the United States. Given the significant increase in promotional activity since the late 1980s when Wells and Wint conducted their research, the more recent study used an approach to estimating effective promotion that would allow for more nuanced estimates of effectiveness. Accordingly, the effectiveness of investment promotion activity was proxied through a promotional variable derived from a questionnaire sent to ten promotional experts around the world in a delphi-like research process. These included individuals working for the

Foreign Investment Advisory Service and the Multilateral Investment Guarantee Agency of the World Bank, and academics, consultants and investment promotion practitioners with experience in providing advice on investment promotion matters in many countries.

The investment promotion experts were requested to assess the effectiveness of promotional activity in each of the countries in the sample using a four-category scale, incorporating the following categories: very effective, fairly effective, ineffective and no knowledge. Nine of the ten promotional experts responded, and their assessments of the effectiveness of promotional activity in each country were aggregated to develop the promotional variable for use in the statistical analysis.

The model was tested on a stratified sample (by geography) of thirty-six developing countries (categorized using the World Bank's categories of low-, lower-middle and upper-middle-income countries). Cumulatively, the variables (interest rates, per capita income, growth rates, current account position, literacy rates and promotion) explained a significant amount of the variance in FDI flows across the countries in the sample (R squared of 0.69 per cent). But by far the most significant contributor to explaining this variance was the per capita income variable. The variables: interest rates, literacy rates and promotion had the expected signs, but were not statistically significant. The current account variable did not record the expected sign, nor was it statistically significant. The per capita growth rate variable recorded a negative sign, but was not statistically significant.

The dominance of per capita income on FDI flows is a most striking finding of this recent empirical study. While per capita income has been recognized as the most consistent predictor of levels of FDI in all previous studies, evidence of the extent to which it dominates all other economic and noneconomic variables is novel.

Previous research had suggested that literacy levels, while having a positive impact on FDI flows, were not statistically significant.[23] But previous research had also suggested that the noneconomic variable of promotional effectiveness would have a statistically significant impact on FDI flows.[24] This recent study did not corroborate those findings.

One possible explanation, for both the dominance of per capita income as a factor explaining FDI flows and the relative insignificance of promotion, is to be found in changes in governmental attitudes towards FDI and a possible convergence among the promotional efforts of developing countries. As countries converge towards best practice in promotion, it becomes more difficult for any particular country to gain a differential advantage in relation to attracting FDI. This recent study does appear to lend support to the notion that there has been a movement down the life cycle of the country-specific effectiveness of special efforts to attract FDI, as captured in figure 6.1, and towards the upper left-hand quadrant of figure 6.2.

Implications for Policy in Small Developing Countries

What then are the implications for policy and action at the level of governments of small developing countries interested in attracting FDI? The first implication is that the findings of a single study should not be interpreted as forming a basis for discontinuing or even reducing special efforts to attract FDI. This is particularly true because of the potential limitations of quantitative research in this area. Quantitative analyses tend not to be the most effective approach to identifying the effectiveness of the role played by institutions. This is why most studies that have sought to assess the effectiveness of countries in attracting and retaining FDI have tended to use qualitative research methods that are more capable of identifying effective institutionally driven strategies.[25]

But even if the conclusions of the statistical analysis generated in this recent study were supported by other analytical approaches, they would not provide a rationale for countries to discontinue their efforts at attracting foreign direct investors. Conceptually, figure 6.1 indicates why such a conclusion is not correct. Even if special attraction efforts do not create for a country differential advantage in the context of convergence towards best practice in policy and promotion, these efforts are likely to lead to an overall increase in investment flows to developing countries. Further, the country that discontinues its special attraction efforts is likely to suffer differential disadvantage in the attraction of FDI. But these findings should, nevertheless, give pause to policy makers in small developing countries who are focused on attracting foreign direct investors.

The trends in FDI inflows suggest that these flows are becoming concentrated in a group of countries with locational advantages in the attraction of FDI. These trends have manifested themselves particularly since the universal reduction of trade barriers among countries during the 1980s and 1990s. As is predicted by the FDI literature, there are three common characteristics that provide countries with a locational advantage in the attraction of FDI: large markets, growing economies, and high income levels.

Any of these characteristics will make countries attractive as destinations for FDI. Obviously, the more of such characteristics a country can boast, the greater the inducement for FDI to enter its market. These characteristics, to some extent, cut across the normal divide between developed and developing countries. It is the existence of two of these characteristics – an obviously large market, comprised of more than 20 per cent of humanity, and a rapidly growing economy that boasted growth rates of 8 per cent per year during the 1980s and 1990s – that has brought China to the position of the second largest recipient of FDI among all countries.

Yet the inverse of the success of large, rapidly growing and affluent markets in attracting FDI is the failure of small, low-to middle-income markets experiencing anaemic growth to attract such investment. When it comes to attracting FDI, I suggest that these countries suffer locational disadvantages. Many such countries have liberalized their investment regimes, created policy environments conducive to FDI, established promotional institutions and engaged in the prescribed promotional activities, and yet have received little FDI for their efforts. For these countries, particularly small countries experiencing slow rates of economic growth, the goal was to attract export-oriented FDI in an effort to initiate a virtuous cycle of increasing exports and growth rates, leading to additional investment, exports and growth.

The models placed in front of these countries by academics and the international development community were those of Singapore and Ireland. While these models are not irrelevant, there are also caveats attached to these models of which countries seeking FDI should be aware. Singapore faced locational challenges at the time that it began its efforts to attract FDI. Although it had economic potential, with its strategic position amid international shipping lanes, it was small, poor, and, at the time, was not experiencing rapid growth. Yet it was able, through export-oriented FDI, to generate the highly sought-after virtuous cycle of export-oriented investment: exports – rapid growth – more investment – more exports – more growth. But the important caveat is that in the late 1960s when Singapore began its drive to attract export-oriented FDI, virtually no other developing country was "in the market" for such investment. Even then, the Singaporean government found it necessary to adopt the innovative, bold, and risky policy of guaranteeing to foreign direct investors a specified rate of return on their commercial activities in order to improve its locational advantages.

Similarly, although Ireland seemed to have a small, domestic market, in reality it did not. Much of Ireland's success in attracting export-oriented FDI came in the wake of its 1973 entry into the European Economic Community. Thus, for foreign direct investors in Ireland the effective market was the world's second largest at the time.

This is not to suggest that the approaches used by Singapore's Economic Development Board and Ireland's Industrial Development Authority in their efforts to attract export-oriented FDI should not be emulated by small developing countries. It is to suggest, however, that imitation alone is an inadequate strategy, because of the differing contextual situations. Given these differing situations, I make the following suggestions for small developing countries seeking to attract FDI, based in part on the experiences of the countries in the Caribbean.

The Elevated Importance of Targeting

Although small developing countries should not be deterred in their efforts to attract FDI, they should recognize that, given the constraints they face, targeting FDI becomes even more important than it is for their locationally advantaged counterparts. There are two critical elements to this enhanced focus on targeting. On the one hand, small developing countries have to offset their locational disadvantages with superior capabilities in the management of investment attraction efforts. Not only are promotional mechanisms more important in order to persuade investors to locate in their countries, but the quality of the promotion effort is critical, since such countries can be less tolerant of inefficiencies in their marketing efforts.

The second element, however, may be even more important. For small developing countries in an environment of fierce competition for FDI, it is critical that promotional agencies target investors for whom the country provides a location with distinct advantages. The Caribbean examples are all cases of promotional efforts grounded on assets that, at least at the time, were distinct. These include Trinidad's success in attracting export-oriented investment requiring the use of natural gas as a feedstock, Panama seeking to attract Taiwanese investment to capitalize on its rare diplomatic relations with Taiwan, and Jamaica attracting quota-hopping garment investment to take advantage of its underutilized garment quotas.

The approach many developing countries have attempted, in which they seek to use promotional efforts to try to diversify the portfolio of investment attracted to their shores, is unlikely to work for small developing countries. These countries do not have the luxury of seeking to use investment promotion efforts to "go against the grain" of investor interest. Rather, their promotional efforts, which theoretically should be designed to overcome market failures, should serve to allow the investment market to function more smoothly, rather than seek to distort that market. For such countries, efforts to diversify the economy through the attraction of investment should be de-emphasized while the focus is placed on attracting investment that will consolidate the economy's position in existing areas of strength.

In essence, for small developing countries in particular, the notion of competing based upon competitive advantage is critical. Such a focus was less important in an era of trade protection, but the trade liberalization that has pushed many developing countries to re-examine their efforts at economic diversification in trade has precisely the same influence on FDI. This focus is also not dissimilar from the call, in an increasingly more competitive world, for firms that had spread their assets and resources widely and thinly to return to their core competence in order to compete effectively.

One of the implications of this approach is that the mandate of promotional organizations in many small developing countries may need re-examination. The typical focus has been to give these agencies the mandate to promote only in "nontraditional" areas of investment. But, in order to complement the market, the mandate for these countries may well need to include, and indeed emphasize, the promotion of investment in traditional areas of investment and economic activity.

Again, the Trinidadian experience is important. The existing approach to the promotion of traditional areas of economic activity is that such promotion is unnecessary since investment in these areas will come automatically. Yet many countries are not receiving such "automatic" inflows of investment. The response of a prospective investor on the initial efforts to promote Trinidad and Tobago indicates one of the potential reasons for this lack of investment.

The investor's response was, "Where's Trinidad?" Promotion in that situation was a very good example of a market-friendly intervention that assisted in overcoming the failure in the market for information.

The Critical Importance of Nondiscrimination Against Indigenous Firms

It is imperative, in small developing countries in particular, that investment activity be broadly defined to include foreign and local investment, and that reforms and promotional efforts be implemented that can serve to unfetter and promote both types of investment. Indeed, investment attraction programmes should ensure that the reform of investment policy is an important element of their portfolio of activities.[26]

This reform process should concentrate on both local and foreign investors. In this way selective interventions targeted at attracting specific foreign firms are complemented by functional interventions that improve investment prospects for all potential investors within the economy. The Caribbean experiences again point to the approaches that are possible in this regard. The focus of liberalization efforts in these countries was on exchange liberalization. This policy fits the model of a reform effort that benefits foreign and indigenous investment simultaneously.

One popular approach in developing countries to investment policy reform has, indeed, been to eschew reform in investment policies that would affect all investors, in favour of concentrating reform efforts only on procedures affecting foreign firms. The notion implicit in this discrimination is that local investors are a captive audience over which the government has monopoly control, while there is a need for the government to compete with other governments for incoming investors.

In fact, of course, in an increasingly integrated world, and with the movement in many countries to exchange liberalization on both current and capital accounts, all capital is footloose, regardless of the nationality of the holder of such capital. With the pendulum swinging towards preferential treatment for foreign investors, developing countries need to recognize that it is in their interests to give all investors "most favoured foreigner" treatment.

Finally, in the small developing countries of the Caribbean, two of the investment institutions, Jamaica's JAMPRO and Trinidad and Tobago's Tourism and Industrial Development Company, were established with a mandate to promote both foreign and local investment. The symbiotic relationship between foreign and local investment, focused on the distinct advantages of countries, can create the economic growth that lends itself to the attraction of additional flows of FDI. This institutional model, therefore, represents yet another example of an approach that recommends itself for other small developing countries seeking FDI.

In sum, recent research and trends in FDI flows suggest that governments of small developing countries, in particular, should create an environment conducive to the entry of foreign investors, and actively seek FDI. But policy makers ought also to be wary about the likely effectiveness of a policy that places too heavy a reliance on attracting FDI as an approach to enhancing the country's level of international competitiveness, given the extraordinary level of competition faced by these countries as they seek to attract export-oriented FDI.

Chapter 7

The Competitiveness of Firms

The preceding chapters in this volume have adopted a macro focus on the question of competitiveness. Such a focus is important because of the critical role that policy, regulation and economic management play in influencing firm-level performance.[1] Chapter 6 began an investigation of the impact of firms on national competitiveness, through an examination of the potential role of foreign investment as a competitiveness driver in small developing countries. But chapter 6 still focused more on the potential of small developing countries to attract FDI than on the characteristics of the operations of these firms. Chapter 6 also pointed to the importance of complementing a focus on attracting foreign investment with one on improving the operations of indigenous firms.

This chapter continues the theme that emerged at the conclusion of chapter 6, but nevertheless represents a shift in analytical focus. Against the background of a national environment common to many small developing countries, this chapter examines the factors important in enhancing the competitiveness of foreign and indigenous firms.

There are two characteristics that are common to the countries that are the subject of this volume. One is their size. The other is that they have encountered periods of low economic growth, contributing to their status as developing countries. This chapter examines the competitiveness of foreign and indigenous firms in one small developing country, Jamaica, which has been affected by a recent period of low economic growth.[2] The chapter seeks to draw lessons for firm-level performance in the context of small developing economies. It does so by examining the performance of Jamaican enterprises during the 1990s, particularly the 1994–1999 period. The research for this chapter involved interviews with executives from several of the enterprises, and the collection of data about their operations. Based upon this investigation, the chapter concludes with propositions about the factors likely to lead to the success of enterprises in small developing economies.

Methodology and Data Collection Approaches

The initial task of the research project reported upon in this chapter was the identification of high-performing enterprises across the Jamaican economy. Often the focus in such studies is the manufacturing and export sectors; the implicit argument is that these are the segments of an economy, particularly in a developing country, for which international competitiveness is most important.

This study took a different approach. It followed the conclusions presented in chapter 1 of this volume in accepting that high performance across all segments of a country's economy is important. It did, however, make one important restriction: this study did not include a search for high performance within the public sector. This is a critical omission, because of the importance of public sector operations to a country's performance. But it was felt that such a critical subject would be more appropriately covered in a separate study. Such a study is reported on in chapter 9 of this volume, which involves an examination of competitiveness of a section of the economy of a small developing country managed by the public sector.

In searching for companies operating in an internationally competitive manner, or moving in that direction, this study used the four, non-mutually-exclusive indicators of internationally competitive operations identified in chapter 1:

- the ability of enterprises to export to an array of countries
- the ability of enterprises to engage in FDI
- the ability of enterprises to operate according to internationally accepted norms of cost, service, operational standards and quality
- the ability of enterprises to earn above-average returns in a market setting which includes domestic competitors and (relatively) unimpeded access for rival enterprises from other countries.

Data on Jamaican-based enterprises that would meet these indicators were sought from several sources. All listed Jamaican companies were sorted by industry, and their profitability was examined over the period 1994 –1999. The Jamaica Exporters Association and Jamaica Manufacturers' Association were contacted for their list of enterprises that received export awards during the 1994–1999 period. Investigations were also conducted on an industry-by-industry basis to identify unlisted companies that had outperformed their peers with respect to at least one of the indicators identified above.

Identifying Competitive Enterprises in Jamaica

The starting point for examining high-performing Jamaican enterprises was an examination of the performance of listed companies, for which data on profitability were readily available. Table 7.1 identifies thirty-six of the thirty-nine Jamaican-based companies that were listed on the Jamaican stock exchange for the entire 1994–1999 period (excluding three utility/infrastructure companies: Cable and Wireless, Kingston Wharves, and Montego Freeport). In table 7.1 these companies are divided into industry categories, and the top-performing companies in each group are identified based upon a composite profitability index. The profitability index used was the mean of average return on sales and average return on equity over the period.

Table 7.1: Profitability of Firms Listed on Jamaican Stock Exchange 1994–1999

Banking	Profitability Index
BNS	33.15
TDB	17.85
CIBC	17.60
MIDA	14.20
DB&G	12.60
Pan Jamaican Investments	7.55
NCB	0.47
Union Bank	-84.85

Insurance	Profitability Index
First Life	18.50
Dyoll	0.30
Island Life	-17.85
Life of Jamaica	-120.35

Tourism/Entertainment	Profitability Index
Pulse Investments	7.95
Pegasus	1.97
Palace	-5.74
Ciboney	-62.72

Retail	Profitability Index
Courts	7.55
Hardware & Lumber	7.55

Manufacturing/Marketing	Profitability Index
Berger	14.98
Seprod	12.99
Goodyear	12.40
West Indies Pulp & Paper	-1.96
CMP Industries	-16.12
Caribbean Cement	-37.35

Agriculture/Food Processing	Profitability Index
Carreras (cigarettes)	36.10
Lascelles de Mercado	12.95
Grace, Kennedy & Co.	9.95
Jamaica Producers	9.85
Montego Bay Ice	8.05
Jamaica Broilers	5.60
Desnoes & Geddes	5.25
Jamaica Livestock Association	0.04
Salada Foods	-31.55
Kingston Ice	-117.35

Communication	Profitability Index
Gleaner	14.40
Radio Jamaica	13.15

Profitability index: Mean of average return on sales and average return on equity over the 1994–1999 period.

Source: Jamaica Stock Exchange, *1999 Year Book* (Kingston, Jamaica: Jamaica Stock Exchange, 2000).

The data from the listed Jamaican companies were complemented by data on companies that had obtained awards from the Jamaica Exporters Association and the Jamaica Manufacturers' Association, in particular, during the period. Other sources were also canvassed for data on award-winning companies, in an attempt to unearth unlisted companies that had performed well during the period under examination. See table 7.2 for a sample of award-winning companies. Finally, an attempt was made to identify Jamaican companies that had been involved in FDI during the period. The Jamaican-based companies that were identified in this regard were: Sandals Hotel Chain, SuperClubs Hotel Chain and Island Grill.

Table 7.2: Sample of Award Winning Jamaican Companies 1994–1999

Jamaica Exporters Association (JEA) Champion Exporter Awards
1994 Grace, Kennedy & Co. Export Trading
1995 United Estates Ltd
1996 JABEXCO Ltd (subsidiary of Jamaica Broilers)
1997 Cifuentes Ltd
1998 Grace, Kennedy & Co. Export Trading
1999 Jamaica Drink Co. Ltd

Jamaica Manufacturers' Association (JMA) Export Awards

1994 GG Award	Dairy Industries Ltd (subsidiary of Grace, Kennedy)
Champion Exporter	J. Wray & Nephew (subsidiary of Lascelles de Mercado)
1995 GG Award	Industrial Commercial Developments Ltd
Champion Exporter	Cifuentes Ltd
1996 GG Award	Mechala
Champion Exporter	LASCO Foods Ltd
1997 GG Award	Desnoes & Geddes Ltd
Champion Exporter	Cifuentes Ltd
1998 GG Award	Desnoes & Geddes Ltd
Champion Exporter	Cifuentes Ltd
1999 GG Award	J. Wray & Nephew Ltd
Champion Exporter	J. Wray & Nephew Ltd

Miscellaneous Awards (Non-listed Companies)

Sandals	World Travel Awards, World's Best All-Inclusive Hotel Resort (1996–2000)
	Travel Weekly, Best Caribbean Hotel Group (1994–2000)
LASCO Foods	JEA, 1997 Trailblazer Award
Super-Plus Foods	CEO recipient of 1999 Observer Business Leader of the Year Award
Starfish Oils	JEA 1997 Best New Exporter; Ernst & Young Emerging Caribbean Entrepreneur Award, 1999.

Based upon these data, the sample of eighteen companies listed in table 7.3 were identified and examined more carefully to identify factors that may have contributed to their relative success.

Table 7.3: Companies Investigated to Elicit Factors Influencing Competitiveness

Banking
1. Bank of Nova Scotia

Insurance
2. First Life Insurance Company

Retail and Distribution
3. Courts
4. Hardware and Lumber
5. Super-Plus Food Stores
6. Island Grill

Agri-Processed Food and Beverage
7. Lascelles de Mercado
8. Grace, Kennedy & Co.
9. Jamaica Broilers
10. Desnoes & Geddes
11. Lasco Foods
12. Jamaica Drink Co. Ltd

Tourism/Entertainment
13. Pulse
14. Sandals
15. SuperClubs

Manufacturing & Marketing
16. Berger
17. Starfish Oils

Communication
18. Gleaner Co. Ltd

Surveying the Experiences of Competitive Jamaican Enterprises

In the following paragraphs we provide information, grouped by industry, from our survey of the enterprises identified in table 7.3.

Banking and Insurance

The period of focus of this study coincided with the most traumatic period in the history of the Jamaican banking and insurance sectors. The profitability of listed companies does not capture the full extent of the trauma. Between 1995 and 2000 the Jamaican government intervened to shore up insolvent and illiquid banks and insurance companies in the amount of about 44 per cent of Jamaica's GDP.

The pervasiveness of governmental intervention is captured in the following data. Of the eleven banks that existed at the beginning of 1995, only four (BNS, CIBC, Citibank and Trafalgar Commercial Bank) did not receive funding from the Financial Sector Adjustment Company (FINSAC), which was the government agency established to rehabilitate the financial sector. Similarly, of the eight life insurance companies that operated in Jamaica in 1995, only two (First Life Insurance and Prime Life Insurance), had not been recipients of financial assistance from the Jamaican government by 2000. This is the context in which the relative profitability of BNS, in the banking sector, and First Life, in the life insurance sector, has to be understood. The key characteristic that seemed to define the relative success of these companies was a conservative approach to financial operations. This focus included strong levels of capitalization and prudent risk management.

Like BNS, First Life Insurance also outperformed its competitors, but it started from a rather different base than BNS. Unlike BNS, which was one of the largest banks in Jamaica and a subsidiary of the Bank of Nova Scotia, First Life was one of the smallest life insurance companies during the financial crisis. But at First Life, from the very outset, there was an effort to ensure high levels of capitalization for the company. This was reflected, by 1995, in a ratio of net worth to total assets that was the highest in the life insurance industry.

First Life, as a relatively small player in the life insurance industry, also sought to learn from the experiences of its larger competitors. In the mid-1990s the Jamaican life insurance industry was operating with high levels of administrative costs, with respect to both central administration and selling new life insurance policies. In the context of an economy experiencing high levels of inflation and interest rates the industry, generally, sought to maintain profitability levels by effectively converting the business of selling ordinary life insurance into one in which many life policies incorporated a fixed interest rate component, thus allowing the life companies to compete against the high interest rates offered elsewhere in the economy. This shift by the industry to deposit-type insurance policies, coupled with its heavy investment in real estate, turned out to be the primary cause for the liquidity and insolvency problems that were to bedevil the life insurance industry in the late 1990s.

First Life took a more conservative posture towards the problems of declining profitability within the life insurance industry. By 1995 the company indicated plans to lower commission rates and marketing expenses, improve policy retention and profitability, increase agent productivity, and lower administrative costs per policy in an attempt to improve the company's viability. The implementation process began in 1996, when the company closed several branches and merged others, initiated severe administrative and marketing cuts, restructured the commission scale, in particular by reducing the heavy up-front commission expenses traditionally associated with life insurance sales in Jamaica, and reduced the agent count. The result was a reduction in new business premium income, but an improvement in profitability.

Tourism and Entertainment

For two decades success in the Jamaican tourism industry has revolved primarily around two entities: the Sandals and SuperClubs hotel chains. The success of these two chains was not interrupted during the period of low growth in the Jamaican economy. The relative success of these chains can be attributed to their innovation; the strong leadership of their founders, Butch Stewart of Sandals and John Issa of SuperClubs; their commitment to high standards; their intense rivalry; and the strategic alliances they have been able to develop.

Retail and Distribution

During the 1990s one of the more dramatic changes in the operations of Jamaican businesses was seen in the ascendancy of retail and distribution establishments and the emergence of supermarket chains. By 2000 the largest such chain in Jamaica was Super-Plus Food Stores, with revenues of approximately US$70 million.

Super-Plus, owned by the Chen family and managed by Wayne Chen, was established as a chain of supermarkets in 1992 when five stores in central Jamaica, which were owned by members of the Chen family who had been in the grocery business for over three decades, were consolidated under common management. The consolidation of these stores was in direct response to the deregulation of the distribution sector by the government. With the opportunity to source goods directly rather than through government-owned trade intermediaries or private traders with exclusive import licences, Wayne Chen saw the opportunity for significant growth in the distribution sector, driven by distributive operations that could benefit from economies of scale in warehousing, transportation and procurement.

By 2000 Super-Plus had grown to include nineteen stores and eleven hundred employees. The success of the group could be attributed to the Chen family's expertise in the grocery-retailing business, the benefits gained from economies of scale in procurement and transportation, and strong leadership, including a vision for development of the group based at least in part on international benchmarking.

With respect to the latter activity, Chen, from the early 1990s, benchmarked Jamaican retailing against developments in Puerto Rico. Although Puerto Rico is clearly a more affluent economy than Jamaica, and has a population 40 per cent larger than the Jamaican population, it was nevertheless deemed significant that the largest supermarket chain in Puerto Rico comprised sixty stores with revenues approaching US$750 million. Benchmarking against international competition, and the view of the world that this created, were par for the course in the Chen family. One of Wayne Chen's siblings, Michael Lee-Chin, for example, was the principal owner, with a 90 per cent shareholding, of AIC, Canada's eleventh-largest mutual fund and the largest privately held mutual fund in Canada, with C$14 billion under management.[3] The year 1999 was an interesting one for these siblings: Lee-Chin won Ernst and Young's Entrepreneur of the Year Award (financial services), while Chen won the Jamaica Observer's Jamaican Business Leader of the Year Award.

Although a rapidly growing player in the Jamaican retailing and distribution sector, Super-Plus Food Stores was not the largest firm in this sector. Its revenues were second to Courts (Jamaica) Limited, the oldest subsidiary, operating outside of the United Kingdom, of the furniture and appliance retailer, Courts (UK) Limited. Courts (Jamaica) had 2000 sales revenues of J$5.2 billion (US$115 million). Courts represented another example of a retailer that had grown dramatically during a period of low growth in the Jamaican economy. The company averaged an annual increase in after-tax profits, denominated in US dollars, of 87 per cent over the same period.

Although Courts had a forty-year-long history of operations in Jamaica, the spurt in its growth and profitability during the late 1990s stood out, in the context of that history. In 1995, the then managing director of Courts (Jamaica) retired and Richard Coe, who had worked with the company as marketing director between 1982 and 1990, returned to Jamaica to take over the leadership of the company as it was struggling with low profitability levels. Coe orchestrated a turn-around plan that recognized the more competitive landscape that confronted the company. Among other elements, the plan featured a strong emphasis on advertising and promotion, revolving around an in-house promotion department designed to take advantage of the global company's considerable promotional expertise.

The two other retail/distribution companies featured in table 7.3 also show the importance of leadership. Hardware and Lumber's profitability reflected that company's investment in bringing a new approach to hardware retailing to the Jamaican consumer, involving much larger retail outlets carrying a wide range of products. Hardware and Lumber was a subsidiary of the Pan Jamaican Investment Trust Company Limited (as was First Life).

Island Grill, although the smallest entity examined in this group, was distinctive in its efforts to engage in FDI. The company was founded by Thalia Lyn in the mid-1990s based upon traditional Jamaican recipes for jerk chicken and jerk fish. The chain's five restaurants in Jamaica are complemented by an overseas branch in Brixton, catering to the Jamaican diaspora in the United Kingdom. In March 2001 Island Grill opened its first US store in Fort Lauderdale, Florida, with plans for a second store in nearby Pembroke Pines scheduled for later in 2001. Island Grill shares a coincidental relationship to Super-Plus: the company's founder, Thalia Lyn, has a brother, Raymond Chang, who has been a leader in Canada's mutual fund industry.

Agri-Processed Food and Beverage

Many of Jamaica's large firms, and several competitive enterprises, operate in the processed food and beverage industrial sector. This study examined the operations of six of these companies (as identified in table 7.3). The companies examined showed evidence of competitive operations based on export success and above-average profitability (tables 7.1 and 7.2).

The six companies can be divided into two categories. The first category comprises those companies with long-established business operations, based largely on import substitution or trade preference, which have sought to transform these operations in the context of trade liberalization and the ongoing erosion of trade preference. The second category comprises companies that have established brand new business operations in response to the changing competitive landscape. These companies include LASCO Foods and Jamaica Drink.

The transforming companies focused on expanding exports and on improving the competitiveness of their export and domestic operations. J. Wray and Nephew, the largest subsidiary in the Lascelles de Mercado Group, for example, is Jamaica's largest producer of rums and spirits. Historically, this company had focused on the UK market, and, indeed, benefited from trade preferences in relation to its sale of bulk rum to that country. The principal focus of the company in recent times, however, has been to build an international reputation with its branded products, de-emphasizing the bulk rum component of its business activity and focusing on improvements in the quality of all of its products, including its branded products. In 1996, for example, the company achieved ISO 9000 certification in record time.

The result is that by the late 1990s J. Wray and Nephew was selling its branded spirit products to more than sixty markets around the world. On the other hand, in relation to the strategy of de-emphasizing bulk rum sales, in 1998 the company withdrew from the commodity bulk rum market in Germany.

J. Wray and Nephew, in addition to developing brand equity, also sought to develop its human resources and transform its workplace relations through a process of continuous re-engineering of its business operations. The company was not unique: the other four (of the top five) food-processing and beverage companies in Jamaica – Grace, Kennedy and Company, Jamaica Producers, Jamaica Broilers, and Desnoes and Geddes – were also engaged in efforts during the late 1990s to transform their workplace relations to make their operations more internationally competitive.

Three of these companies had explicit transformation programmes that led to improvements in short-term financial performance and organizational productivity, as detailed in chapter 8 of this volume. An assessment of the transformation efforts of these three companies indicates that transformation efforts among firms in developing countries that are seeking to improve their competitiveness should recognize the importance of democratizing traditionally hierarchical work environments (see chapter 8).

The second category of firms in the agri-food and beverage cluster are those which established or significantly expanded operations during the 1990s in response to changes in the competitive landscape in Jamaica. LASCO Foods illustrates. This company, owned by Jamaican businessman Lascelles Chin, grew during the 1990s to become the largest private company in Jamaica in the food-processing and distribution business, selling more than ninety brands locally and internationally, and with 2000 sales revenue estimated at J$3 billion (US$68 million).

Chin began business in 1961 running a commission agency that imported black pepper and peas. After investing in a range of industries, by the late 1980s Chin's focus was on distribution, with the creation of LASCO Foods. The company's most significant growth, particularly as it relates to exports, has come from the events that took place in 1993–1994.

In 1993, Chin purchased Jamaica Soya Products from the Jamaican government. The venture was unsuccessful, as the company was soon to collapse in the face of trade liberalization. By 1993–1994, however, Chin was in dialogue with Dupont Chemical Company in an effort to identify nutritious and affordable products for Jamaicans. This dialogue led to the sourcing from Dupont of soya protein isolate, which LASCO has used in the creation of a range of soy-based protein drinks. Operating on low margins, the company prices its products competitively.

The line of soy-based drinks has facilitated a rapid expansion in export sales by LASCO. By 2000 LASCO was the largest purchaser of soya protein from Dupont and the company was exporting its soy-based drinks to the Caribbean, Central America, Latin America, Europe and in African-American markets in the United States. The company continued to invest heavily in distribution and processing facilities, and marketing and promotion in the Jamaican market.

Investment in processing facilities was a main area of competitive advantage for another successful Jamaican exporter in the food and beverage sector, Jamaica Drink Company. This company was a subsidiary of the Wisynco group of companies, and produced the popular Jamaican soft drink Bigga. The Wisynco group of companies was involved in the establishment of the first PET (polyethyl phtheraphalate) bottling manufacturing operation in Jamaica. It used its processing capacity to compete with the market leader in soft drinks, Desnoes and Geddes, in the mid-1990s, at a time when Desnoes and Geddes operated only a glass bottling line.

Manufacturing and Marketing

Outside of food and beverage processing, the operations of two manufacturing/marketing companies that have shown evidence of competitiveness were examined. Among listed companies, the profitability leader in this category is Berger Paints. Berger Paints was incorporated in Jamaica in 1953. It was listed on the Jamaican stock exchange in 1992, and since then has shown consistent increases in sales and profitability through the financial year ended December 1999. This was a record year for the company, with profits, sales, production volumes, export revenue, productivity and customer satisfaction all experiencing significant improvement. In 1998 the company achieved ISO 9000 certification.

Since 1993 Berger Jamaica has focused on expanding capacity, investing in equipment, improving skill levels of workers and penetrating niche export markets for special paints. The group focused on these areas in anticipation of the imminent reduction in the common external tariff on paints imported into the CARICOM region.

In terms of worker relations, in 1999 64 per cent of Berger's workers had been with the company for ten years or more, and in that year, 90 per cent of workers strengthened their professional skills through specialized training programmes. Early in 2001 Berger Jamaica's exceptional performance within the Berger International Limited group of companies was recognized. The Jamaican company won the inaugural Berger International Limited award presented to the best operating company in the Berger International Limited Group, which comprises twenty-five companies in fourteen countries.

A much more recent entry to the Jamaican manufacturing sector is Starfish Oils. This company, under the leadership of Sharon Cooke, began operations in 1996 as a manufacturer of aromatherapy body, bath and massage oils, scented candles and handmade soaps. By the end of 1996 Starfish was exporting to twelve countries. This company may well be Jamaica's first "new economy" manufacturer. A supplier to local hotels, Starfish boasts a state-of-the-art website, through which it processes most of its export orders. The company utilizes a US-based website order fulfilment service that provides round-the-clock responses to web inquiries, arranges the logistics of distribution of web-ordered products, and conducts all the web marketing and servicing activities for the company, in exchange for a 30 per cent margin.

Communications

The final subsector considered in this survey was communications. In this category the profitability leader among listed companies was the Jamaican *Gleaner* newspaper. Competition in this industry, as in so much of the Jamaican economy, has changed in the last two decades. By 2001 there were three national Sunday newspapers, two national daily newspapers, several regional papers, a score of radio stations, three national television stations and the ubiquitous access to cable television. Yet the Gleaner Company has continued to operate profitably.

The Gleaner Company has benefited from strong leadership during the entire period of liberalization of the communications industry, and it has not been complacent in its responses to the new competitive environment. One example was its response to new entrants to the market that introduced colour newspaper printing. Gleaner executives could have relied complacently on superior editorial capabilities, well-known columnists and the benefits of an extremely strong brand. They did not, and immediately matched the colour-printing capabilities of their competitors in order to maintain their own competitive position in this industry segment.

Lessons from the Survey of Competitive Jamaican Enterprises

It is possible to distil from this chapter's survey of competitive Jamaican enterprises a number of competitiveness drivers. Table 7.4 summarizes these drivers for each sector of economic activity examined in the survey.

A number of these competitiveness drivers recur from sector to sector. These common drivers are identified below, using examples from the enterprises surveyed. Collectively, they appear to represent the key factors that have contributed towards enterprise competitiveness.

Responsiveness to Liberalization, Deregulation and Competition

One of the competitiveness drivers common to most sectors was the extent to which firms were able to respond to liberalization, deregulation and increasing

Table 7.4: Competitiveness Drivers by Sector

Sector	Competitiveness Drivers
Banking and insurance (First Life, Bank of Nova Scotia)	Focus, risk management, industry knowledge, leadership, international benchmarking
Tourism and entertainment (Sandals, SuperClubs, Pulse)	Innovation, leadership, factor conditions, responsiveness to competition, quality focus, industry knowledge, benchmarking
Retail, distribution and communication (Courts, Hardware and Lumber, Super-Plus Food Stores, Island Grill, Gleaner)	Responsiveness to liberalization and competition, international benchmarking, leadership, risk management, aggressive marketing, industry knowledge, quality focus
Manufacturing and marketing (Berger, Starfish Oils)	Leadership, training, international benchmarking, strategic alliances, risk management, quality focus
Agri-processing, food and beverage (Lascelles, Grace, Kennedy, Jamaica Broilers, Desnoes & Geddes, LASCO Food, Jamaica Drink)	Leadership, branding, work transformation, international benchmarking, responsiveness to deregulation, quality focus, innovation, technology focus, marketing and distribution, industry knowledge, risk management

levels of competition. Super-Plus Food Stores illustrates. That chain of super-markets began in direct response to the Jamaican government's deregulation of the food trade. As the two most successful indigenous hotel chains in the Caribbean, Sandals and SuperClubs are forced to respond to intense competitive pressures and, it can readily be argued, both have become more successful in the process. Grace, Kennedy and Company's entry into the financial services industry, through its remittance operation, is another example of a firm responding to liberalization, in this case of the Jamaican foreign exchange market. Yet another is the Gleaner Company's effort to respond quickly and decisively to competition.

International Benchmarking

The survey of competitive enterprises provided several examples of companies that responded to competition as a result of a process of international benchmarking.

International benchmarking activity was one of the competitiveness drivers that was common for competitive enterprises in all sectors.

In banking and insurance, BNS and First Life benchmarked capital adequacy and prudential ratios against international rather than local competitors. In the case of BNS, this process was facilitated by the standards imposed by its corporate headquarters in Canada. The success of Sandals in winning major international awards provides an indication of the world view exhibited by that company.

In the retail sector, the survey reported in this chapter provided an example of Super-Plus benchmarking the chain's growth prospects against a Puerto Rican standard. As will be noted in chapter 8, Jamaica Broilers benchmarked explicitly against chicken processors throughout the Western Hemisphere, and Desnoes and Geddes initiated a process of international benchmarking against other breweries in the Guinness global network after the company's acquisition by Guinness in 1993. Berger also benchmarked, with great success, against other companies in the Berger International Limited group of companies. The benchmarking activity was aided by the fact that the leaders of the companies themselves had a significant reservoir of industry knowledge.

Yet this survey also hints at another dimension of international benchmarking and competitive response. One might describe it as the "Reunion Effect". Douglas Orane, CEO of Grace, Kennedy, was a Baker scholar (graduating in the top 5 per cent of his 1981 class from Harvard Business School). Under Orane's leadership, Grace, Kennedy enunciated its 2020 Vision plan and also articulated a goal of having the company listed on the US NASDAQ Stock Exchange, in addition to being the first Caribbean company to list on all three major exchanges in the anglophone Caribbean (Jamaica, Trinidad and Tobago, and Barbados).

It does not stretch the limits of credulity to hypothesize that Orane's world view and competitive drive would be influenced by attending reunions with highly successful classmates from Harvard Business School, some of whom were probably running Fortune 500 companies by the late 1990s. Similarly, it is a rather interesting coincidence that both Wayne Chen, CEO of Super-Plus Food Stores, and Thalia Lyn, CEO of Island Grill, had siblings who were extremely successful players in the Canadian mutual fund industry. Again, it seems possible that sibling reunions at Christmas dinners would assist in the development of an internationally competitive world view.

A Focus on Innovation, Marketing, Quality and Technology

The survey also pointed to competitive firms engaging in business practices that are likely to create value in any type of business environment. Innovation was a noticeable activity in many firms, from the continued innovation of the Jamaican-based all-inclusive hotel chains, to LASCO's innovative approach to the development of soy-based drinks.

The aforementioned companies also complemented innovation with a focus on marketing as a source of competitive advantage. Such a focus was also evident in the turn-around plans for Courts, in the branding activities of J. Wray and Nephew, and at Grace, Kennedy, which relaunched the Grace brand during the late 1990s. Quality was an important focus of business activity, and several of the companies featured had symbolized their quality focus with a movement towards ISO 9000 certification (Grace, Kennedy, J. Wray and Nephew, and Berger, for example). Enhancing processing capabilities through technology acquisition and adaptation was also a feature of the activities of companies, as illustrated by Jamaica Drink Company.

Workplace Transformation and Human Resource Development

Another competitiveness driver common to companies in several sectors was an effort to transform the workplace and focus on the development of all human resources within the enterprise. There were several examples of explicit workplace transformation programmes. These were particularly evident in the context of companies responding to the imperative of enhancing competitiveness based on the onset of trade liberalization and integration into global enterprise networks. The programmes of Grace, Kennedy, Jamaica Broilers, and Desnoes and Geddes illustrate. Further, Berger's achievement of having 90 per cent of its workforce undergoing professional development during one year is a striking testament to the importance placed on human resource development.

Effective Risk Management

Yet another competitiveness driver that characterized the operations of companies within several sectors was the careful management of risk. Entrepreneurs have been widely viewed as risk takers, yet studies have recognized that they

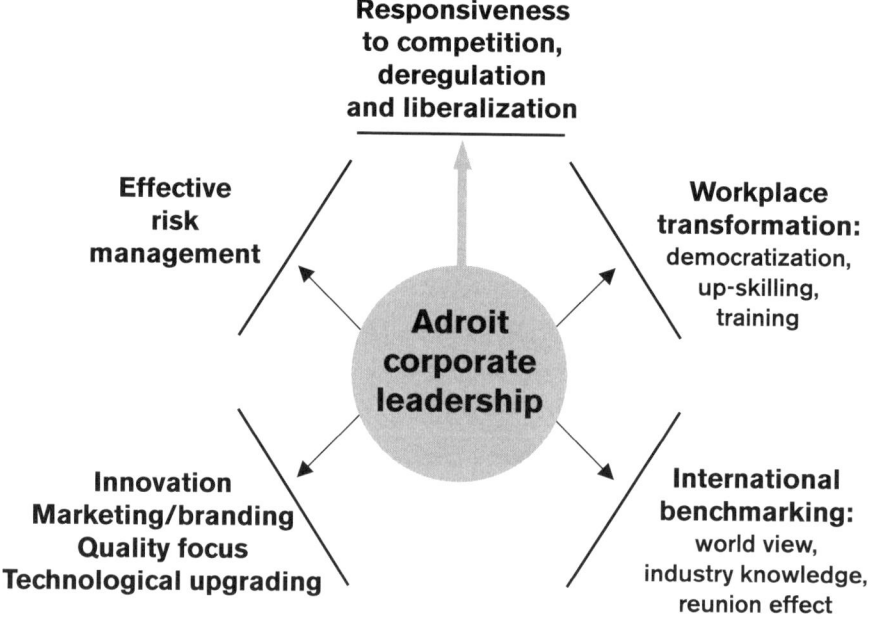

Figure 7.1: Competivenesss Drivers in Small Developing Countries

are, in fact, risk managers.[4] The competitive companies in the banking and insurance sectors illustrate. Recognizing the nature of the Jamaican environment of the 1990s, it was critical that financial institutions manage their risks carefully. In the case of these institutions it was important to focus their operations in order to ensure an appropriate balance between the time profile of their assets and liabilities.

But risk management does not necessarily involve pursuing highly focused activities. Grace, Kennedy sought to manage corporate risks through the time-honoured risk management strategy of diversification. By diversifying into the financial services industry, the company's financial services division benefited from liberalization of the Jamaican financial sector, even while its traditional trading and processing operations initially faltered as they encountered increased competition resulting from Jamaica's trade liberalization efforts. In the mid-1990s a significant share of the conglomerate's profitability was generated from financial services.

Similarly, J. Wray and Nephew's geographic market diversification and movement away from commodity rum to branded products reflected an effort to manage the risk of a reduction in preferential access to the European market for bulk rum and the sugar produced by the company. Starfish Oils' strategic alliance with a US-based web service and order fulfilment company was yet another example of risk management.

Adroit Corporate Leadership

Importantly, however, these efforts to respond to new competitive landscapes; benchmark against international competition; focus on innovation, marketing, quality and technology; transform workplaces and upgrade human resources; and manage risks did not occur in a vacuum. Uniformly, across these companies, adroit corporate leaders drove these activities. This study has found, like others before,[5] that leadership matters a lot. Figure 7.1 seeks to capture the common competitiveness drivers around the central, organizing force of adroit leadership.

Chapter 8

Workplace Performance and Competitiveness

This chapter continues the focus on the operations of foreign and indigenous firms in small developing countries begun in the previous chapter. In response to the globalization challenge identified in the introductory chapter of this volume, firms in small developing countries are recognizing the critical importance of improving the competitiveness of their operations. These firms recognize that moving to levels of operational performance that meet international standards is likely to require a new culture of workplace performance, which will include a fundamental transformation in the ordering of relationships between workers and managers.

There is a burgeoning literature on changes in workplace relations, but it is a literature that tends to be dominated by the experiences of firms in developed countries. While these experiences are certainly relevant to firms operating in small developing countries, they do not fully capture the set of challenges that confronts this latter group of countries.

The study reported on in this chapter represented an attempt to examine the specific challenges confronting firms operating in small developing countries that are seeking to reorder their workplace relations in an effort to meet the critical challenges of international competition. The remainder of this chapter examines the research methodology used in the study, surveys the management of changes in workplace relations globally, and examines these change efforts through the lens of each of the companies investigated in this study. The chapter concludes with the lessons for other small developing countries seeking to reorder their workplace relations in an effort to improve competitiveness.

Research Methodology and Data Collection

Given the importance of understanding the nuances of the approaches used to modify workplace relations, this study examined the management of workplace relations in three firms in one developing country, Jamaica. The Jamaican environment is a useful one for examining this subject because it captures many of the elements that are likely to drive change efforts in other small developing countries.

With a population of just 2.5 million people, Jamaica is a relatively open economy, with trade in goods and services representing 53 per cent of GDP. Recognizing the continued need for openness, the government has been involved in a series of trade liberalization efforts that began in the early 1980s, as pointed out in chapter 6. These efforts have increased the degree of international competition to which local firms are subjected. Yet Jamaica, like most other developing countries, historically pursued a development strategy of import-substitution industrialization. Accordingly, most companies in the goods-producing segment of the economy were spawned in the context of high levels of import protection. These firms would have to pursue different strategies to cope with liberalization.

For this study, the focus was on three firms in the processed food and drink subsector of the Jamaican manufacturing sector. This subsector is particularly subject to competitive pressures. It is also the only subsector of the Jamaican manufacturing sector that was created based on an import-substituting philosophy, and yet is believed by the Jamaican government to have a potential competitive advantage in an era of global competition (as reported upon in chapter 4 of this volume, in a discussion of the country's industrial policy).[1]

The three companies – Grace, Kennedy and Company, Desnoes and Geddes, and Jamaica Broilers – were three of the top five processed food and drink companies, by market value and revenue, listed on the Jamaica Stock Exchange at December 1999, with ranks of one, four and five respectively.[2] The companies ranked two and three were Jamaica's largest banana and rum companies, both of which benefited from preferential access to the European market.

Grace, Kennedy and Company is an indigenously owned diversified conglomerate, which has been operating in Jamaica since 1922. The group is comprised of subsidiaries operating in a number of industries, including finance, shipping and information technology, but the core operation of the group is in the area of trading and agri-processing.

Desnoes and Geddes, prior to 1993, was also an indigenously owned Jamaican company. The country's largest brewer of beer, it had been in operation since 1918. Over time, Desnoes and Geddes diversified into the manufacturing of soft drinks and assorted industries. In 1993 the company was sold to the Irish-based company Guinness, and several years later, with the acquisition of Guinness by the Diageo Company, based in the United Kingdom, Desnoes and Geddes became a part of the Diageo Group. By 2001 Desnoes and Geddes had sold its soft drink business to Pepsi-Cola, and divested other businesses to become a focused beer processor.

Jamaica Broilers was another indigenous Jamaican conglomerate, which began operations in 1958. It was a vertically integrated meat-processing company with operations in beef, fish and chicken. The largest segment of its operations, however, comprised chicken processing and marketing, an industry segment in which it was the market leader in Jamaica.

The research project reported on in this chapter involved studying each of these companies with a view to understanding the processes used in their efforts to change workplace relations. The research involved interviewing managers in these firms who had been involved in change efforts, interviewing officers of the unions that represented these companies, interviewing former workers through a focus group, and interviewing an individual who had sought to mediate relations between the company and the union, in the company that experienced the most traumatic attempt at workplace change.

Managing Change in Workplace Relations

The considerable literature on the management of change in workplace relations is captured schematically in figure 8.1.

The contracting out of production activities and services is gaining momentum around the world as firms seek to increase workplace flexibility.[3] Although various approaches are captured in the contracting-out phenomenon, they all involve some shift from the traditional process of managing workforces in vertically integrated bureaucratic structures to one in which workers are no longer directly employed by companies, but their working relations with companies are mediated through contractual agreements, sometimes with the assistance of labour market intermediaries.[4] These arrangements allow firms to operate more flexibly, but they also are likely to create the problems often associated

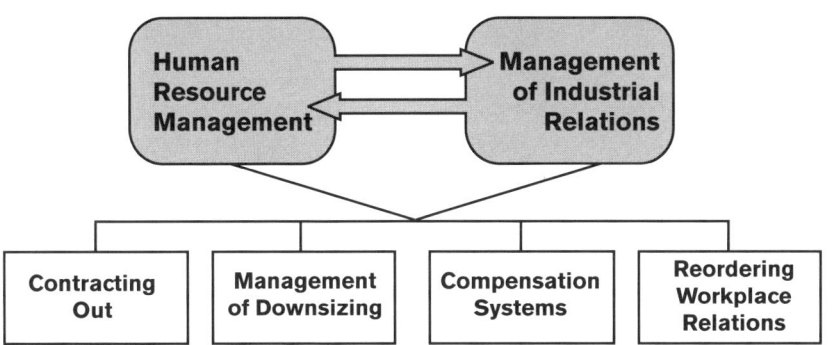

Figure 8.1: Managing Change in Workplace Relations

with contractual relationships, namely information impactedness, uncertainty, gaming and opportunism.[5] Such problems could well have an impact on organizational commitment and motivation.

While there is nothing new about the down-sizing phenomenon, the incidence of organizations down-sizing has increased considerably in recent years. Not surprisingly, so has the academic commentary on this subject. Much of the focus of this commentary has been on the challenges created by down-sizing. In particular, commentators warn of the potentially damaging effect of downsizing and redundancy programmes on the survivors and on the culture of the downsized organization.[6]

Changes in compensation systems have often complemented other types of organizational changes as companies seek to respond to competitive pressures. The most significant element of these changes has been a shift towards payment and recognition based upon performance, replacing recognition based upon status, which operated through mechanisms such as executive dining rooms and private parking spaces.[7]

A critical set of changes employed by many organizations seeking to change workplace cultures is through reordered workplace relations. Organizations have been democratizing workplaces, flattening organizational hierarchies and blurring the distinctions between different categories of workers as they focus on flexibility and creativity in the workforce, performance-based recognition and self-controlled and motivated employees. Self-controlled employees become critical, since key desired results such as world-class quality, superior customer service, continuous innovation and flexibility are not easily achieved through traditional "Fordist" methods of top-down managerial control.[8]

Figure 8.1 indicates that the various workplace changes have to be managed appropriately if these changes are to have their intended effects. In this context, much of the literature on workplace transformation appropriately places the onus on the management of human resources. This literature places emphasis on the importance of a process of organizational transformation which creates a new type of empowered employee.[9] The process of empowering employees often requires a complete re-engineering of the organizational environment, in which there is a fundamental redesign and rethinking of organizational processes.[10]

Out of this process of redesign a work environment is created in which there is a new moral contract between managers and employees, incorporating a role-responsibility reversal. In this new moral contract, empowered employees are responsible for the company's competitiveness and their own learning, and top managers support an employee's entrepreneurial initiatives.[11] This approach requires a perspective that sees human resource management as the key element of the strategic operations of companies, rather than traditional, more myopic approaches to the human resource managerial function.[12]

In unionized work environments, the management of human resources has to be complemented by the appropriate management of industrial relations. The various changes identified in figure 8.1 are areas in which unions are likely to have a significant interest, since they all involve important changes in the terms and conditions of employment. The literature on the management of industrial relations indicates the extent of union involvement in efforts at workplace transformation.[13] The ability of a union to influence the outcome of workplace transformation depends on several factors. These include the union's ability to: access information from its membership; educate and mobilize the workforce around a vision of workplace reform; access decision making at multiple levels in the employing organization. Also important to the degree of influence a union exercises in this process is its ability and willingness to balance co-operation with conflict.[14]

Against the backdrop of global efforts at workplace transformation, the efforts of the three aforementioned firms were examined in order to understand the management of workplace transformation in the setting of a small developing country.

Managing Workplace Changes in the Caribbean

In extending global findings on workplace change to the context of a small developing country, one must recognize that there are key elements which are peculiar to small developing country environments. In the Caribbean environment in which this study was based, for example, an important element has been, historically, a significant level of distrust between workers and managers, arising from the region's history as a plantation-based economy.[15] The contemporary nature of these attitudes of distrust within Caribbean organizations is reflected in recent research suggesting that almost half of the workforce in Jamaica describe decision making in their organizations as exploitative and authoritative, and as a process in which managers make decisions unilaterally without providing prior information to workers.[16]

It was against the background of this historical organizational culture that the companies studied sought to effect workplace change. The change efforts of the three companies studied involved a competitive trigger point, a transformation plan and the actual transformation action, which included a combination of changes in workplace relations, compensation systems, and contractual relations, including contracting activities and redundancies.

Competitive Trigger Points

The need to improve the competitiveness of a firm's operations has been the rationale for many efforts at transforming workplaces in companies around the world. This is also true in small developing countries, but because firms in many of these countries have been sheltered from international competition, the recognition of the need to improve levels of competitiveness may well await a trigger point.

In the cases of both Grace, Kennedy and Company and Jamaica Broilers the competitive trigger point for re-examining workplace relations was the indication from the Jamaican government that the protective tariffs enjoyed by processed food companies in Jamaica would be reduced. By 1995 the Jamaican government had advised the local meat-processing industry that it had signed agreements with its counterpart countries in CARICOM to reduce duties on processed meat (which amounted to 86 per cent in the 1990s) to the level of 20–25 per cent.

In addition, by 1995 the trade liberalization process in Jamaica had already ensured that Grace, Kennedy was facing far more competition than it had historically faced in its trading and merchandising activities. Against this backdrop, by the mid-1990s Grace, Kennedy and Jamaica Broilers made a public commitment to the goal of enhancing the international competitiveness of their operations. In the case of Grace, Kennedy, international competitiveness was to be demonstrated not only by the ability to compete on Jamaica's market, but also by the extent to which the company could generate revenues from international business activity.

For Desnoes and Geddes, the competitive trigger point came two years earlier, in 1993, with the Guinness acquisition. The previous management team had initiated improvements in production equipment and processes, but the acquisition by Guinness brought a greater sense of urgency to the need to improve the productivity of the Jamaican facility. It was immediately apparent to the new owners that the Jamaican brewery was far less efficient than other Guinness operations around the world.

The Transformation Plans

In all three cases, transformation plans were developed. In 1995 the CEO of Grace, Kennedy unveiled a plan to transform the company by the year 2020 – the 2020 Vision. In introducing this vision to staff members of Grace, Kennedy on 27 July 1995, CEO Douglas Orane made the following statements:

> Our goal is to double the productivity of every person in the Grace, Kennedy organisation from the messenger to the chairman. In order to accomplish this goal we will have to increase significantly the proportion of our earnings that derives from international activities from the current level of 11 per cent of profits to a level of 50% of profits by the year 2020.

The transformation plan for Desnoes and Geddes was introduced in the same year as Grace, Kennedy's 2020 Vision. In 1994 Guinness appointed a vice-president for human resource development for Desnoes and Geddes. This was the first such appointment in the company's history. A Guinness executive with considerable experience in human resource and industrial relations management came to Jamaica to take up this position. Within one year of his arrival, as team leader he had spearheaded the preparation, by the top twenty-five executives in the company, of a Vision 2000 plan for Desnoes and Geddes. This plan was to reduce the cost base of the company's operations through a 50 per cent reduction in operation and technical headcount, while increasing productivity (measured by hecto-litres per person) by at least 50 per cent, in addition to improving key performance indicators, such as quality. The plan also involved shifting the company's orientation from a supply-led to a demand-led business operation.

In the case of Jamaica Broilers, the transformation plan initially focused on the company's adoption of the goal of enhancing its international competitiveness. In 1998 the company's number one objective was as follows: "To secure our future, we must achieve customer satisfaction through a motivated and productive workforce committed to international competitiveness and the development of new products." After attempts to achieve this objective with the company's unionized workforce broke down in early 1998, the executive-level human resource management team working at the group's chicken-processing plant developed "Operation Revalorize". The objective of this transformation plan was to meet average performance standards for chicken-processing plants in the Western Hemisphere by effecting a 50 per cent savings in wage costs and an increase in worker productivity and motivation through the introduction of a team-based approach to production activities.

The Change Programmes

Workplace Change at Grace, Kennedy and Company
The change programme in Grace, Kennedy focused on planned improvements in productivity through the reordering of workplace relations, shifts in the contractual relations of workers, redundancies and changes in compensation systems. The starting point in understanding efforts at change within Grace, Kennedy is with the planning efforts among senior staff, pushed by the CEO and chairman. The company began weekly luncheons to develop teamwork among senior managers. An executive council was formed, later transformed into a strategy council, and a director was placed in charge of strategic planning, to demonstrate the attention the company planned to place on this area. Out of this process came the development of the first group mission statement, which was notable because of the diversified nature of this conglomerate's operations.

The transition from planning to action became most evident in 1996, when the company embarked on its first major restructuring exercise at its Grace Canning subsidiary. It was clear that this company had no future in a world of liberal trade unless it was fundamentally reconfigured, because the operation was quite inefficient. Indeed, even with the levels of protection that continued to obtain in the mid-1990s, this subsidiary was losing money. The company embarked on a transformation exercise, in conjunction with the unions, with whom it had historically had very cordial relations. The company was closed and all workers were made redundant; workers had been provided with notice about closure. The company and union also engaged in discussions on the types of services that could be provided to redundant workers to cushion the effects of the redundancy, with the unions providing suggestions in this regard.

Some six weeks after the company was closed it was reopened, with Grace, Kennedy engaging a placement service to provide the company with the staff required, under contract. The new workforce represented about 60 per cent of the old workforce, numerically. One of the requirements of obtaining employment was a minimum of secondary-level education, which had not been required in the previous production force. In the early stages of implementing the new workforce arrangements, office workers at the facility were required to man the production lines. The compensation system was also changed to include an element of performance-linked compensation, although a fixed salary component was also retained. The company placed emphasis on training in teamwork and production processes. The new workforce was considerably more productive than its predecessor.

The company used a similar template for restructuring another subsidiary, Dairy Industries, a cheese processor. In the case of Dairy Industries, the company was profitable but was not operating at world-class levels. Grace, Kennedy was particularly aware of this because it owned Dairy Industries as a joint-venture partner with the New Zealand Dairy Board. Also, Dairy Industries had been through the process of gaining ISO 9000 certification in the mid-1990s, and in this context had benchmarked its operations against dairy-processing facilities elsewhere and realized that it was far off the mark of international best practice. A shift to contracted workers operating under new terms and conditions of employment, including a performance-based compensation system, also resulted in significant productivity changes at the company. As in the Grace Canning template, office workers at Dairy Industries manned production lines during the initial phase of the start-up operations of the new workforce. These workers continue to operate production lines during the lunch-time break provided for production workers.

The blurring of the distinction between categories of workers was a hallmark of other efforts at transformation within the company. At the launch of the 2020 Vision, the CEO had stated,

> We can no longer run the company as a medieval monarchy with a monarch at the top. Instead, we should seek to run the organisation as a professional football team. On such a team, it does not matter who scores as long as we score. And we must all be capable of changing positions quickly.

The CEO of Grace, Kennedy sought to demonstrate the movement from monarchy to team by, among other things, leading a transformation of workspace at the group's headquarters. During refurbishing, large offices for senior managers, including the CEO, were replaced by far more modest offices, with an open floor arrangement complemented by strategically located meeting rooms.

Workplace Change at Jamaica Broilers

The change efforts at Jamaica Broilers focused on efforts to improve productivity through a process of contracting more highly educated workers under a performance-based compensation system, while changing workplace relations to emphasize improved worker responsibility for the production process, and a team-based approach to production.

Jamaica Broilers had operated its chicken-processing plant in the Spring Village district in Jamaica since the company's inception. The company was by far the most significant economic actor in the village, and close relations had developed between residents of the village and the company's owners. By the mid-1990s the production workforce at the processing plant comprised a network of workers, including many family members, from the village who were long-standing employees of the company, and who were well paid by the standards of Jamaican manufacturing industry. Over time employment relations at the company had deteriorated, and wild-cat strikes were not unusual, with employees leaving the production lines uncleared of perishable products, and the management almost conceding the running of the processing plant to a powerful set of employees from the village.

The need for change became clear as employment relations continued to deteriorate, profits declined, and the company contemplated the impact of this position on its operations in a more liberal trade environment. The company was acutely aware of its poor productivity and high cost levels because it utilized an international agricultural statistics company, Agristat, whose data showed that the company was one of the highest-cost chicken-processing facilities in the Western Hemisphere. In 1997 the president reported that the company was the highest-cost chicken plant in Jamaica, Barbados, Trinidad and Tobago or the United States.

Against this background the company sought to work with the unions in improving work relations and workplace practices at the company. While engaged in this attempt at restoring relations, the company experimented with new workplace relations by transferring to the cold room facility of the processing plant a group of workers who had been trained to operate using a multiskilled, multifunctional, team approach to production. The new workers in this section of the plant significantly outperformed their predecessors.

With the breakdown of an attempt at union-management mediation in early 1998, and the success of the "cold room" project in improving productivity levels, the company decided to embark upon Operation Revalorize. The operation involved recruiting and training a new set of better-educated workers from outside the Spring Village area to operate the processing plant. The existing workers were made redundant. The union was not involved in the redundancy exercise, and the workers were not given notice of the impending redundancy. The Jamaica Industrial Dispute Tribunal was later to find against the redundancy programme but did not order reinstatement in most cases, since most workers had accepted redundancy payments.

The company entered into a contractual arrangement with a placement company to provide the staffing for the production facility, with the proviso that 30 per cent of the new workforce could be staffed from the group of existing employees, and with the understanding that compensation levels would be performance based. The arrangements led to considerable hostility between the company and residents of Spring Village, to the extent that few of the former workers continued working at the new company, despite the 30 per cent reservation. Most of the production supervisors and the contractors, however, were from the old workforce, and these individuals were taken on study and benchmarking trips to broiler plants in the United States. They returned with ideas, which they had the latitude to implement, about how to improve processing operations at Jamaica Broilers.

Workers retained from the old workforce indicated that the new workforce showed considerable improvements over its predecessor in productivity and workplace attitude and discipline. New workers are expected to be multiskilled, and are given the opportunity to engage in different tasks. After the redundancy programme the company continued to provide assistance to former employees who needed assistance with training. Current workers who gained acceptance into a tertiary educational institution would also be assisted. In addition the company committed to involvement in job placement for workers who were interested in employment change, including seasonal work in US poultry firms. All workers would be expected to participate in a skill-upgrading programme with company assistance.

Workplace Change at Desnoes and Geddes
The change efforts at Desnoes and Geddes focused on improving productivity through a reduction in an overstaffed operation and increased compensation for those remaining workers. The exercise also sought to flatten the organizational hierarchy and increase the multifunctionality of workers.

The starting point for these efforts at Desnoes and Geddes was the Vision 2000 plan. This plan was spearheaded by a new vice-president of human resource management who came to Desnoes and Geddes with considerable experience, having being involved in transformation efforts in heavily unionized environments elsewhere in the worldwide Guinness family of companies. At the outset it was clear that the Jamaican operation was "over-crewed" and inefficient by the standards of other Guinness facilities of similar size and operational scope.

In concert with the development of the Vision 2000 plan, the new human resource management team developed the company's first industrial relations negotiating strategy; this was viewed as important to the success of the Vision 2000 plan, which called for changes in workplace relations. The strategy had three principal pillars: the pursuit of the high moral ground in negotiations; transparency in all negotiations and operations of the company; and an unwillingness to concede to force or coercion. In this regard, the strategy differed from previous negotiating practice in which capitulation to the threat of industrial action had been a regular practice of the company. As a consequence of the implementation of this new negotiating strategy, when the company and its union failed to agree on a new contract, a ten-day strike ensued around Christmas of 1995. In earlier periods, the company would have ensured that no strike took place during the busiest season of the year.

Thereafter, the Vision 2000 transformation efforts gathered momentum. The company sought to reduce the level of hierarchy at the workplace. One action that demonstrated the company's resolve in this area was the consolidation of the firm's three canteens into one canteen in which all workers were entitled to dine. Prior to this change the three canteens had corresponded to different categories of workers. One, nicknamed the "Executive", was restricted to the firm's senior managers; another, named the "Pegasus" after one of Jamaica's luxury hotels, catered to middle managers; the third, nicknamed "Rock Bottom" by the workers, was the dining place for the firm's production workers, who would have to wait in long lines for lower-quality fare. Another action was the elimination of reserved parking spots for managers. A third was the movement to bi-weekly, rather than weekly, pay-cheques for production workers; the cheques were transferred directly to employee bank accounts, thereby eliminating the practice of employees lining up on a weekly basis to receive their pay.

In line with these changes, the company sought to improve the multifunctionality of workers by consolidating the nuanced and numerous job categories of workers. Historically, workers in each category were restricted to the specific job functions that corresponded to the twenty-five work categories that existed at the company. The union was the University and Allied Workers Union, which had a history of focusing on worker democracy and was particularly aware of the need for improving competitiveness. Both the union and the company recognized the need to consolidate worker categories. The result was a reduction to only five categories of production workers by 2000. The reduction in categories of workers became one of the factors that contributed to a process of redundancies at Desnoes and Geddes, which was quite challenging for a company that had never reduced its workforce during its seven-decade history.

Clear criteria were developed for determining which positions would be made redundant, and which workers would be separated from the company. All individual cases of worker separation were discussed with the union before workers were informed. The company provided four weeks' notice to each employee, union-negotiated redundancy packages that were twice as generous as legal requirements, post-redundancy counselling for eight weeks and financing for training, in some instances. Redundancies were implemented across the board, and included individuals among the management as well as production workers. Indeed, towards the end of the Vision 2000 planning period, a higher proportion of managers were made redundant than production workers.

The widespread process of redundancy throughout the company created concerns about the responses of "redundancy survivors". The company and union agreed to deal with this problem through transparency in decisions, communication about the reasons for the need to change the workforce, and explicit processes of change management. In this latter area, the company measured employees along a change curve that spanned categories such as denial, immobilization, acceptance, hope and vision. It cumulated individual measurements to compute the organization's point along the change curve. Careful attention was paid to the psychological state of managers at meetings, and to the company's leadership. In so doing, Desnoes and Geddes benefited from change processes developed at its parent company, the UK firm Diageo.

Further, efforts were made to involve the entire workforce in the change process. The vice-president, human resources since 1997 was a Jamaican who had received training in Guinness's overseas operations. In 1999 he spearheaded a process by which the company's entire workforce was brought together to discuss the company's vision and strategy for the 2000–2005 period. The efforts at employee involvement were also reflected in the company's benchmarking activity. For example, during the Vision 2000 period, at the suggestion of the union, twenty company workers, including the chief union delegate, were taken to the Canadian brewery Labatts. There they observed production processes at a plant that operated 30 per cent more efficiently than Desnoes and Geddes, but with fifty people. This workforce contrasted to the approximately five hundred–person workforce of Desnoes and Geddes, which, in turn, was down from a level of fourteen hundred persons in brewing operations at the beginning of the Vision 2000 period.

Short-Term Results

Generally, the results from the transformation plans in all three companies were positive, in that they led to improved levels of productivity within the various organizations in the short term. Grace, Kennedy's 2020 Vision transformation plan focused on improving the productivity of all employees of the organization. One of its key success indicators in this regard was after-tax profits per employee, denominated in US dollars. This indicator increased by 107 per cent between 1995 and 2000.

At Jamaica Broilers, in the aftermath of Operation Revalorize, the chicken-processing plant moved from the bottom third of broiler plants in the Western Hemisphere to the top third of plants, in terms of cost and efficiency. Indeed, by 2000 the plant had moved, in some productivity categories, to become the lowest-cost processor among plants monitored by Agristat, the company involved in producing international agricultural statistics. At the same time, the company reported an increase in staff morale, based upon its annual measurements.

The brewery at Desnoes and Geddes also experienced improvements in productivity subsequent to the implementation of Vision 2000. Whereas the company had ranked in the lowest quartile among similarly sized breweries internationally, by 2000 it ranked in the middle (between the second and third quartiles). The company had made critical investments to enhance productivity levels, but an important element of the improvement in ranking was based on skills upgrading for workers and changes in work relations. Table 8.1 summarizes the workplace change programmes at these three companies.

Lessons for Firms in Small Developing Countries

The experiences of these three firms operating in Jamaica, coupled with the findings of the literature on the management of workplace change, primarily in developed countries, provide lessons for firms in small developing countries seeking to reorder workplace relations in their enterprises in pursuit of international competitiveness. Figure 8.2 indicates important factors to be considered in the management of such efforts.

Recognition of Competitive Trigger Points

For companies operating from small developing countries, it is particularly important to recognize, and respond to, competitive trigger points. In the companies in this study, a critical trigger point was impending international competition arising from a reduction in trade barriers.

Table 8.1: Elements of Workplace Change Programmes

Elements of Programme	Desnoes & Geddes	Grace, Kennedy & Co.	Jamaica Broilers
Competitive trigger point	Acquisition by multi-national corporation; need for improved profitability; impending international competition via lowering of duty levels.	Need for improved profitability; impending international competition via lowering of duty levels.	Need for improved profitability; impending international competition via lowering of duty levels.
Transformation Plan	Vision 2000	2020 Vision	Operation Revalorize
Transformation action	Significant redundancy of production workers and managers, with union involvement; worker up-skilling and multi-skilling; reordering of relations via organizational democratization and flattening of hierarchies.	Mass redundancy of production workers, replacement with performance-paid contractors, with union involvement; worker up-skilling and multi-skilling; organizational flattening and democratization.	Mass redundancy of production workers and replacement with performance-compensated contractors; worker up-skilling and multi-skilling with employee participation in decision making; no union involvement.
Short term transformation results	Improvement from bottom quartile to middle of comparator international companies in terms of productivity levels.	Significant improvement in productivity as indicated by 107 per cent increase in US$ profits (after tax) per employee measure.	Significant improvement in productivity from bottom third to top third of comparator international companies in cost and efficiency.

Even if the pace of trade liberalization slows, as is suggested by the resistance of developing and many developed countries to further trade liberalization and the possibility of a retreat from market integration following the inflexion points discussed in the introduction to this volume, many firms in small developing countries are so far from internationally competitive levels that there can be no complacency in relation to the need for improved competitiveness.

International Benchmarking in Transformation Efforts

Although companies may be aware that they face a problem of international competition, a recognition of the precise extent of the problem involves close assessment of the company's position in relation to international counterparts. The three companies in this study engaged in such international benchmarking

Figure 8.2: Management of Changes in Workplace Relations in Developing Countries

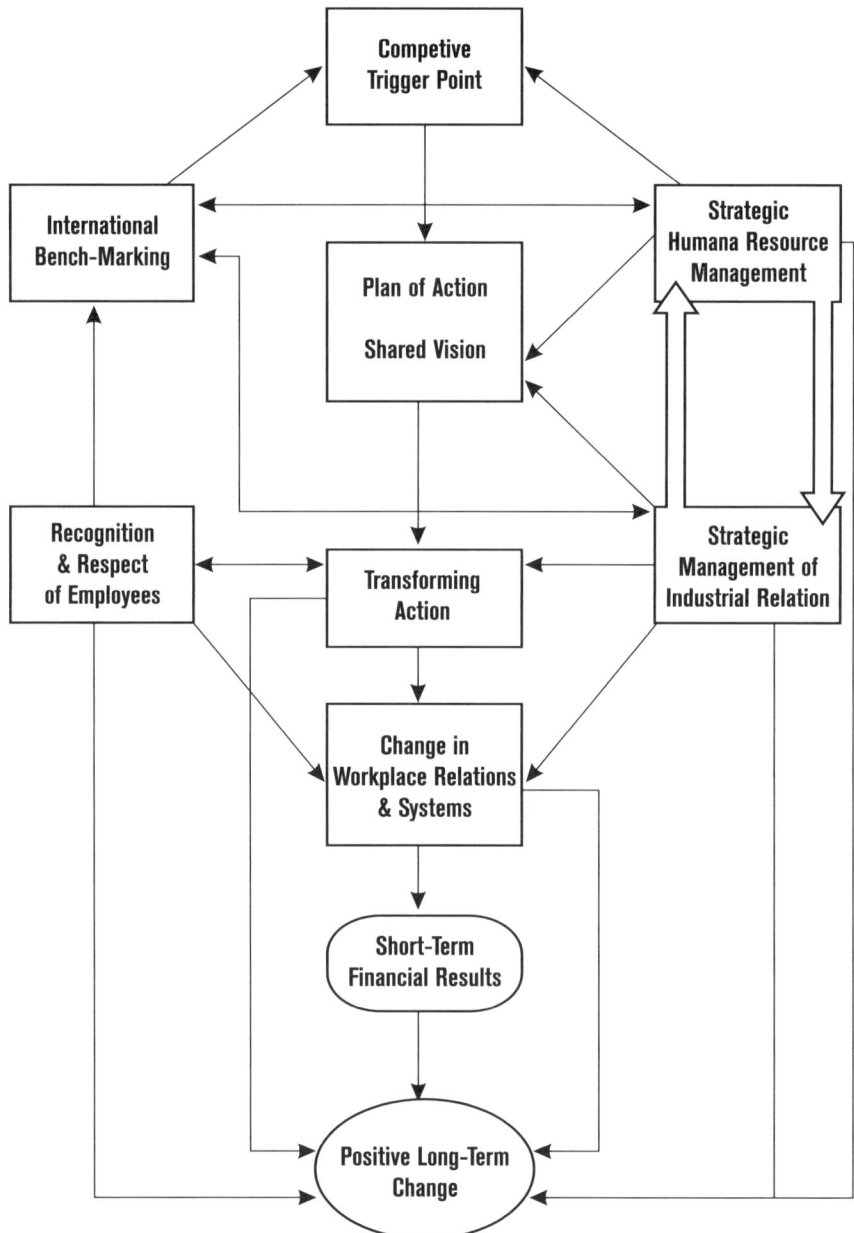

activity. Indeed, at Desnoes and Geddes, even after an increase in productivity associated with efforts at transformation, the company's international benchmarking exercise suggested that it was still a considerable distance from international best practice. These benchmarking efforts, on a continuous basis, are critical to the ability of companies in developing countries to initiate the radical workplace reforms necessary for corporate survival.

Sharing a Vision of the Need for Corporate Competitiveness

But there is little point to a process in which the senior managers of the company are the only ones aware of the competitive challenges brought on by changes in the global economy. The challenges of competition must be shared. A transformation plan is an important ingredient for sharing the need for corporate competitiveness with all those within the company who will be needed for a successful process of transformation. The Vision plans at Desnoes and Geddes and Grace, Kennedy and Company represent examples of a process of shared vision for corporate competitiveness. The chairman of Grace, Kennedy, at the launch of the 2020 Vision plan, indicated that from now on it would be "business as unusual" at the company, capturing the spirit of change that was communicated to the employees.

Strategic Human Resource Management

It is noteworthy that all three of the workplace transformation efforts designed to improve competitiveness were initiated by top-level management within these organizations. Desnoes and Geddes's transformation process, for example, began as an initiative of the company's first vice-president of human resources. Firms in developing countries do not have a tradition of placing the human resource function at the apex of the organization. In the environment of scarcity and, consequently, supply-driven companies which has dominated developing countries, emphasis has not been placed on strategic human resource management. Instead, management of human resources has been viewed as synonymous with a "personnel" function, which has been relegated, at best, to a mid-level position within corporate hierarchies. These cases imply that in a more competitive environment, firms will need to recognize the importance of a senior-level strategic human resource management function.

The Convergence of Human Resource
and Industrial Relations Management

In a related vein, the experiences of these companies suggest that in the new competitive environment there needs to be a convergence between the management of human resources and industrial relations. There are traumatic elements to the process of workplace transformation. Attempting to transform unionized work environments without the involvement of unions leads to even greater trauma. Yet it may be necessary for a company to engage in such action if it cannot gain the co-operation of the union in implementing changes that are critical for organizational viability in a more competitive environment.

At issue is the fact that the management-union rivalry that has dominated the workplaces in many developing countries is increasingly a vestige of an outdated business environment. To the extent that firms in small developing countries competed in settings of limited competition, industrial action in the form of a strike did little irreparable damage to the organization. Sales lost during the strike period were easily recaptured with the return of industrial relations normalcy. This state of affairs will not obtain in an environment of heightened international competition.

For firms and unions in small developing countries, co-operative relations will have to replace conflictual relations if the organizations in which both entities have a considerable stake are to compete effectively. This new environment calls for a new attitude to workplace relations, involving recognition of mutual interdependence on the part of both sets of players. In Jamaica these efforts were afoot, beginning in the late 1990s with the creation of an informal group (ACORN) comprising leaders from key private-sector firms and the country's leading unions dedicated to shifting the industrial relations in the country to a more co-operative mode. This period also saw enhanced communication between the Jamaica Employers' Federation and the Joint Confederation of Trade Unions, an umbrella union organization.

Recognizing and Respecting the Value of the Firm's Intellectual Assets

A critical element of this new attitudinal process will require that both managers and unions respect the value of employees as the firm's intellectual assets and principal source of competitive advantage. This new-found respect will be reflected to the extent that both parties attempt to improve skill levels, involvement in decision making, accountability and productivity-based compensation for all categories of workers within the organization. If redundancies are necessary as a part of the workplace transformation process, this respect should also extend to the management of the redundancy process. The movement to contracting out workforces can easily militate against intellectual contributions from employees to the extent that these contactual arrangements are accompanied by significant reductions in employee loyalty to the organization. Firms need to carefully consider the long-term impact of workplace changes on employee and organizational productivity.

Understanding the Implications of Changing Organizational Power Relations

In implementing processes of workplace change, the firms studied all sought to shift the power relations within the organization. The literature notes five sources of power within organizations: legitimate, coercive, reward, expert and referent.[17] The firms sought to shift power relations in the direction of enhancing the coercive, reward and legitimate power of managers, while reducing the focus on expert and referent power of management and the coercive power of employees, through their union representatives.

The challenge faced in these shifts in organizational power relations is that the various power sources all influence behaviour, but with varying levels of motivational effectiveness. Thus, coercive and legitimate sources of power tend to be the least motivational, while reward, expert and referent sources of power tend to translate into high levels of motivation. The shift towards power sources with lower motivational effects could easily result in reduced long-term organizational commitment on the part of employees.

It is against this background that workplace transformation processes that involve activities such as redundancies and contracting out of employment need to be complemented with other changes such as democratization of the workplace, increased empowerment of employees through involvement in decision making, skills upgrading and performance-based compensation systems. These processes serve to assist in rebalancing power relations somewhat, by introducing expert and reward power elements to employee activities. These companies recognized the need for complementary action along the lines discussed.

Managing Change and Post-Action Survivor Morale

The potential for reduced organizational commitment associated with a process of workplace transformation also emphasizes the need for careful management of change processes within the organization and attention to issues of employee morale for those employees who have been through traumatic change processes. The efforts to manage change and measure its effects at Desnoes and Geddes, and the measurement of employee morale and efforts to increase organizational commitment at Jamaica Broilers through assistance with the personal development of workers, illustrate the importance of these matters.

Efforts at changing workplace cultures in small developing countries must ultimately be judged not only on the short-term financial results of firms, but on the ability of these firms to demonstrate improved competitiveness over the long term based upon a motivated workforce producing at international standards. To achieve this goal will require a movement to international best practice within all segments of organizations in these countries.

Chapter 9

Competitiveness and Rarely Traded Products: Health in Jamaica

The preceding two chapters examined the operations of enterprises seeking to improve their levels of competitiveness in the context of a demanding national and international environment. But there was an important omission in the set of enterprises examined: none was located in the public sector, although effective management of public sector–based institutions is also critical to the overall competitiveness level of a country.

This chapter remedies that omission, while also examining international competitiveness in the context of sectors of the economy often ignored in such analytical efforts: nontradeable or rarely traded sectors. The study upon which this chapter reports sought to assess competitiveness outside the context of export activity and outside of an exclusive focus on the operations of private firms. In the context of a small developing country, this study examined the performance of a sector the products of which are rarely traded: the health sector of the Jamaican economy.

The study examined the productivity and performance of the Jamaican health sector by assessing the relationship between the inputs to, and outputs from, the system. In order to provide a point of reference against which this relationship between inputs and outputs can be assessed, input-output relationships in other countries were also examined. It is in this sense that the study assesses the competitiveness and, indeed, the international competitiveness of the Jamaican health sector.

The Jamaican health service is a rarely traded product as opposed to a non-tradeable product because there is, in fact, trade. This occurs when Jamaican patients cross borders in search of treatment unavailable at home, and when Jamaican health workers move to other countries in search of professional opportunities. The issue of international benchmarking of rarely traded products is likely to become ever more important, due to the changing nature of competition consequent upon the trend towards globalization. Health services, for example, are likely to be traded more frequently as diagnostic, computer-based medical services cross borders as a result of the market convergence created by information technology.

The remaining sections of this chapter identify the research methodology used in the performance assessment, assess the performance and structure of the Jamaican health system, seek to identify the factors responsible for the relative performance of the system and determine whether these factors are idiosyncratic to Jamaica, locate the Jamaican health system in competitiveness analysis, and examine challenges associated with enhancing the performance of the Jamaican health system.

Methodology

This study used the criteria identified in the introduction to this volume and in chapter 7 to identify a competitive industry. The indicator most relevant to the study was the "ability of enterprises to operate according to internationally accepted standards of cost, service and quality". Like the other indicators of international competitiveness, it covers entities that are involved in the production of tradeable products, are amenable to cross-border investment and operate on a for-profit basis. This indicator also, however, is relevant to products that are never, or rarely, traded, and are produced by enterprises that may or may not be operating on a for-profit basis.

This study employed two approaches to the research goal of identifying the level of international competitiveness of the Jamaican health system. The international competitiveness of the Jamaican health system was assessed using secondary data that compared the inputs into the system with the outputs achieved. Comparisons were then made with similar input and output relationships in other countries to determine Jamaica's ranking among comparator countries, including a statistical analysis to assess the factors that accounted for differential levels of health performance across a range of countries.

The research process also involved interviews with CEOs of different types of Jamaican health facilities (types A, B and C) and executives from the Jamaican Ministry of Health (including the health sector reform unit), the regional health authorities and the Medical Association of Jamaica, in an effort to understand the structure of the Jamaican health system, challenges confronting the system and the key factors driving performance levels in the system.

Assessing the Performance of the Jamaican Health System

The Jamaican health system can be evaluated at several levels. At the macro level, the system can be evaluated based on its ability to maintain the population at large in a healthy state of being, relative, of course, to the extent to which health systems in other countries are able to maintain the well-being of the citizenry whose care is their responsibility. Such macroindicators of performance, however, do not reveal how well the system is structured, or its likely ability to respond to the changing financial circumstances of the country and the future health needs of the population. Consequently, a closer evaluation of system performance and structure is necessary.

Macrosystem Performance Evaluation

Jamaica's health system performs well relative to other countries at its income level in terms of life expectancy levels and infant mortality rates. Jamaica falls into the category of a lower-middle-income economy. But, as pointed out in table 9.1, it has macro health performance indicators more typical of upper-middle-income economies than lower-middle-income economies. Indeed, its life expectancy and infant mortality levels are close to the levels of high-income economies. Jamaica's health indicators are much higher than those of other lower-income developing countries.[1]

Jamaica's health system also performs well relative to the resources the country has available to devote to health. Since available resources influence inputs, this is an important measure of performance because it speaks to the issue of productivity: that is, outputs relative to the level of inputs.

Table 9.1: Comparative Health Statistics 1997

	Life Expectancy at Birth (years)		Infant Mortality Rate (per 1,000 live births)
	Male	Female	
Costa Rica	74	79	12
Dominican Republic	69	73	40
Ecuador	68	73	33
El Salvador	67	73	32
Guatemala	61	67	43
Haiti	51	56	71
Honduras	67	72	36
Jamaica	**72**	**77**	**12**
Panama	72	76	21
Paraguay	68	72	23
Peru	66	71	40
Uruguay	70	78	16
Low-income countries	62	64	69
Middle-income countries	66	72	33
Lower-middle-income countries	65	71	38
Upper-middle-income countries	67	74	27
High-income countries	74	81	6
Latin America and the Caribbean	66	73	32
World average	65	69	56

Source: World Development Report, 1999/2000.

Data on the link between the resources available to a health system and the performance of that system have, for some time, illustrated the complex relationships that lie therein. The 2000 report from the World Health Organization (WHO) focused particularly on the issue of health system performance and the link between resources and performance. The report both accepts the seemingly logical link between resources and performance, and also considers the most interesting issue to be the case where such a link does not obtain:

It is achievement relative to resources that is the critical measure of a health system's performance. Thus, if Sweden enjoys better health than Uganda – life expectancy is almost exactly twice as long – that is in large part because it spends exactly 35 times as much per capita on its health system. But Pakistan spends almost precisely the same amount per person as Uganda, out of an income per person that is close to Uganda's, and yet it has a life expectancy almost 25 years higher. This is the crucial comparison; why are health outcomes in Pakistan so much better, for the same expenditure?[2]

The 2000 World Health Report also provides, for the first time, a framework that allows comparison among health systems in terms of performance along several performance-related dimensions, and includes the juxtaposition of these performance indicators against per capita expenditure on health.

Performance is based on the disability-adjusted life expectancy (DALE) of the country's citizens. DALE adjusts traditional measures of life expectancy to capture the period of life spent in disability. For the individual who spends no portion of his or her life in disability, DALE and traditional life expectancy measures are identical. Other indicators include the responsiveness of the health system (based upon dignity, autonomy, confidentiality, prompt attention, quality of basic amenities, access to social support networks and choice of care provider), and fairness in financial contribution to the health system. Also included is a composite measure of overall goal attainment. In addition to average levels of DALE and system responsiveness across each country, the framework measures distributional issues within the population (that is, the differences among individuals and groups within the population in relation to these measures).

Table 9.2 shows the ranking (out of 191 WHO member states) of several countries, including Jamaica, in relation to DALE and health expenditure per capita. The data allow for interesting comparisons. Japan has the world's highest level of DALE, but its health system is outspent by the world's highest spender on health, the United States. The United States, in turn, ranks only twenty-fourth in the world in terms of average DALE levels. The data on Jamaica are interesting, in that Jamaica has the second-largest (positive) gap (of 53 ranks) between its DALE ranking and its per capita health expenditure among all WHO member countries (The DALE ranking used is the average level; Jamaica ranks much lower [eighty-seventh] using the distribution ranking of DALE.)

In order to identify the factors driving performance in the Jamaican health system and those challenges confronting the system, this study turned to an examination of the system's structure.

Table 9.2: Health Outcome and Expenditure Ranking among Select Countries

Country	DALE	Health Expenditure Per Capita
Bahamas	109	22
Barbados	53	36
Haiti	153	155
Jamaica	36	89
Japan	1	13
Pakistan	124	142
St Lucia	54	86
South Africa	160	57[a]
Switzerland	8	2
Sri Lanka	76	138[b]
Uganda	186	168
United Kingdom	14	26
United States	24	1

[a]Highest negative gap between DALE and health expenditure ranking among all countries.
[b]Highest positive gap between DALE and health expenditure ranking among all countries.

Source: World Health Report 2000, Health Systems: Improving Performance (Geneva: World Health Organization, 2000).

Structure of the Jamaican Health System

The Jamaican health system is a mixed system in which public and private sectors play critical and complementary roles.

Public and Private Roles in Health Provision

The private sector's principal involvement in the health care system is in the capacity of provider of ambulatory health care services and pharmaceutical supply. The public sector's main role is in the funding and delivery of primary and inpatient health care services. Estimates of health sector activity, for example, suggest that 95 per cent of inpatient days, 25 per cent of ambulatory visits and 18 per cent of pharmaceutical purchases are routed through the public sector, with the remaining proportions handled by the private sector. Although only 5 per cent of inpatient days are accounted for by private sector health institutions, inpatient expenditure at these institutions comprises 35 per cent of total expenditure, illustrating the differing cost structure between public and private sector facilities.[3]

Overall, estimates suggest that a greater proportion of health care expenditure is directed towards private provision of medical services (60–65 per cent) than is spent by the public sector in its support of public health care institutions (30–35 per cent).[4]

The public sector's greater involvement in the provision of inpatient care is reflected in the distribution of hospitals in Jamaica. There are thirty-two hospitals in the country, with twenty-three operated and funded by the Ministry of Health, one partially funded by the ministry and serving as the teaching hospital of the University of the West Indies, and eight operated and funded privately. The distribution of beds, however, heavily favours the public sector. While hospitals operating in the public sector, cumulatively, are host to about five thousand beds, those within the private sector collectively represent about three hundred beds. As in other countries, hospitals are divided into various categories based upon the nature of the treatment that is provided.

Types and Capacity of Hospitals

There are three types of hospitals in the Jamaican health system. First, there are the type A, or general (secondary/tertiary) hospitals. There are three in Jamaica (Kingston Public, Cornwall Regional and the University Hospital of the West Indies – the teaching hospital of the University of the West Indies), and they collectively have some one thousand beds available, and provide a full range of medical services. Second, there are the type B or general secondary hospitals, of which there are five (Mandeville, Sav-la-Mar, May Pen, Spanish Town and St Ann's Bay). Third, there are the type C, district or community hospitals. These are host to over nine hundred beds, but are unable to provide acute medical care.

Finally, there are six specialist hospitals in Jamaica, providing services in paediatric medicine and surgery (Bustamante Hospital for Children), psychiatric medicine (Bellevue), obstetrics and gynaecology (Victoria Jubilee), cardio-pulmonary and respiratory care (National Chest), oncology (Hope Institute), and rehabilitation (Sir John Golding Rehabilitation Centre). These six hospitals have eighteen hundred beds.

Spatial Distribution of Jamaican Medical Facilities

The hospital facilities in Jamaica are spread across the country, but with a concentration in the Kingston Metropolitan Area, which is the most intensively populated section of the country. Two of the type A hospitals are in Kingston, with the other located in the nation's second city, Montego Bay. The five public type B hospitals are distributed across the country. The private hospitals are concentrated in the Kingston Metropolitan Area. The Jamaican health system also incorporates a comprehensive, nationwide network of some 366 primary health care clinics (or health centres). Table 9.3 identifies the spatial distribution of hospitals, including bed capacity, and health centres in Jamaica.

The Public Financing Challenge in Health Care

As indicated above, the Jamaican health system involves a mix of public and private sector funding and delivery mechanisms. In the public funding of health care, Jamaica is not unusual. No country leaves its health care system completely up to the vicissitudes of the marketplace because of the public-good nature of primary health care and the notions of societal compassion that feature, virtually universally, in the provision of emergency health care. Health care has consistently been one of the three sectors of the Jamaican economy, alongside education and security, that dominate non-debt-related government expenditure.

But in spite of health representing a significant proportion, about 8 per cent, of the Jamaican government's recurrent expenditure between 1997 and 2000,[5] the actual resources available for health spending were inadequate by the standards of developed countries. Further, of concern in a Jamaican context was the fact that resources devoted to health were declining because of the debt crisis confronting the Jamaican economy in the late 1990s.[6]

In terms of health spending, during the late 1990s Jamaica was at the world average, slightly above the average for lower-middle-income countries (within which category Jamaica falls), and slightly below the average for Latin America and the Caribbean (see table 9.4).

As indicated in table 9.4, whereas low-income economies spend, on average, 1 per cent of their GDP on health, middle-income countries spend 2.4 per cent and high-income economies, in striking contrast, spend 6 per cent of GDP on

Table 9.3: Spatial Distribution of Medical Facilities in Jamaica

Parish	Health Centres	Hospitals	Type	Beds	Beds per Parish
St Catherine	26	Spanish Town	Public	295	
		Linstead	Public	52	347
Kingston	–	Kingston Public	Public	373	
		Victoria Jubilee	Public	197	
		Bellevue	Public	1,190	
		St Josephs	Private	66	
		Maxfield Medical	Private	10	
		Bustamante	Public	253	2,089
St Andrew	49	National Chest	Public	100	
		Sir John Golding Rehab.	Public	72	
		Hope Institute	Public	44	
		University	Public	450	
		Andrews	Private	30	
		Medical Associates	Private	NA	
		Norwood	Private	NA	
		Nuttall	Private	NA	696
St Thomas	19	Princess Margaret	Public	98	98
Portland	21	Port Antonio	Public	117	117
St Mary	32	Annotto Bay	Public	119	
		Port Maria	Public	89	208
St Ann	27	St Ann's Bay	Public	139	139
Trelawny	21	Falmouth	Public	80	80
St James	26	Cornwall Region	Public	316	
		Doctors	Private	10	326
Hanover	19	Noel Holmes	Public	52	52
Westmoreland	22	Sav-La-Mar	Public	189	189
St Elizabeth	30	Black River	Public	97	97
Manchester	28	Mandeville	Public	168	
		Hargreaves	Private	27	195
Clarendon	46	May Pen	Public	97	
		Percy Junor	Public	120	
		Lionel Town	Public	60	277
National Totals	**366**			**4,910**	**4,910**

Source: Ministry of Health Annual Reports, 1998.

Table 9.4: Expenditure on Health in Selected Countries

Country/Category	Health as a Proportion of GDP (1990–1997)
	%
Costa Rica	6.0
Ecuador	2.0
El Salvador	2.4
Guatemala	1.7
Haiti	1.2
Honduras	2.8
Jamaica	**2.5**
Panama	4.7
Paraguay	1.8
Peru	2.2
Uruguay	1.9
Low-income countries	1.0
Middle-income countries	2.4
Lower-middle-income countries	2.2
Upper-middle-income countries	3.0
High-income countries	6.0
Latin America and the Caribbean	2.6
World average	2.5

Source: World Development Report, 1999/2000. The data provided were the latest available between 1990 and 1997.

health. These comparisons slightly overstate the disparity in total expenditure on health across countries of different income levels because, paradoxically, the share of private health financing, which is not as easily measured as public expenditure, tends to be higher in countries where income levels are lower. Jamaica is illustrative of this relationship; it is estimated, as indicated earlier in this chapter, that 60–65 per cent of total health expenditure in Jamaica is directed towards private provision of health services.

Nevertheless, this overstatement is not nearly sufficient to reconcile the extreme variation in per capita public expenditure on health between low- and middle-income developing economies, on the one hand, and high-income developed economies, on the other. Low-income economies have per capita public health expenditure of US$5, middle-income economies, US$70, and high-income economies, US$1,500.[7] Per capita health expenditure in the United States is estimated at US$4,500.[8]

These financial resource challenges are the most significant factor contributing to related deficiencies in the area of physical and technological infrastructure and health system staffing. Constrained financial budgets typically place greatest strain on medical facilities and equipment. The constrained budgets are directed towards the payment of salaries, leaving little in the way of a capital budget that could be utilized to construct new facilities, upgrade existing facilities, or procure new medical equipment. Indeed, even medical supplies are likely to become a casualty of underfunded health system budgets. But even as constrained budgets are directed towards remuneration of medical personnel, the levels of remuneration made possible by limited budgets are inadequate to retain many categories of health personnel.

Human Resource Staffing in the Jamaican Health System

One of the implications of the restricted funding available to the health sector in Jamaica has been relatively low levels of pay among certain health professionals, particularly reflected in the salaries of nurses.[9] This problem, coupled with the highly attractive salaries offered by North American health care institutions, and the relative ease with which nurses can legally migrate to North America, have contributed to very high levels of vacancies among nurses in the health system, leading Jamaica to be grossly "under-nursed".

This has been less true with respect to physicians, where there is a much lower vacancy rate. The differential vacancy situation can likely be attributed to the fact that the compensation gap between Jamaica and North America, the most sought-after destination for potential medical migrants, is much lower for physicians than it is for nurses. In 1998, for example, median (official) compensation for Jamaican public sector doctors was estimated at 66 per cent of median physician salaries in the United States, while median compensation of Jamaican public sector nurses was 37 per cent of US nursing salaries.[10] In relation to both categories of staff there have been improvements in the vacancy rate over time, although in the case of registered nurses it is noteworthy that one component in the improvement in the vacancy rate has come through a reduction in the cadre of nurses in the health system (see table 9.5).

Migration of health professionals not only leads to personnel shortages, but also typically creates training cross-subsidies from poor countries to their richer counterparts. Most nurses in developing countries, for example, are trained at

Table 9.5: Selected Human Resource Staffing in Health System 1996/1998

Category of Staff	Cadre		In Post		% Vacancy	
	1996	1998	1996	1998	1996	1998
Physician	439	544	421	504	4.1	7.0
Public health nurse	246	260	147	234	40	10
Registered nurse	2,639	2,191	1,005	1,682	62	23
Enrolled assistant nurse	1,090	1,090	587	622	46	43
Public health inspector	499	425	276	262	45	38

Source: Ministry of Health Annual Reports, 1996, 1998.

the expense of the public purse. It is estimated, for instance, that the 111 registered nurses who resigned from government service in Jamaica in 1990 and migrated took with them US$1.7 million in training and education funded by the Jamaican government.[11]

The ability of the Jamaican health system to maintain close to a full complement of doctors is noteworthy. Indeed, with respect to physician coverage, Jamaica is relatively well doctored. In 1999 the Medical Association of Jamaica estimated that there were 2,800 doctors in the country, of whom an estimated 1,000 were in general practice.[12] This estimate suggests that Jamaica had a ratio of about 900 persons per doctor. Although most doctors were concentrated in the largest population centre of Kingston, doctors were also in private practice in all parishes across the country.

The Jamaican ratio compares with the average for industrial countries of one doctor per 300–400 persons. It also compares with averages of one doctor per 1,400 persons in developing countries with high levels of human development, one doctor per 3,471 persons in countries with medium levels of human development (a category into which Jamaica falls), and one doctor per 7,700 persons in countries with low levels of human development.[13] These data suggest that Jamaica has up to three times as many doctors per person as other countries in its income category.

In summary, the Jamaican data suggest that Jamaica performs quite well in macrohealth statistics in relation to other countries at its income level, and given the resources it devotes to health. Its most distinctive area, relative to other countries, appears to be linked to the breadth of its clinical activity, and its human resource staffing activity, which is particularly evident in relatively high levels of doctoral coverage. This brief survey of Jamaican health system performance and structure suggests testable hypotheses about the factors important in macrohealth system performance.

Explaining Differential Macrohealth Performance among Countries

Based upon the data from the assessment of Jamaica's macrohealth performance, the three factors influencing health performance were national income, proportion of resources spent on health and levels of doctoral coverage. Of these, the latter would appear to have the greatest impact on health performance. This was the principal area in which Jamaica appeared to differ from comparator countries. To test whether this result was idiosyncratic to Jamaica, this study was broadened to include a statistical test of factors affecting health performance across countries.

Statistical Test on Factors Affecting Macrohealth Performance

For this statistical test, the dependent variable used was DALE, as computed by the WHO. The independent variables that were used include per capita income (on a purchasing-power-parity basis), doctors per 100,000 of population, and proportion of GDP spent on health. These variables are summarized in table 9.6, with their expected signs and significance levels.

Table 9.6: Variables for Regression Analyses on Sample of 70 Countries

Variable	Proxy	Hypothesized Sign	Data Source
Health system performance	DALE[a] (1999)	Dependent variable	WHO, *World Health Report, 2000*
Doctoral level coverage	Physicians per 100,000 population (1990–1999)	Positive	United Nations *Human Development Report, 2001*
Health resources	Total expenditure on health as % of GDP	Positive	WHO, *World Health Report, 2000*
National income level	Per capita income (PPP) (1998)	Positive	World Bank, *World Development Report, 2000*

[a]DALE – Disability adjusted life expectancy

Based upon the WHO's analysis, one would expect per capita income and proportion of GDP spent on health to have positive signs and to be significant. Based upon the data implicit in the performance level of the Jamaican health system, the level of doctoral coverage would be expected to have a significant influence on health performance. The analyses were conducted on a stratified random sample of seventy countries across all income levels.

The data from the regression analysis are provided in tables 9.7a and 9.7b. The health expenditure and doctoral coverage variables explained almost 61 per cent of the variation in DALEs for these seventy countries, with the doctoral coverage indicator being highly statistically significant, while the proportion of GDP spent on health did not have the expected sign, but was not statistically significant.

Table 9.7a: Results of Regression Analysis on Sample of Seventy Countries

Variable	Beta Coefficient	Standard Error	T Statistic
Doctoral coverage	0.09228	0.011336	8.140755[a]
Proportion of GDP on health	-0.43420	0.572283	-0.758720

Dependent variable: DALE; R^2 (Adj.) = 0.609632, F = 54.87814
[a]Statistically significant

Table 9.7b: Results of Regression Analysis on Sample of Seventy Countries

Variable	Beta coefficient	Standard error	T statistic
Income	0.000891	0.000172	5.170562[a]
Proportion of GDP on Health	0.665616	0.640849	1.038648

Dependent variable: DALE; R^2 (Adj.) = 0.444975, F = 28.6594
[a]Statistically significant

Note that another regression was also run using proportion of GDP spent on health and per capita income (PPP basis), as explanatory variables (table 9.7b). This regression produced inferior explanatory results (R squared of 44 per cent), with positive and statistically significant results for the income variable. All three independent variables were not shown in a single regression model because of problems of multicollinearity between the doctoral coverage and income variables, as demonstrated by the pairwise correlations, and the fact that including all three variables changed the explanatory power of the regression by only one percentage point, from 61 per cent to 62 per cent.

Discussion of Findings

There are a number of features of the Jamaican and international health sectors that emerge from the foregoing analysis. In relation to Jamaica, foremost among these is the fact that the Jamaican health system is one of high relative productivity. The outputs of the health system in terms of life expectancy, including DALE and infant mortality levels, are relatively high by the standards of Jamaica's comparators. On the other hand, the principal input, in terms of proportion of GDP spent on health, is equivalent to the world average and to the level that applies in other lower-middle-income economies.

There are two areas in which the inputs into the Jamaican health system are higher than international norms. One area in which Jamaica is distinctive is in its network of health clinics. The other area in which Jamaica is distinctive, relative to countries at its income level, is in the extent of doctoral coverage of the population. The analysis reported in this chapter also suggests that the Jamaican situation is not idiosyncratic, and that for countries around the world, doctoral level coverage is a significant variable in explaining differential levels of health performance. Although the WHO accepts a logical link between health system performance and income level, the analysis reported here suggests that doctoral level coverage is a better indicator of health system performance than is income level.

In the Jamaican context, in addition to high levels of doctoral coverage, the country had an impressive national network of clinics. The interesting element of both of these areas of distinctiveness is that they impact significantly on the system of primary health care across the country. During the 1997–1999 period primary health care comprised 18–21 per cent of the budget for the health service. Yet this considerably underestimates the amount spent on primary health care and ambulatory visits.

Recall that estimates of the total health spending in Jamaica indicate that 60–65 per cent of expenditure was routed through the private sector, which was also responsible for 75 per cent of ambulatory health visits. Considered from that perspective, at least 50 per cent of total health spending in Jamaica is probably located in the primary care segment of the health care continuum. The private sector expenditure occurs primarily through the offices of general practitioners strategically located throughout Jamaica.

It is fair to deduce, therefore, that Jamaica's health system has performed relatively well, and is reasonably competitive, because the structure of the health system places a greater emphasis on primary care than systems that are more driven by a hospital and secondary/tertiary care focus.

Locating the Jamaican Health System in Competitiveness Analysis

In this respect the relative competitiveness of the Jamaican health system is driven largely by variables that would be familiar in competitive analyses of the sector of any economy.

Porter's work on the determinants of national competitiveness leads to a model in which competitive industries in countries can usually be linked to a combination of appropriate factor conditions; demand conditions; related and supporting industries; and firm strategy, structure and rivalry.[14] To the extent that the competitiveness of the Jamaican health system can be linked to the relatively high doctoral coverage within the country, a Porterian perspective explains this phenomenon well, as illustrated in figure 9.1.

Jamaica's relatively healthy level of doctoral coverage must be related directly to the fact that since 1948 the medical faculty of the University of the West Indies (covering most of the anglophone Caribbean) has been located in Jamaica. Indeed, this university began with a class of medical students, and medicine has long been the institution's most prestigious faculty. In 2001 the medical faculty graduated over seventy-five students with MBBS degrees. Many of the Jamaican students, and a significant proportion of non-Jamaican students, stay on in Jamaica to practise medicine. A significant majority of the practising physicians in the country are University of the West Indies graduates.

Further, Jamaica has not expanded the supply of doctors by lowering admission standards for entry into medical school at the University of the West Indies, as appears to have occurred in other countries that have sought to expand levels of doctoral coverage. The World Bank, for example, reports that the number of doctors in Mexico increased from about 21,000 in 1960 to 166,000 in 1990. But this was achieved through open enrolment policies at some of the largest medical schools. This led to a decline in the quality of

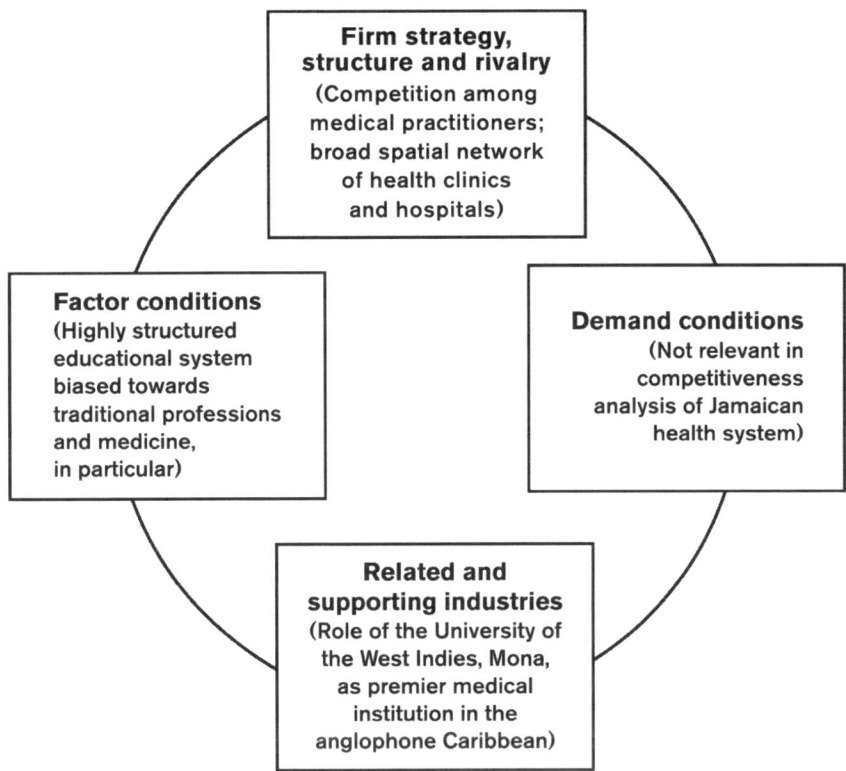

Figure 9.1: Locating the Jamaican Health System in Competitiveness Analysis

Source: Adapted from Michael Porter, *The Competitive Advantage of Nations* (New York: Free Press, 1990).

medical education and unemployment among medical practitioners, although ironically, unlike the Jamaican situation, doctors were still not attracted to rural areas.[15]

In the context of competitiveness, the linkage between the Faculty of Medicine at the University of the West Indies and the competitiveness of the Jamaican health sector mirrors the "related and supporting industry" element of Porter's model of national competitiveness. The significant number of medical practitioners operating throughout Jamaica is also likely to contribute to improved medical practice through the lens of competition, linked to the "firm rivalry" element of the Porter competitiveness diamond. Finally, the unusually strong demand pressures for entry into the Faculty of Medicine of the University of the West Indies, and the high calibre of applicants, was linked in part to the highly structured Jamaican educational system, which helped to produce many graduates with the analytical and memorization capabilities strongly emphasized in basic medical studies. These demand pressures were also influenced by the Jamaican educational system's bias towards the traditional professions. These elements are strongly linked to Porter's "factor conditions" variable.

Addressing Challenges to Health System Performance in Jamaica

Yet, despite its relative competitiveness, there were problems in the Jamaican health system at the turn of this century. Indeed, there was a strongly held view in Jamaica that conditions within the health system had deteriorated by the 1990s.[16] The funding constraints of the Jamaican government created challenges for both primary and secondary/tertiary health care. The 1999–2000 preliminary estimates for expenditure on primary health care, for example, represented a 37 per cent reduction relative to the revised estimates for fiscal 1998–1999. Yet the role of the expansion of primary care, which had accelerated during the early 1970s, in enhancing the performance of the Jamaican health system was widely recognized.

Another critical challenge confronting the Jamaican health system was that associated with control of the HIV epidemic. At the turn of the century, the Caribbean had the second-highest incidence of HIV infection among all regions of the world. By this time, the epidemic had already led to a significant deterioration in life expectancy levels in sub-Saharan Africa, and would have to be carefully managed to ensure that a similar result did not beset the Caribbean region.[17]

Finally, against the background of the success of the Jamaican health system being linked to the well-structured primary and secondary health systems, there was cause for both optimism and pessimism in the elements of a health care reform process that was underway in Jamaica at the turn of this century. The reform process was likely to improve the functioning of the overall system to the extent that accountability was instituted at the hospital and clinic level through a consensual process that did not lead to a lowering of morale of any of the key components of the system, and that ensured that health administration was complementary to, and did not substitute for, on-the-ground delivery of health care.[18]

Further, it was clear that there was a need for managerial attention at the level of medical facilities. There is, for example, evidence that suggests significant variation in performance across medical facilities, with managerial performance accounting for some component of this variation.[19] Variation is observable with respect to both funding mechanisms and to the effective management and deployment of resources. The act of simply instituting twenty-four-hour fee collection in some hospitals, for example, has significantly improved fee collection and avoided the incidence of patient registrations taking place after the cashier's office has closed for the day. Similarly, some, but not all, hospitals examined during the course of this study were developing comprehensive mechanisms for obtaining community grant financing.

The central plank of the reform process was one of decentralization, which also, if sensitively implemented, should augur well for the continued integration of the nation's primary and secondary health system. In the decentralized structure, positions of parish manager were created to supervise the health system at the parish level. An important component of the parish manager's responsibility is to ensure integration between the many primary facilities in each parish and the one or two public hospitals. This responsibility involves both ensuring efficient resource allocation across the primary and secondary level, and also developing mechanisms for integrating patient referrals between the primary and the secondary/tertiary system.

On the less optimistic side, the reform also involved a recommended National Health Insurance Plan that, as pointed out in a critique of the plan by the Medical Association of Jamaica, had a very heavy orientation towards hospital care. This could easily create a situation in which individuals, having been informed that they have paid for a standard package of inpatient and diagnostic services, seek to take advantage of those services, thus raising the overall costs of medical provision. This, in turn, in the absence of additional resources, would be likely to lead to a rationing exercise in which citizens would probably become disaffected with the system.

This possibility has to be linked to the general disaffection of the Jamaican citizenry with taxes such as the education tax which, although initially intended to support education, was then relegated to the general revenue fund of government as budgetary vices tightened. It is not implausible that an improperly structured National Health Insurance Premium, used to finance national health insurance, could begin as a health insurance premium, revert to a health tax, analogous to the education tax, and end up as a general tax.

Conclusion

The Jamaican health system has performed at a competitive level in the past, in relation to the inputs into the health system relative to the outputs of that system. The data suggest that this high relative performance is related to the system's focus on primary health care, operating through a comprehensive national network of clinics and physicians in both private and public practice. Jamaica's level of physician coverage is considerably higher than that of countries of similar income levels and similar levels of public sector health expenditure.

Nevertheless, despite past relatively high performance, it is likely that the continuation of, and improvement upon, past trends will require an ongoing process of health reform. This reform process will need to improve the productivity and competitiveness of the health system. That is, the reform process will have to maintain at least the current level of health performance with fewer resources, in the context of the likelihood of a decline in resources available for health, as the Jamaican government grapples with an extremely difficult budgetary situation associated with high levels of debt servicing.

Yet, while seeking to improve the productivity of the system, it is critical that the reform process build upon the past successes of the Jamaican health system, while recognizing its current elements of vulnerability. Thus, while the process of managerial reform should continue, it is also important that the focus on a structure of primary care not be neglected. The mix of private and public delivery with joint and integrated primary and secondary foci should continue to be important aspects of the Jamaican health care delivery system, and of health systems in other small developing countries eager to enhance the competitiveness of their health systems. Indeed, the Jamaican experience suggests that small developing countries, with tightly limited health budgets, need not have low-performing health systems.

Chapter 10

The Role of Microenterprise Support and Social Policy

mall developing countries are quick to point to the differences between small and large countries. Indeed, the countries of the Caribbean region, which feature prominently in the analyses of the preceding chapters, have been at the forefront in indicating to the world community the importance of recognizing the particular vulnerability of small economies. Based largely on the lobbying efforts of the Caribbean countries, for example, issues of small state vulnerability have been placed on the agenda in the trade discussions directed at creating a Free Trade Area of the Americas, and in the context of the Cotonou Agreement discussions. The particular vulnerability associated with the specialized economies of small states is likely to be raised with ever more intensity in any post–September 11 trade, aid and adjustment discussions.

But even within small economies there is a tension of size among economic actors. One such tension is between small and large firms: between, if you will, the micro- and macroenterprises in small developing countries. It is easy to focus only on the largest firms in small countries, on the assumption that all efforts must be made to ensure that they can be positioned to compete with larger rivals elsewhere. But ignoring the smallest firms, and not tapping into the potential of all capital holders in these countries could have serious negative implications for social stability and capital generation. This risk is particularly high in small developing countries because, as pointed out in chapters 4 and 5, these countries have potential capital constraints because of the extent to which their residents like to diversify their capital holdings. This chapter focuses on the appropriate role for government and the extent to which governmental assistance of microenterprises is consistent with the development focus of a small economy seeking to compete in a global marketplace.

The following sections of the chapter examine three elements that are critical in understanding the appropriate role for government in relation to microenterprises. The first is the rationale for government support of microenterprises; the second is the necessary support mechanisms, assuming there is an appropriate rationale; and the third is whether the pace of globalization has an impact on the rationale or the necessary support mechanisms.

The Rationale for Government Support of Microenterprises

The rationale for government support of microenterprises falls into the dual categories of economic and social reasons.

Economic Reasons for Microenterprise Support

A critically important rationale for government support of microenterprise is the economic potential represented by this segment of an economy. Even without getting into the tortuous discussion of how to define a microenterprise, it is clear that those relatively small enterprises in an economy, although of low individual visibility, collectively have a significant economic impact.

Reports on economy after economy have shown that small and microenterprises constitute the most significant employment-generation component of these economies. To take one example of this employment-generation effect, note that in 1994 the Mexican National Statistics Institute made an attempt to measure the number of informal "micro businesses" in the entire country, and came up with a figure of 2.65 million. The employment-generation effect of 2.65 million businesses in a country with a population (at that time) of ninety million speaks for itself. Taking another example, in Jamaica 60 per cent of the employed labour force works in firms employing fewer than ten workers.[1]

A less examined element of microenterprise lies in its potential rather than its actual economic impact. This potential is most graphically represented in the work of Peruvian social scientist Hernando De Soto. De Soto estimates that the total value of real estate held but not legally owned by the poor of the Third World and former communist nations is at least the equivalent of

US$9.3 trillion.[2] He seeks to put this number into perspective by pointing out that it is almost as much as the total value of all the companies listed on the main stock exchanges of the world's twenty most developed countries, and that it is twenty times more than all the foreign direct investment into all Third World and former communist countries in the 1989–1999 period. To quote an example from a particular country, he points to the fact that in Haiti, the poorest nation in Latin America, the total assets of the poor are more than 150 times greater than all foreign investment received since Haiti's independence from France in 1804.[3]

Admittedly, these last two statistics represent the somewhat unreasonable comparisons of flows with stocks of capital, but they nevertheless provide an indication of the magnitude of this capital that has been accumulated by individuals in developing countries. But the economic potential of these assets is muted because they represent dead capital: they cannot be translated into financing because of the absence of legal title. De Soto concludes that "eighty per cent of the world is undercapitalised: people cannot draw economic life from their buildings (or any other asset) to generate capital".[4]

Yet in developed countries buildings, in particular, are a critical element of the capital support for new business formation. It is estimated that 70 per cent of the capital used to support new business formation in the United States is collateralized by mortgages on the homes of owners.

Not only are microenterprises in developing countries often undercapitalized, but this undercapitalization has some link to the nature of governmental legal and regulatory systems. Again, De Soto's research team helps us to understand the factors surrounding the tremendously high incidence of informality and extralegality in enterprise activity in developing countries.

The first, much publicized, field research activity involved the team seeking to open a small garment factory on the outskirts of Lima, Peru. The research team spent six hours a day and finally got all the appropriate permits some 289 days later. The garment factory was established to employ only one worker, but the cost of legal registration was thirty-one times the monthly minimum wage. Obtaining legal authorization to build a house on state-owned land took six years and eleven months and required 207 administrative steps in fifty-two government offices. Obtaining legal title for the land took 728 steps.[5]

The research team repeated these experiments in many developing countries. The experiments resulted in the identification of similar, if not even more formidable, barriers to the legal establishment of business. Furthermore, not only were there barriers to becoming legal, there were fundamental challenges associated with staying legal.

The prohibitive, and unnecessary, regulatory costs that lie behind the high incidence of extralegality among microenterprise sectors in many developing countries provide a strong rationale for government intervention to support microenterprise. Many governments assume that the driving force behind extralegality is tax avoidance and, consequently, seek either to enforce tax compliance or write off the sector as incorrigible. Again, this perspective on the sector, which can comprise as much as 50–80 per cent of the individuals in developing countries, does not accord with research.

De Soto's research team concludes that most people do not operate in the extralegal sector because of a desire to avoid taxation. The team designed a programme in Peru for bringing small, extralegal entrepreneurs into the legal system, and 276,000 of those entrepreneurs recorded their businesses voluntarily in new registry offices designed for them, with no promise of tax reductions. Their underground businesses paid no taxes. Yet, four years later, tax revenues from formerly extralegal business totalled US$1.2 billion. In drawing conclusions from this research De Soto writes:

> Contrary to popular wisdom, operating in the underground is hardly cost-free. Extralegal businesses are taxed by the lack of good property law and continually having to hide their operations from the authorities. Because they are not incorporated, extralegal entrepreneurs cannot lure investors by selling shares; they cannot secure low-interest formal credit because they do not have legal addresses. They cannot reduce risks by declaring limited liability or obtaining insurance cover. The only "insurance" available to them is that provided by their neighbours and the protection that local bullies or mafias are willing to sell to them. Moreover, because extralegal entrepreneurs live in constant fear of government detection and extortion from corrupt officials, they are forced to split and compartmentalize their production facilities between many locations, thereby rarely achieving important economies of scale.[6]

The rationale for government support in assisting these enterprises to convert significant quantities of dead capital into a living, breathing form is clear. Beyond the employment-generation effect and the fact that governments can assist in translating the dead capital of microenterprises into a living form, the economic rationale for governmental support to microenterprise rests in the linkages that can be created between these enterprises and the formal, larger and more established segments of developing country economies.

Efforts to create linkages between enterprises in the separate segments of dualistic economies have been examined particularly in the context of foreign-owned enterprises and those operating with indigenous capital.[7] Of course, much of the early literature on economic development also focused on the importance of linkages between advanced and backward segments of dualistic economies.[8] In all of this research, a key observation has been the importance of both sectors of the economy to overall economic development.

The work on linkages between multinationals and indigenous firms has particular relevance to the issue of linkages between micro-and macroenterprise in developing countries. It suggests that efforts to create such linkages, which are critical to the deepening and sustainability of the development process, are far more effective when placed in a promotional and facilitatory context, as opposed to situations where efforts are made to institute linkages through government fiat or regulation.[9]

A final economic rationale for government support for microenterprise is linked to the likelihood of continued dynamism in economic development patterns in the twenty-first century. Unless a Luddite philosophy overtakes the world, demanding the cessation of technological development, it is likely that change will be the order of the day. This change has the potential to be quite disruptive to developing economies, making it very difficult to forecast which sectors can be counted on to power economies. Against this background, the nimbleness of microenterprises is likely to be an important element of the adjustment imperatives likely to be demanded of the peoples of developing countries.

Social Rationale for Government Support of Microenterprises

In addition to the economic reasons for promoting governmental support of microenterprises, as identified in the section above, there are social reasons for advocating such support, which often lie only one step removed from economic reasons. Macroeconomic stability is widely held to be a critical element in any programme of economic development and growth. This chapter takes no issue with that perspective, but adds the equally obvious point that social stability is also critical to such efforts, as is also to be inferred from the analyses in chapter 1 of this volume.

Microenterprise activity has the potential to improve levels of social stability by converting individuals from the ranks of the unemployed to those of the gainfully employed, even if there continues to be a degree of underemployment associated with some microenterprise activities. These activities have the potential to provide individuals who might otherwise have only a limited role in the society with a stake in the affairs of a country.

As an example, the importance of all members of a society having a stake in that society is an appropriate justification for governmental efforts to expand access to land to as wide a cross-section of the population as possible. In the many societies that have not progressed in the area of gender-neutral policies, it is also critical that such support efforts have an explicit gender focus. Indeed, it is to the variety of mechanisms available to governments in their justifiable goal to provide support to microenterprises that we turn in our next section.

Mechanisms for Supporting Microenterprises

Paul Streeten suggests that "the approach to improving the conditions of human and social well-being and of human capital can be considered under the headings of eight policy instruments and government interventions: incentives, input, innovation, information, infrastructure, institutions, initiative and independence". Government intervention in support of microenterprises can be assessed to include all of these policy instruments.[10]

Incentives are critical to the emergence of the true potential of these enterprises. For policies towards enterprises to be most effective, the input of the players must be sought. Microenterprises are an important source of innovation. But to maximize their innovative capabilities, policies need to be implemented that create the appropriate information base, through the necessary infrastructure and institutions. Finally, such a programme can unleash personal initiative and the independence of action that lies at the heart of successful capitalism.

The most effective mechanisms for government support of microenterprises lie in activities that respond to the most pressing challenges confronting these business concerns. Chief among these, following the conclusions of De Soto's research, is improvement in the laws, regulation and bureaucracy that affect the formation of microenterprise and the integration of these businesses into legal commercial frameworks.

Development of Comprehensive National Property Law Infrastructure

A key task of a government that is desirous of engaging in the critically important goal of assisting the microenterprise sector is the development of a comprehensive national property law infrastructure. The operative term in the preceding sentence is "comprehensive". Every developing country has a formal property system; the problem is that in many countries this system is relevant to a decreasing proportion of the population.

In seeking to correct this problem, the focus is often on surveying, mapping and sorting property. While these activities are obviously important, the focus must be on recording the property owned by all individuals, including that owned extralegally, in a manner that allows individuals to extract surplus value from the property, at least in part to finance micro business activity. Otherwise, it is possible that significant sums spent surveying, mapping and developing computerized recording systems for property will not have their intended effect. De Soto reports, for example, the conclusions of a government property manager in Brazil during that country's abortive efforts to create new property systems: "lots of new maps and computers, but few new formal owners".[11]

Avoiding such an unintended effect requires that efforts to incorporate the extralegal sector into the formal mainstream (or minor slipstream in many developing countries) respect the extralegal relationships that preceded these efforts. De Soto, once again, articulates this position powerfully:

Extralegal social contracts on property underpin nearly all property systems and are part of the reality of every country . . . property is socially constructed . . . [T]his means that property arrangements work best when people have formed a consensus about the ownership of assets and the rules that govern their use and exchange . . . . Any attempt to create a unified property system that does not take into account the collective (social) contracts that underpin existing arrangements will crash into the very roots of the rights most people rely on for holding onto their assets. Efforts to reform property rights fail because officials in charge of drafting new legal rules do not realize that most of their citizens have firmly established their own rules by social contract.[12]

Of course, one might question whether or not social contracts, which can be used as a basis for formalizing property, do in fact exist in many developing countries. Again, we borrow from the research of De Soto and his team:

Extralegal activity in developing and former communist countries is rarely haphazard. In the course of issuing formal title to hundreds and thousands of home and business owners in Peru, my organization never found an extralegal group that did not comply with well-defined consensual rules. Whenever we visited an undercapitalised area, whether in Asia, America or the Middle East, we never stepped into a wilderness. By observing carefully, we were always able to distinguish patterns of (ownership) rules. In the worst cases, we found a neglected garden – never a jungle.[13]

It is important to distinguish these consensual ownership rules that form part of the ownership social contract in a society. Once this task is achieved, a bridge is required between what in many countries is the minority formal ownership structure and the majority extralegal ownership structure. These activities have to be championed by the government.

In creating new comprehensive legal systems of property ownership, it is also critical that governments "engender" these systems of property ownership, particularly if one hoped-for result is the capitalization of microenterprises, not to mention the resolution of critical issues of social equity that surface. This is because, as reported by the World Bank, the land titling process in many countries is often rife with inequities and has often, thereby, reduced the access that women have to land.[14]

The impact of denying women's access to formal land ownership needs to be considered and condemned for its inherent inequity, but its implications also need to be understood in the context of a situation where women are the principal micro-entrepreneurs in many developing countries. A study in Southern Africa, for example, concludes that women own by far the majority of small, informal sector businesses: 67 per cent in Zimbabwe, 73 per cent in Lesotho, and 84 per cent in Swaziland.[15]

The World Bank makes two recommendations to assist in responding to the problems of gender inequity in formal land ownership systems, which are worthy of note. The first is to make joint titling of land to couples mandatory. Joint titling guarantees to married women property rights to jointly acquired land. The second is to foster partnerships between government departments and nongovernmental organizations that defend the rights of women, in order to increase women's awareness of their rights and support them in claiming title to land in the face of a possibly hostile bureaucracy or family.[16]

Governments would need to be champions of any mandatory land titling provisions, and to be supportive of relationship building with nongovernmental organizations involved in defending the rights of women. Again, these approaches are critical to ensuring that all citizens of a country have a stake in its development and growth.

Training and Promotion

Linking extralegal and legal property systems represents a critical level of linkage if the microenterprise sector is to develop to its fullest potential. There are, however, other areas of linkage. Microenterprises are likely to be most successful to the extent that they are able to develop linkages with other players, including macroenterprises within the economy. Governments in developing countries have much experience in seeking to nurture linkages between dual sectors of an economy. Unfortunately, however, much of the experience is one of failure.

Small developing countries, in particular, have long struggled with the challenges of dualistic economies. Dualism has been manifested in different ways, but an important one has been that created by the parallel existence of multinational corporations and local enterprises. The lessons learnt from governmental efforts to establish linkages between these two sets of economic actors are relevant to governmental efforts to establish linkages between micro- and macro-enterprises within a national economy.

As indicated earlier, a key lesson learnt has been that linkage by regulation and fiat has been unsuccessful. Very few programmes of domestic content legislation, for example, have elicited the intended result. On the other hand, explicit programmes of assisting in the training of indigenous entrepreneurs, the promotion of technological upgrading and assistance in the efforts of such firms to migrate towards international best practice in their operations have been more successful. This is evidenced in the success of explicit linkage programmes geared to create links between indigenous firms and multinational corporations in Ireland, Taiwan and Singapore.[17]

Governments in developing countries seeking to upgrade the operations of microenterprises and link their operations with those of macroenterprises in the country that are themselves focused on improving the international competitiveness of their operations need to develop explicit programmes of training and enterprise development.

The Role of Macropolicy

There is a critically important point to be made in relation to the impact of government's macropolicy on the development and success of microenterprises. It is the obvious point that microenterprises operate largely based on cash transactions. Those elements of an economy whose assets are largely denominated in cash are particularly vulnerable to macropolicy that erodes the earning power of cash.

It is now well established that the control of inflation has a salutary effect on the poorest sections of a society, and those with least access to noncash assets. Macropolicy that has inflation control as one plank of its activities is likely to be of benefit to the development and growth of microenterprises.

The Role of Government Financing

A final mechanism for government support of microenterprises is financial support. There is a case for financial support, to the extent that microenterprises represent public goods, whose existence provides positive externalities to the society at large. But two caveats are in order. The first is that a strong case can be made that government support in the form of developing the legal infrastructure to provide a platform from which capital can be more easily channelled to the micro sector is likely to lead to greater access to capital than may be available from government coffers.

Further, such capital may well be more appropriately used than direct government funding. This is the burden of De Soto's calculations about the extent of dead capital in developing countries, exceeding by wide measure funds that would be allocated through aid, government subvention or FDI. Linked to legal infrastructure are other types of physical and training-based infrastructure that can assist microenterprises unleash their potential.

The second caveat is that government efforts that serve a catalytic role with respect to financing of the microenterprise sector may be even more effective than direct funding. This is because, with government operating as a catalyst through a process of indirect funding, a greater level of market testing is likely to be retained in the financing activity. Clearly, the presence of market failures suggests that reliance on the market is suboptimal. But experience has also suggested that complete ignorance of the market in government's financing role is also likely to result in problems of expenditure effectiveness.

Evidence on this point comes from an examination of the most successful micro-financing programmes. The best known of these, the Grameen Bank programme in Bangladesh, relies on governmental and international support, but does not involve direct government management of the funding activity. In some programmes, whereas repayment rates on direct government funding are extremely low, repayment rates on consensual, peer-managed micro financing schemes, which are developed around social norms of property protection, are extraordinarily high. In the case of the Grameen Bank programme, for example, repayment rates have historically hovered at 98 per cent.[18]

In the small developing country of Jamaica, a series of efforts conducted by the government and the private sector illustrate the range of institutional approaches to the provision of support for the microenterprise sector.

Microenterprise Support in Jamaica

One of the funding mechanisms was the Jamaican government's Self-Start Fund. This was a fund that provided direct government financing to the microenterprise sector. It was financed by the capital development fund, which in turn was funded primarily from tax revenue from the bauxite and alumina sectors. Self-Start was one of a menu of funding and training activities provided by the Jamaican government to this sector. Other funding activities included the small-business credit programme financed by the government and the European Union, through which funds were wholesaled to a private development bank (Trafalgar) and the National Development Foundation of Jamaica (a public financing entity) for on-lending to small firms.

Other microenterprise credit programmes included funds directed through the Micro Investment Development Agency and a MicroFin credit programme, through which the Ministry of Industry, Commerce and Technology contracted a private company (Development Options) to develop a network of small, private microfinance organizations throughout the island. This private company was also involved in the administration of a "Jump-Start" fund to facilitate microenterprise start-ups. To enhance repayment prospects, the ministry also established a medium and small enterprise credit bureau.

These funding activities were complemented by the government's facilitation of a business incubator programme, established at the University of Technology, geared towards accommodating small, technology-based businesses. And the ministry worked with the Jamaica Business Development Centre to provide marketing outlets to showcase products produced by small firms.

An important element of the support process was the streamlining of business facilitation services throughout the country. For example, the Office of the Registrar of Companies was converted to an executive agency and assigned international best-practice targets for the maximum time that customers would wait for company registration and related matters.

The government also supported export-oriented microenterprise activities. Indeed, the experience from export-linked micro-financing programmes supported by the Government of Jamaica and the World Bank, but managed by the Jamaica Exporters Association, lends additional credence, beyond the experience of the Grameen Bank, to the potential of consensually managed credit programmes. As in the case of the Grameen Bank programme, the programmes managed by the Jamaica Exporters Association were noncollateralized lending programmes, reflecting the limitations confronting many micro-entrepreneurs with respect to collateralizable assets. The Jamaica Exporters Association programmes have performed well, with repayment rates in excess of 90 per cent.[19]

The Jamaica Exporters Association programme was highly reliant on social capital in the form of bonds of trust between this organization and its members, with careful monitoring of the activities of the firms by the association. Evidence from informal financing in Jamaica, operating through the Jamaican version of rotating savings and credit associations (roscas), known in Jamaican parlance as "partners", also shows the importance of high levels of social capital to the success of these arrangements.[20]

Microenterprise Support – A World Bank Perspective

Excerpts from the World Bank's *World Development Report, 2000/2001: Attacking Poverty* summarize much of the preceding discussion on the mechanisms available to governments for assisting in the development of micro-enterprises:

> Special measures are frequently essential to ensure that micro enterprises and small businesses, which are often particularly vulnerable to bureaucratic harassment and the buying of privilege by the well-connected, can participate effectively in markets. Such measures include ensuring access to credit by promoting financial deepening and reducing the sources of market failure; lowering the transactions costs of reaching export markets by expanding access to internet technology, organizing export fairs, and providing training in modern business practices; and building feeder roads to reduce physical barriers.[21]
>
> Women also need more equitable access to credit and associated productivity-enhancing services. Studies of the effect of networking schemes, such as group-based micro-credit, suggest that these schemes have enormous potential for reducing poverty. Some of these credit programmes, such as Grameen Bank in Bangladesh, are targeted more to women than to men. Critical to these programmes are services that complement credit and savings facilities, such as training in entrepreneurial skills – especially for women, who are typically cut off from the normal paths for acquiring such skills.
>
> Governments can improve financial intermediation for the poor by providing complementary public goods and improved regulation that recognize the special needs of micro-finance schemes. For example, better investment in rural infrastructure and literacy promotion can help expand the reach of micro-finance organizations, and credit information registries can lower informational costs and allow borrowers to build reputational collateral.[22]

The Impact of Globalizing Trends on Microenterprise Support

I conclude this chapter with a reference to the debate on the impact of globalization that was first discussed in the introduction to this volume.

Two of the classic positions suggesting support for a system in which the forces of global market opening would benefit developing countries were captured in the 1991 *World Development Report*, which spoke to a consensus among countries around a "market friendly approach to development",[23] and John Williamson's well known summary of the Washington Consensus,[24] with its focus on opening countries to global capital, goods and to the diminution of government's direct involvement in productive activity. Coming as these documents did on the heels of the collapse of communism, they heralded to many the end of debate on developmental approaches.

But this supposed consensus among countries supporting a market-friendly approach to development has not been able to improve development levels in many countries around the world, including the countries of the former Soviet Union. Consequently, this has contributed to a resurgence of debate about development approaches. Contributing to this renewed debate was the East Asian crisis, which punctured the aura of the inevitable success of outwardly oriented development approaches.[25]

As pointed out in our introductory chapter, the demonstrations surrounding meetings of global institutions have been a clear manifestation of this continued debate. And it is widely accepted that the terrorist attacks of 11 September 2001 on the United States will lead to a further rethinking of the implications of economic systems that are open to the movement of goods, capital and people from around the world.

Already, one outcome of what is a healthy debate on developmental approaches has been a rethinking of the Washington Consensus. The World Bank, in particular, either corporately or through the work of staff members, has been at pains in recent years to articulate a position that recognizes the importance of state intervention in the development process,[26] and that seeks to focus its role on enhancing development through the alleviation of poverty.[27]

This new consensus among analysts from various centres of thought, on the critical importance of a focus on directly alleviating poverty and liberating all segments of the societies of developing countries, provides greater urgency to support for microenterprise. I conclude with a quote from De Soto that captures the link between microenterprise support and the challenges of globalization:

> Capitalism is in crisis outside the West not because international globalization is failing but because developing and former communist nations have been unable to "globalize" capital within their own countries . . . [T]he promoters of capitalism, still arrogant over their victory over communism, have yet to understand that their macroeconomic reforms are not enough. By stabilizing and adjusting by "the book" the globalizer's macroeconomic programmes have dramatically rationalized the economic management of developing countries. But because their book does not address the fact that most people do not have property rights, they have done only a fraction of the work required to create a comprehensive capitalist system and market economy. Their tools are designed to work in countries where systematized law has been "globalized" internally, when inclusive property rights systems that link up to efficient monetary and investment instruments are in place – something these countries have yet to achieve.
>
> Too many policy makers have taken an Olympian view of the globalization process. Once they stabilized and adjusted at the macro level, allowing legal business and foreign investors to prosper and orthodox economists to control the treasury, they felt they had fulfilled their duty. Because they concentrated only on policies dealing with the aggregates, they did not inquire whether people had the means to participate in an expanded market system. They forgot that people are the fundamental agents of change. They forgot to focus on the poor. And they made that enormous omission because they do not operate with the concept of class in mind . . . . As a result the assets of the majority of their citizens have remained dead capital stuck in the extralegal sector . . . . If extralegal property rights are not accommodated, these societies may muddle along with their dual economies – with the so called law-abiding sector on one side and the impoverished extralegal sector on the other. But as information and communications continue to improve, and the poor become better informed about what they do not have, the bitterness over legal apartheid is bound to grow.[28]

Conclusion

Determinants of
Competitive Advantage
in Small Developing Countries

What, then, are the factors that enhance competitiveness in small developing countries? The research presented in this book has provided some tentative answers to this question.

One of the clearest of these answers lies in the recognition that small developing countries face a dilemma. Smallness leads to an absence of a diverse range of factors of production, forcing a reliance on world markets for many of the products the society needs to consume. Yet, at the same time, smallness also leads to an absence of scale economies, which make it more difficult for resident firms to produce goods and services for world markets. And the smallness of the domestic market presents a severe impediment to the ability of these economies to attract embodied international capital.

In the context of this dilemma, the research presented in this volume, particularly in chapter 1, suggests that it is critical for such economies to seek to offset their inherent scale-based risks with a level of stability and a quality of infrastructure which will serve to encourage investment activity, both from residents and from the international capital markets.

The stability needed in the context of these economies is comprehensive; it includes macroeconomic, social, political and policy stability. The experiences of Caribbean economies, which provide much of the fodder for the empirical analyses that anchor this volume, provide eloquent testimony to the role of macrostability in differentiating among small economies in relation to their level of economic performance. In this regard, chapters 2 and 3 in this volume speak to the importance of macroeconomic stability, and point to the critical importance of fiscal prudence as the most important element of macroeconomic stability in a small economy.

In anchoring their programmes of macroeconomic stability, many Caribbean economies have demonstrated their fiscal responsibility through a commitment to fixed exchange rates with open foreign exchange windows. Fixed exchange rates have fallen out of favour around the world. And for good reason, since such exchange rates do create the likelihood of exchange rate misalignment, with its corollary of distorted prices that reduce the export competitiveness of the country's resident firms. This likelihood is made even more certain in the context of "competitive" exchange rate depreciation by neighbouring countries.

Yet, for many high-performing Caribbean economies, the macroeconomic stability that has been demonstrated through the conservative fiscal policy demanded by a commitment to fixed exchange rates with open foreign exchange windows has been paramount. It has been of more importance to these economies than the marginal improvements in export competitiveness, and the greater latitude in monetary and fiscal policy, that would have been afforded through a flexible exchange regime.

Indeed, one of the clearest lessons from an examination of efforts to enhance competitiveness in Caribbean economies has been the importance of the state. While the international academic community, at large, has vacillated in its perspective on the role of the state, those interested in questions of development have always recognized the important role that the state plays in the development process. Possibly, the state's role is nowhere as important as it is in small economies, in part because these economies are unique in the extent to which their success rests on macrostability and high-quality infrastructure, both of which are largely public goods. The role of the state in small developing countries in reducing the risks associated with internationally competitive activity is explored in detail in chapter 4 of this volume, focusing on the experiences of the four largest anglophone Caribbean countries.

Although the state in small countries performs such a critical role, the irony is that this role may be performed most effectively by ceding activities normally considered to be responsibilities of the state apparatus to other institutions. There are two factors that drive this process of transfer of state functions in small economies. One is the same factor that forces economic specialization in small economies: the issue of operational scale. Small states could have the same potential for functional spread as their larger counterparts, with activities in regulation, promotion, negotiation, defence, economic management and so forth. But with a much more constrained set of human resources, it may well be prudent to share some of these functions with others in the context of regional groupings, or other forms of international collaboration.

But the more critical factor in the ceding of some of the traditional responsibilities of state lies in the importance of the stability which rests at the heart of many of the competitiveness enhancement concerns in small economies. In this regard, the ceding of monetary policy to supranational institutions, or indeed to other countries, at times, has been an important pillar in the efforts of governments of small economies to insulate their economies from the temptation of fiscal indiscipline. This issue takes on special significance in the context of small economies because politicians in these economies face greater pressures to adopt a paternalistic approach to governance than their counterparts in larger countries. Inevitably, this paternalism is converted to fiscal profligacy unless determined steps are taken to insulate political authorities from the temptation of fiscal overreach.

Interestingly, the pattern of ceding monetary policy to supranational institutions is gathering steam in unions that incorporate much larger economic actors. This is, of course, an important element of the integration process in Europe, and by 2001 was being posited as an option for consideration in the economic integration effort of the Southern Common Market (MERCOSUR), following, in part, on the problems that Brazil and Argentina, the two largest countries in that regional grouping, were experiencing in co-ordinating their exchange and monetary regimes.

One of the consequences of the option of ceding some normal activities of the state to other institutions is that it has lowered the MES of an economy. While this certainly appears to come at the cost of lost sovereignty, it is increasingly clear that sovereignty is the ability of the residents of an economy to decide on their own approaches to governance. If, in so deciding, they choose to cede particular elements of their governance activity to other institutions, this is not necessarily a diminution of their sovereignty.

Increasingly, it is clear, as advocated in chapter 5, that the concept of sovereignty needs to depart from a focus on the historical "trappings of sovereignty" in favour of recognizing the importance of self-determination. In this regard, many in developing countries have become frustrated with an emphasis on political sovereignty, which brings with it economic impoverishment, destitution and dependence. Politicians and the elite in many developing countries tend to be most concerned with the maintenance of historical notions of sovereignty. But then, they tend not to be the individuals who are impoverished and destitute.

One indicator of the new thinking on issues of sovereignty in developing countries is captured in the new attitudes towards FDI. Where once foreign investors were reviled, particularly in the immediate aftermath of the pride generated from success in independence struggles, they are now welcomed with open arms and, indeed, are sought after by developing countries, especially small developing countries.

To the extent that these investors are operating at internationally competitive levels, which is likely to be the case if they are export-oriented, or competing in domestic markets that are not sheltered from international competition, and they do not generate undue negative externalities, small developing countries are right to welcome them. They bring with them potential benefits of market access and international best practice in areas such as technology, management and employment relations. Small developing countries are particularly likely to benefit from these investors, given the challenges that these economies face in nurturing internationally competitive indigenous firms.

Unfortunately, as pointed out in the research reported in chapter 6 of this volume, the bargaining power of such countries in relation to the attraction of internationally competitive FDI is not high. They face locational disadvantages, in that they lack one of the key ingredients important in the attraction of FDI: a large domestic market.

Consequently, small developing countries eager to attract FDI in pursuit of their objectives of increasing the level of international competitiveness of resident firms have to offset their locational disadvantages with inducements. Many have turned to inducements such as fiscal incentives, in cases accompanied by aggressive programmes of investment promotion and reforms that create liberal investment environments. The most successful cases of attracting export-oriented FDI, however, have made sure to accompany a package of incentives, liberal investment policies and active promotion with the enduring elements of a stable macroenvironment and high-quality physical and intellectual infrastructure.

The reality for small developing countries, however, is that, relative to the number of such countries in the market for export-oriented FDI, there is an inadequate supply of export-oriented foreign direct investors willing to use small developing countries as a platform to produce for regional or global markets, in a manner that would have a significant impact on investment flows in each country. Further, the almost universal movement among small developing countries to similar programmes of investment policy and promotion has made it more difficult for countries to distinguish themselves in the crowded investment attraction marketplace.

In light of this scenario, small developing countries, while continuing their promotional efforts, should concentrate on ensuring that their overall economic environment is conducive to all types of investment, and not discriminate against local investors in pursuit of relatively scarce foreign investment. They also need to be careful about their approach to the provision of financial incentives. Attracting FDI is not a goal that should be achieved regardless of the cost to the national treasury. There is a cost-benefit analysis that must be carefully assessed in the provision of financial incentives to investors, particularly direct grants, as opposed to fiscal incentives in the form of foregone taxes.

Finally, in this regard, it is important that small developing countries consider carefully the approach that many have adopted to the attraction of FDI. The implicit, and in cases explicit, approach adopted has been that the national promotional authority should seek to attract FDI that aids in diversifying the economy away from areas of existing strength to new areas of economic activity that can serve to reduce the country's exposure to the vagaries of world markets.

This is a laudable goal, but it may be impractical. It is the rare small developing country that has an industry so distinctive that it faces no international competition. Thus, even in areas of existing strength, there is typically much opportunity for a country to increase its level of competitiveness. And the right foreign investors are likely to be able to assist a small developing country in this regard. Promotional efforts should not be handicapped by being required to go against the grain of investor interest, in pursuit of economic diversification. The competitiveness of the investment attraction market suggests that FDI attraction efforts need to be anchored in areas of competitive strength within a small economy.

The reality of small economies is that their levels of economic diversification are much lower than is the case of their larger counterparts. Investment attraction efforts can expand the range of competitive industries in these countries, but the range of industries is still likely to be narrow. The inevitable vagaries in world markets are probably best managed in small developing countries by diversifying across markets within an industry, and by adopting an approach of economic prudence, inclusive of fiscal prudence and high foreign-exchange reserve levels. This is more appropriate than seeking widespread industry diversification, including efforts to channel investment into areas in which the country offers no underlying competitive advantage to export-oriented investors.

The public-good nature of investment attraction efforts suggests that these are likely to be most effectively handled by the state. The state bears a fundamental role in the efforts of small developing countries to increase levels of international competitiveness. But, as important as is the role of the state, it is not the only actor that has a role to play. The very visible hands of the state need to be complemented by the rolled-up sleeves of enterprise managers in order to increase levels of competitiveness in small developing countries.

Chapter 7 reports on a study of enterprises in Jamaica's national environment of the late 1990s. This environment was one of low growth, which is a challenge confronting many other small developing countries. This study placed a critical premium on the attitudes and approaches of the leadership of firms. It suggested that adroit corporate leadership is an indispensable element in the process of improving firm-level performance in the direction of increased international competitiveness. This leadership needs not only to wax evangelical in the area of transforming the operations and systems of the firm, but also has to be sufficiently integrated into world markets to be aware of the standards that have to be met to ensure the survival of the firm in the face of aggressive international competition.

One of the clear examples of the role of enterprise management in small developing countries arises from the area of the management of employment relations, as indicated in chapter 8 of this volume. This area of management calls for special attention because of the particular circumstances of many small developing countries. These countries typically have cultures deeply anchored in historical inequity, discrimination and exploitation. In some cases, as in the countries of the Caribbean region, this derives from a legacy of slavery, onto which was fashioned colonial administrations that continued slavery's legacy of inequity. Indeed, most such countries have colonial legacies that were not noted for the practice of egalitarianism.

Deep-seated mistrust among classes lives on in these societies because, for the most part, post-colonialism and independence have done little to address fundamental issues of social hierarchy within these societies. And, indeed, many of the local elite, management and administration in these countries have gone even further than colonial administrations in their attitudes of social stratification and hierarchy.

It is against this background that firms in small developing countries encounter challenges as they seek to create a motivated workforce that can improve firm-level productivity in an era of substantially greater international competition. The need to democratize workplaces, and the challenge of this democratization process, becomes ever more significant in the context of small developing economies. Workers, managers and unions in these countries, in particular, have to reorder their relations, recognize their trilateral dependency, and move from a dominant paradigm of conflict to one of co-operation in their relations if their enterprises, or those to which they are affiliated, are to survive.

Finally, chapters 9 and 10 of this volume point to the critical importance of expanding considerations of international competitiveness beyond the traditional focus of macropolicy and the performance of firms involved in the formal and tradeable segments of a national economy. Issues of international competitiveness need to be applied to sectors in which trade takes place infrequently or not at all. Such issues are considered in chapter 9, in a case study of the rarely traded products of the Jamaican health system.

As importantly, the social stability that is important to the success of a small economy is unlikely to be achieved if significant swathes of an economy are allowed to remain outside of the formal sector. Moreover, as pointed out in chapter 10, enterprises and individuals operating in these segments of an economy have tremendous underutilized economic potential that, if realized, can serve to enhance the overall competitiveness of the economy, and the ultimate well-being of its citizenry. It is, of course, the ultimate well-being of all residents that is the goal of efforts to enhance and sustain levels of international competitiveness in small developing economies.

Sustaining Competitiveness in Small Developing Economies

This volume has focused on identifying the factors that differentiate economic performance among and within small developing economies. The lessons that can be drawn from an elucidation of these factors are important to the efforts of these countries to adapt best recognized practice in their competitiveness enhancement efforts.

Yet it is myopic to focus an analysis of competitiveness enhancement efforts in small developing countries on the practices in other such countries, even ones that are outperforming their counterparts. Surely, there is a need to assess the activities in these countries against the more competitive developed countries of the world, which is nothing more than the benchmarking exercise in which the more successful firms in small developing countries are continually engaged.

There are elements of the analyses recorded in this volume that included developing and developed countries. Recall that the analysis of the competitive advantage of small economies captured in chapter 1 of this volume was not restricted to an analysis among small developing economies. That analysis involved a sample of small economies across all income levels.

Nevertheless, it is useful to focus explicitly on the extent to which the analyses and conclusions of this volume relate to competitiveness analysis models developed from an examination of competitiveness in the context of more developed economies. The most popular such model is the Porter model of national competitiveness,[1] referred to in the introductory chapter of this volume and tested in the context of the competitiveness assessment of the Jamaican health system in chapter 9.

Porter makes two fundamental arguments in his analysis of competitiveness as it applies to the nation state. The first is that the international competitiveness of industries in a country is driven by a collection of variables including factor conditions, related and supporting industries, firm strategy, structure and rivalry, demand conditions, the role of chance and the role of government, with the latter two being subsidiary to the first four variables that, together, combine to create the diamond of national competitive advantage.

The second point is that countries operate at different stages of a competitiveness continuum, inclusive of factor-driven, investment-driven, innovation-driven and wealth-driven, with the various elements of the diamond taking on greater significance depending upon a country's stage of competitiveness. Thus, at the factor-driven stage of competitiveness, most of a country's competitive industries would be internationally competitive based upon the country having a configuration of factors of production that is particularly relevant to the requirements of those industries. In this stage, such a country's competitiveness would be readily explained by a classical and neoclassical model of comparative advantage.

On the other hand, a country in the innovative stage of competitiveness would find that the most important factor driving competitiveness would be the sophistication of home-country demand, which demand creates the conditions for innovation. This approach to the performance of nations is not represented at all in classical or neoclassical economic theory, but it does follow the work of international business scholars, in particular the intellectual pedigree of Ray Vernon's product cycle theory.[2]

Importantly, to understand a Porterian perspective, it is useful to recognize that the stage of a country reflects the area in which the majority of industries, but not all, derive their competitive advantage. Thus, it is possible for countries in a factor-driven or investment-driven stage to have industries that derive their competitive advantage from demand conditions.[3] But most competitive industries in these countries would not derive their competitive advantage from the sophistication of consumer demand. Similarly, it is likely that an innovation-driven country will have competitive industries deriving demand from factor-conditions, in addition, of course, to having industries that are not at all internationally competitive.

The analyses reported in this volume find consonance with a Porterian perspective on national competitiveness. Internationally competitive industries in most small developing countries can be traced to a combination driven by factor conditions, but supported by firm strategy, structure and rivalry, and related and supporting industries, as illustrated by the analyses of chapter 9. It is the very rare industry in a small developing country that has become internationally competitive driven by the sophistication of a home market. One possible exception is Jamaica's reggae music industry, but even this industry did not achieve respectability in mainstream Jamaica until it had developed an international appeal, and that industry continued to be driven by institutions largely external to the country for many years, even as it relied on Jamaican recording artistes.[4]

The research of this volume, however, does not provide complete support for a Porterian perspective on national competitiveness. In small developing countries, the role for government, which Porter views as marginal, is far more important. This difference in focus is not surprising. The least developed countries that Porter examined in his ten-country study were Singapore and South Korea. Thus, the countries he studied could take for granted well-managed economies. This is clearly not the case in many developing countries. For small developing countries, the competence of government plays a critical role in differential performance, in much the same way as government-related activities play such an important role in the variation in growth rates among nations.[5]

In this respect, the Porterian perspective of classifying virtually all countries outside Western Europe, the United States and Japan as in the factor-driven stage of national competitiveness also does not resonate with the results of this study. Clearly some of these countries, and Singapore represents the obvious example among small countries, are better classified in an investment stage. This classification is driven, in the Singaporean context, by its tremendous success in attracting export-oriented FDI. And, further, the lessons of this volume suggest that a more fine-grained categorization of countries is needed within this factor-driven stage, possibly to include basic factor, intermediate factor and advanced factor stages.

Other analysts concerned with either developing country competitiveness, or the competitiveness of small, open economies, have expressed concern about the explanatory power of a Porterian perspective in the context of small or developing countries. In terms of the applicability to small and open economies, Rugman and D'Cruz, based largely on the experiences of the Canadian economy, advocate a double diamond, in which the competitiveness of a multinational firm is linked not only to the diamond of its home country, but also to that of its host country, particularly focused on the infrastructure, government and resources of that country.[6]

In this regard, this double diamond model, in the context of a small economy, places greater emphasis on the role of government and of infrastructure than a Porterian perspective, and in that respect accords with the findings of the analyses of this volume. Barclay also finds support for the double diamond model in the context of the competitiveness of firms based in the anglophone Caribbean.[7] There is, however, an extent to which these models speak past each other, since it might be argued that the elements in the double diamond model are implicit in a factor-driven explanation of competitiveness.[8] And, further, that the elements of the double diamond do not provide for sustainable competitive advantage, nor indicate clearly where competitive advantage is derived.

In terms of the applicability of the Porterian perspective, Kapur and Ramamurti[9] suggest, in the context of the competitiveness of the Indian software industry, that a virtual diamond, which links Indian national conditions to the demand conditions of the United States and the role of overseas Indians in the United States, more adequately explains the success of that industry than a Porterian perspective.

Kapur and Ramamurti are certainly correct in noting the particularly important role that overseas Indians have played in the competitiveness of the Indian software industry, in a manner equivalent to the role that overseas Chinese networks have played in enhancing the manufacturing competitiveness of various South East Asian economies. But the generalizability of their findings to other developing countries is surely constrained by the peculiar circumstances of India and China, which together constitute 40 per cent of humanity, and are likely, therefore, to have diasporic communities that can play a critical role in creating and sustaining national competitiveness.

It is in the area of sustaining competitive advantage that a Porterian perspective on national competitiveness is critical to considerations of competitiveness in small developing countries. Porter advocates a dynamic process to the enhancement of national competitiveness. The vulnerabilities that are inherent in the characterization of small developing economies suggest that, among all types of economies, they can least afford complacency. And, of course, the key challenge of factor-driven competitiveness is that competitive advantage is easily lost, to the extent that similar factors are found or made available elsewhere. Porter advocates for countries, including those in the factor-driven stage of competitiveness, a constant upgrading of factors of production through the application of technology, and a focus on the principle that, ultimately, competitive advantage is created, not inherited.

There is no more effective way for small developing countries to seek to sustain their levels of competitiveness than by recognizing the importance of the application of technological and managerial effort to the dynamic upgrading of competitive advantage in industries where they already exhibit competitive strength. Laudable efforts to seek out new economic opportunities in niche markets and industries where they can offer to world and national markets a distinctive product should complement, not displace, the former focus.

It is the combination of such efforts, while recognizing, as detailed in this volume, the structural constraints confronting small developing economies, and the opportunities these economies provide for nimble action, which will lead to the enhancement and sustaining of competitiveness in small developing economies, for the ultimate benefit of all of their citizenry.

Notes

Introduction

1. See Theodore Levitt, "The Globalization of Markets", *Harvard Business Review* (May–June 1983): 92–102.

2. Several of the analysts who argue that there is nothing special about the current situation give insufficient credence to this distinction. Alan Rugman, for example, argues that the world is regionalizing, not globalizing, using as evidence the tendency of multinational enterprises to concentrate their production activities in the Triad Regions of North America, Europe and Japan. He also suggests that "foreign direct investment is the engine that drives globalisation". For Rugman's perspective, see "Multinational Enterprises and the End of Globalization", in his *The End of Globalization* (London: Random House, 2000).

3. For a comprehensive account of the information technology revolution's impact on the globalization of markets, see Frances Cairncross, *The Death of Distance: How the Communications Revolution Will Change Our Lives* (Boston: Harvard Business School Press, 1997).

4. See Levitt, "Globalization".

5. See Cairncross, *Death of Distance*; Thomas Friedman, *The Lexus and the Olive Tree: Understanding Globalization* (New York: Farrar Straus and Giroux, 1999); *Economist*, "A Survey of Globalization", 29 September 2001, 3–30; Joseph Stiglitz, *Globalization and Its Discontents* (New York: W.W. Norton, 2002); David Dollar and Aart Kraay, "Spreading the Wealth", *Foreign Affairs* 81, no. 1 (January–February 2002): 120–33.

6. For several articles written by developing country scholars on the adverse consequences of globalization, particularly from the perspective of developing countries, see Denis Benn and Kenneth Hall, eds., *Globalisation, A Calculus of Inequality: Perspectives from the South* (Kingston, Jamaica: Ian Randle Publishers, 2000). For a discussion of the concerns about the impact of globalization on developing countries, with proposals for how these countries can increase the likelihood of reaping benefits from open markets, see Dani Rodrik, *The New Global Economy and Developing Countries: Making Openness Work* (Washington, DC: Overseas Development Council, 1999).

7. Norman Girvan, quite appropriately, characterizes these options as a "walking on two legs strategy", with one leg involving a strengthening of the bargaining position and negotiating capacity of Caribbean states, and the other involving strengthening the productive and competitive capacities of regional producers. For his useful analysis, see "Globalisation and Counter-Globalisation: The Caribbean in the Context of the South",

in *Globalisation, A Calculus of Inequality: Perspectives from the South,* ed. Denis Benn and Kenneth Hall, 65–86 (Kingston, Jamaica: Ian Randle Publishers, 2000).

8. See, for example, Michael Porter, *The Competitive Advantage of Nations* (New York: Free Press, 1990); and Alan Rugman and J. D'Cruz, "The Double Diamond Model of International Competitiveness: The Canadian Experience", *Management International Review* 33 (special issue; 1993): 17–39.

9. Paul Krugman has been quite critical of the loosely drawn analogies between companies and countries, and the notion that countries are engaged in head-to-head competition. See, for example, Paul Krugman, *Pop Internationalism* (Cambridge, Mass.: MIT Press, 1996).

10. See Krugman, *Pop Internationalism*, 22.

11. On this point, for example, Krugman takes exception to both the title and the content of Lester C. Thurow's *The Coming Economic Battle among Japan, Europe and America* (New York: Morrow, 1992). See Krugman, *Pop Internationalism*, 22.

12. See Krugman, *Pop Internationalism*, 5.

13. The World Economic Forum, for example, devotes an annual publication to an assessment of the extent to which national environments create a platform that increases or decreases the level of competitiveness of their resident firms. See the joint effort of the World Economic Forum and Harvard University's Centre for International Development, *The Global Competitiveness Report* (New York: Oxford University Press, 2000).

14. Krueger's proposal was motivated, in large part, by the 2001 Argentina crisis. See Anne Krueger, "Should Argentina Be Able to Declare Bankruptcy?", *New Perspectives Quarterly* 19, no. 2 (Spring 2002): 86–87.

15. For a critique of Krueger's proposal, which concludes that if implemented correctly it could lead to an improvement in the world's financial system, see Richard N. Cooper, "Chapter 11 for Countries?", *Foreign Affairs* 81, no. 4 (July–August 2002): 90–104.

16. The first two of these indicators is used by Michael Porter. See his *Competitive Advantage*.

17. See Porter, *Competitive Advantage*.

18. See Rugman and D'Cruz, "The Double Diamond Model"; and Lou Anne A. Barclay, *Foreign Direct Investment in Emerging Economies: Corporate Strategy and Investment Behaviour in the Caribbean* (London: Routledge, 2000).

19. See Devesh Kapur and Ravi Ramamurti, "India's Emerging Competitive Advantage in Services", *The Academy of Management executive* 15, no. 2 (2001): 20–33.

20. See, for example, Deena Khatkhate and Brook Short, "Money and Central Banking Problems of Mini-States", *World Development* 8, no. 12 (1980): 1017–25.

21. For a recent survey of scholarly thought about the Caribbean, see Brian Meeks and Folke Lindahl, eds., *New Caribbean Thought: A Reader* (Kingston, Jamaica: University of the West Indies Press, 2001).

Chapter 1

1. See William Easterly and Aart Kraay, "Small States, Small Problems? Income, Growth and Volatility in Small States", *World Development* 28, no. 11 (2000): 2013–27.

2. See Commonwealth Secretariat, *Vulnerability: Small States in the Global Society*

(London: Commonwealth Consultative Group, Commonwealth Secretariat, 1985.)

3. See, for example, Lino Briguglio, "Small Island Developing States and Their Economic Vulnerabilities", *World Development* 23, no. 9 (1995): 1615–32; and Lino Briguglio, *Alternative Vulnerability Indices for Developing Countries*, Report for UN Department of Economic and Social Affairs (Malta: Foundation for International Studies, University of Malta, 1997).

4. See, for example, *The Vulnerability of Small Island Developing States in the Context of Globalisation* (Geneva: UNCTAD, 1997).

5. See, for example, *World Development* 8, no. 12 (1980); and *World Development* 21, no. 2 (1993).

6. See Briguglio, "Small Island Developing States and Their Economic Vulnerabilities".

7. See Paul Streeten, "The Special Problems of Small Countries", *World Development* 21, no. 2 (1993): 197–202; and Charles Farrugia, "The Special Working Environment of Senior Administrators in Small States", *World Development* 21, no. 2 (1993): 221–26.

8. See Commonwealth Secretariat, *Vulnerability*.

9. See Briguglio, "Small Island Developing States and Their Economic Vulnerabilities".

10. See, for example, Briguglio, "Small Island Developing States and Their Economic Vulnerabilities".

11. For evidence on this point, see T.N. Srinivasan, "The Costs and Benefits of Being a Small, Remote, Island, Landlocked or Mini-State Economy", *World Bank Research Observer* 1 (1986): 205–18; C. Milner and T. Westaway, "Country Size and the Medium-Term Growth Process: Some Cross-Country Evidence", *World Development* 21, no. 2 (1993): 203–12; and H. Armstrong et al., "A Comparison of the Economic Performance of Different Microstates and between Microstates and Larger Countries", *World Development* 26, no. 4 (1998): 639–56.

12. See Paul Streeten, "Special Problems"; and Geoffrey Bertram, "Sustainable Development in Pacific Micro-Economies", *World Development* 14, no. 7 (1986): 809–22.

13. See, for example, William Demas, *The Economics of Development in Small Countries with Special Reference to the Caribbean* (Montreal: McGill University Press, 1965); Commonwealth Secretariat, *Vulnerability*; John Kaminarides and Edward Nissan, "The Effects of International Debt on the Economic Development of Small Countries", *World Development* 21, no. 2 (1993): 227–32; Armstrong et al., "A Comparison of the Economic Performance"; and Easterly and Kraay, "Small States, Small Problems?".

14. See, for example, Andrew Downes, "On the Statistical Measurement of Smallness: A Principal Component Measure of Size", *Social and Economic Studies* 37, no. 3 (1988): 75–96.

15. See Demas, *The Economics of Development in Small Countries*; and Kaminarides and Nissan, "The Effects of International Debt".

16. See John Caldwell, Graham Harrison and Pat Quissin, "The Demography of Micro-States", *World Development* 8, no. 12 (1980): 953–67.

17. On this point, see Percy Selwyn, "Smallness and Islandness", *World Development* 8, no. 12 (1980): 945–51.

18. See Caldwell, Harrison and Quissin, "The Demography of Micro-States".

19. See Briguglio, "Small Island Developing States and Their Economic Vulnerabilities".

20. See Paul Krugman, *Pop Internationalism* (Cambridge, Mass.: MIT Press, 1996).

21. See Alvin G. Wint, "International Competitiveness and Public Policy in the Caribbean", *Journal of Eastern Caribbean Studies* 25, no. 1 (2000): 39–57.

22. See P. Aghion and P. Hewitt, *Endogenous Growth Theory* (Cambridge, Mass.: MIT Press, 1998).

23. For support, see Kwabena Brempang-Gyimah and Samaria Munoz de Camacho, "Political Instability, Human Capital and Economic Growth in Latin America", *Journal of Developing Areas* 32 (Summer 1998): 449–66.

24. See Deena Khatkhate and Brook Short, "Money and Central Banking Problems of Mini-States", *World Development* 8, no. 12 (1980): 1017–25; and A.R. Caram, "The Repercussions of Financial Imbalances in Suriname", *World Development* 21, no. 2 (1993): 291–99.

25. For example, note the concerns of Intel when considering its widely publicized investment in Costa Rica. For a detailed account of the investment attraction process, see Debora Spar, *Attracting High Technology Investment: Intel's Costa Rican Plant,* Foreign Investment Advisory Service Occasional Paper, no. 11 (Washington, DC: 1998).

26. See Brempang-Gyimah and Munoz de Camacho, "Political Instability"; and Spar, *Attracting High Technology Investment.*

27. See Easterly and Kraay, "Small States, Small Problems?"; and Armstrong et al., "A Comparison of the Economic Performance".

28. See Commonwealth Secretariat, *Vulnerability.*

29. See, for example, Srinivasan, "Costs and Benefits"; Milner and Westaway, "Country Size"; Armstrong et al., "A Comparison of the Economic Performance"; and Easterly and Kraay, "Small States, Small Problems?".

30. See Robert Barro, *Determinants of Economic Growth: A Cross-Country Empirical Study* (Cambridge, Mass.: MIT Press, 1997).

31. See, for example, Rodney Cole, "Economic Development in the South Pacific: Promoting the Private Sector", *World Development* 21, no. 2 (1993): 233–43; Bertram, "Sustainable Development"; and World Bank, *Enhancing the Role of Government in the Pacific Island Economies* (Washington, DC: World Bank, 1998).

32. See Armstrong et al., "A Comparison of the Economic Performance".

33. For an interesting set of data on this point, see Lorraine Eden and Jun Li, "Black Holes in Tax Space? Tax Havens and Inward Foreign Direct Investment" (paper presented at Annual Conference of Academy of International Business, Sydney, Australia, November 2001).

34. See Spar, *Attracting High Technology Investment.*

35. For a discussion of the concept of "brain circulation" and a computer model of the impact of migrant remittances on developing countries, see Mina Yoo and Klaus Webber, "Brain Circulation, International Capital Flows, and the World Order: A Computer Simulation of Migrant Economic Activity" (paper presented at Annual Conference of Academy of International Business, Sydney, Australia, November 2001).

36. As examined, for instance, in Michael Porter, *The Competitive Advantage of Nations* (New York: Free Press, 1990) or in *The Global Competitiveness Report 2000* (New York: Oxford University Press, 2000).

Chapter 2

1. See M. Klein and N. Marion, "Explaining the Duration of Exchange Pegs", *Journal of Development Economics* 54 (1997): 387–404.

2. For useful analyses of the discipline linked to fixed exchange rates, see Pierre Richard Agenor, "Credibility and Exchange Rate Management in Developing Countries", *Journal of Development Economics* 45 (1994): 1–16; and Berthold Herrendorf, "Importing Credibility through Exchange Rate Pegging", *Economic Journal* 107 (1997): 687–94.

3. See Graham Norton, "Bermuda's Independence Referendum", *The World Today* 51, no. 10 (1995): 68–70.

4. See Norton, "Bermuda's Independence Referendum".

5. See Susan Collins, "On Becoming More Flexible: Exchange Rate Regimes in Latin America and the Caribbean", *Journal of Development Economics* 51 (1996): 117–38.

6. See Delisle Worrel, "Role Models for Monetary Policy in the Caribbean: Comparing CARICOM Central Banks", in *Central Banking in Barbados: Reflections and Challenges,* ed. Harold Codrington et al., 37–55 (Bridgetown, Barbados: Central Bank of Barbados, 1997).

7. See the pioneering work of Mundell in this area; R.A. Mundell, "A Theory of Optimum Currency Areas", *American Economic Review* 51 (1961): 657–65.

8. See Paul Krugman, "A Model of Balance of Payments Crises", *Journal of Money, Credit and Banking* 11 (1979): 311–25.

9. See, for example, John Williamson, foreword in *Exchange Rate Misalignment: Concepts and Measurement for Developing Countries,* by Lawrence Hinkle and Peter Montiel (New York: Oxford University Press, 1999); and Guillermo Calvo and Reinhart Carmen, *Fear of Floating* (2000), available at www.bsos.umd.edu/econ/ciecrpn.pdf.

10. See Chris Canovan and Mariano Tommasi, "On the Credibility of Alternative Exchange Rate Regimes", *Journal of Development Economics* 54 (1997): 101–22; and Maria Luiza Falcao Silva, "The Rules-Versus-Discretion Debate Revisited: What Can Be Learnt From Argentina's Quasi-Currency-Board Regime?", *Social and Economic Studies* 46, no. 1 (1997): 111–34.

11. Silva describes Argentina's system as a "Quasi Currency Board Regime". See Silva, "The Rules-Versus-Discretion Debate Revisited". Another dissenting voice is that of Kurt Schuler, who argues that the Argentine "convertibility system" was an "awkward combination of currency board and central banking features". See Kurt Schuler, "Keeping Argentina Afloat", letter to the editor, *Foreign Affairs* 81, no. 4 (2002): 184–85.

12. See, for example, Martin Feldstein, "Argentina's Fall", *Foreign Affairs* 81, no. 2 (March–April 2002): 8–14, for the views of a noted economist who argues that the fixed exchange rate regime was an important proximate cause of the Argentine crisis. Also note the debate between Feldstein and Schuler on the causes of the Argentine crisis. See Schuler, "Keeping Argentina Afloat"; and "Martin Feldstein Replies", *Foreign Affairs* 81, no. 4 (2002): 184–85.

13. For this view, see Miguel A. Kiguel, "Structural Reforms in Argentina: Success or Failure?", *Comparative Economic Studies* 44, no.2–3 (Summer 2002): 83–102.

14. See Claudius Emmanuel and Alvin G. Wint, "Choice of Exchange Regime in the Caribbean" (Department of Management Studies, University of the West Indies, Kingston, Jamaica, February 2001, mimeo).

15. In a useful critique of this paper, Damien King suggested that the paper's use of official foreign exchange data, as opposed to market data, might have had an impact on the results.

16. See J. Frankel, "PPP: Doctrinal Perspective and Evidence from 1920s", *Journal of International Economics* 8 (1978): 169–91.

17. See Collins, "On Becoming More Flexible".

18. See Emmanuel and Wint, "Choice of Exchange Regime".

19. See International Monetary Fund, "Exchange Rate Regimes in an Increasingly Integrated World" (2000), available at www.imf.org/external/np/exr/ib/2000/062600.htm.

20. See John Williamson, *Exchange Rate Regimes for Emerging Markets: Reviving the Intermediate Option* (Washington, DC: Institute for International Economics, 2000).

Chapter 3

1. Interestingly, Barbados also experienced robust growth during this period (1973–1980), averaging real growth of 5 per cent per year. This might be compared with growth rates in the other two CARICOM-MDC non-oil-exporting countries of Jamaica and Guyana, which experienced comparable growth rates of -2.4 per cent and 2 per cent respectively over this period.

2. For a full discussion of these views, see Delisle Worrel, "Role Models for Monetary Policy in the Caribbean: Comparing CARICOM Central Banks", in *Central Banking in Barbados: Reflections and Challenges*, ed. Harold Codrington et al., 37–55 (Bridgetown, Barbados: Central Bank of Barbados, 1987). Worrel also draws on early research on Caribbean central banking which suggests that monetary policy is ineffective in small, open economies with a high degree of capital mobility, and that open market operations are less effective in thin financial markets. See, for example, Clive Y. Thomas, *The Structure, Performance and Prospects of Central Banking in the Caribbean* (Kingston, Jamaica: Institute for Social and Economic Research, 1972).

3. See Courtney Blackman, "The Practice of Central Banking in Barbados: An Interpretation of the First Fifteen Years", in *Central Banking in Barbados: Reflections and Challenges*, ed. Harold Codrington et al., 15–35 (Bridgetown, Barbados: Central Bank of Barbados, 1987).

4. While recognizing the caution from Collins about drawing causal links between exchange rate regimes and levels of economic growth in cross-sectional comparisons across countries (see Susan Collins, "On Becoming More Flexible: Exchange Rate Regimes in Latin America and the Caribbean", *Journal of Development Economics* 51 [1996]: 117–38), it seems reasonable, nevertheless, to take a cursory longitudinal look at economic growth levels after the implementation of a stabilization programme. Economic growth in Barbados after the adjustment process following the 1981 crisis averaged close to 3 per cent per annum over the 1983–1990 period.

5. See R.A. Mundell, "A Theory of Optimum Currency Areas", *American Economic Review* 51 (1961): 717–25.

6. Worrel makes this point and adds that the experiences of the Netherlands, Austria, Denmark and the European principalities confirm that even for prosperous industrial countries the best strategy for small economies in proximity to large dominant countries is to fix their currency to that of their dominant neighbour. See Worrel, "Role Models for

Monetary Policy", 51.

7. There is now a burgeoning literature on the problems involved in managing flexible exchange rates and exchange rate change. See, for example, Thorvaldur Gylfasona and Marian Radetzki, "Does Devaluation Make Sense in the Least Developed Countries?", *Economic Development and Cultural Change* 40, no. 1 (1991): 1–25; Sebastian Edwards, "Exchange Controls, Devaluations and Real Exchange Rates: The Latin American Experience", *Economic Development and Cultural Change* 37, no. 3 (April 1989): 457–95; Pierre-Richard Agenor et al., "Macroeconomic Effects of Anticipated Devaluations with Informal Financial Markets", *Journal of Development Economics* 42 (1993): 133–53; and Richard Barnett and Mun S. Ho, "Sunspots, Currency Substitution and Inflationary Finance", *Journal of International Economics* 41 (1996): 73–93.

8. The two options that are most effective in institutionalizing endogenous money supply growth (currency boards and dollarization), however, do have the symmetrical disadvantage of also allowing for no degrees of policy freedom in the event of a temporary exogenous shock. See Maria Luiza Falcao Silva, "The Rules-Versus-Discretion Debate Revisited: What Can Be Learnt from Argentina's Quasi-Currency-Board Regime?" *Social and Economic Studies* 46, no. 1 (March 1997): 111–34, for a discussion of credibility and flexibility issues in the context of Argentina's currency board system.

9. See Worrel, "Role Models for Monetary Policy".

10. See, for example, George A. Akerlof et al., "The Macroeconomics of Low Inflation", *Brookings Papers on Economic Activity*, no. 1 (1996): 1–76.

11. For evidence on this point, see William Easterly and Klaus Schmidty-Hebbel, "Fiscal Deficits and Macroeconomic Performance in Developing Countries", *World Bank Research Observer* 8, no. 2 (1993): 211–37; and Edwards, "Exchange Controls, Devaluations and Real Exchange Rates".

12. For a classic work on the subject of social capital, or social networking that enhances trust and cooperation among a nation's citizenry, see R.D. Putman, "Bowling Alone: America's Declining Social Capital", *Journal of Democracy* 6, no. 1 (1995): 65–78. For a comparative analysis of social capital development in Barbados and Jamaica, see Havelock Brewster, "Social Capital and Development: Reflections on Barbados and Jamaica", 1996, manuscript. I acknowledge useful discussions with Mark Figueroa and Norman Girvan on the importance of social capital in the Barbadian case of exchange rate management.

Chapter 4

1. When the principal regional integration effort in the Caribbean, the Caribbean Community (CARICOM), was established in 1973, the four most populous members of the regional grouping were referred to as the more developed countries (MDCs).

2. As an example of work in this genre, see Stan Reid, "The Decision-Maker and Export Entry and Expansion", *Journal of International Business Studies* (Fall 1981): 100–111.

3. See chapter 6 for a discussion of this issue and a sampling of the research in this area.

4. For an excellent account of the process of attracting Intel to Costa Rica, see Debora Spar, *Attracting High Technology Investment: Intel's Costa Rican Plant,* Foreign Investment Advisory Service Occasional Paper, no. 11 (Washington, DC: 1998).

5. It is important to note that a programme such as the Trinidadian one, in which incentives are targeted preferentially toward exporters, is unlikely to be possible in the future with the more aggressive implementation of WTO rules against the use of export subsidies.

6. See *National Industrial Policy: Growth and Prosperity – The Way Forward* (Kingston, Jamaica: Jamaica Information Service, 1996).

7. The extent to which foreign exchange reserves were acquired in the immediate aftermath of liberalization of the foreign exchange system was significant. Jamaica's net international reserves grew by at least US$700 million between 1990 and 1993. The sterilized acquisition of these reserves over the period would have involved very significant budgetary transfers.

8. One might well question, in retrospect, a goal of such rapid achievement of macroeconomic stability, given the levels of inflation and interest rates in Jamaica prior to the promulgation of the industrial policy. The policy crafters, and key institutions in the Jamaican government, also underestimated the impact that stabilizing the economy would have on a financial sector whose performance was positively impacted by the instability of the foreign exchange markets, in particular, in the period subsequent to the liberalization of the financial sector and the financial markets.

9. For an account of the privatization of telecommunications in Jamaica, see Alvin G. Wint, "Pioneering Telephone Privatization: Jamaica", in *Privatizing Monopolies: Lessons from the Telecommunications and Transport Sectors in Latin America*, ed. Ravi Ramamurti, 49–71 (Baltimore: Johns Hopkins University Press, 1996).

10. The absence of compensation was important. The Hong Kong government, for example, had to pay Cable and Wireless US$1 billion to extricate itself from a similar monopolistic arrangement.

11. For an outline of the government's expectations from the new agreement, see "Jamaica's Information Technology Vision", a paper presented by the Hon. Philip Paulwell, minister of commerce and technology, to the Jamaican National Planning Council on 1 December 1999.

12. Cable and Wireless had become a victim of a well-known problem in international investment: "the obsolescing bargain". See Raymond Vernon, *Sovereignty at Bay: The Multinational Spread of US Enterprises* (New York: Basic Books, 1971), for the initial explication of this concept. The concept suggests that the bargaining power of international investors fades after they have committed to fixed investments. The breakthrough for the Jamaican government in this case, however, was its ability to arrange a negotiated settlement, with the associated reduced impact on perceptions of risk, as opposed to a unilateral abrogation of Cable and Wireless's fifty-year exclusive licence. This was important for Jamaica, since in 1974 the government, with good and understandable intentions, had unilaterally abrogated a taxation agreement with the bauxite and alumina sector, through the introduction of a tax on the production of bauxite, replacing the income-based taxation regime that had applied previously. This action prompted a claim to the Overseas Private Insurance Corporation by these firms, and contributed to lower levels of investment in the sector for two decades. For a discussion of the obsolescing bargain in relation to investment in infrastructure in developing countries in the 1990s, see Louis T. Wells, Jr and Eric Gleason, "Is Foreign Infrastructure Investment Still Risky?" *Harvard Business Review* (September–October 1995): 45–55.

13. For an insightful account of the problems of implementing economic reform in Jamaica, see Damien King, "The Evolution of Structural Adjustment and Stabilisation Policy in Jamaica", *Social and Economic Studies* 50, no. 1 (March 2001): 1–53.

14. Nominal interest rates on Government of Jamaica securities peaked at over 50 per cent in the mid-1990s. Real interest rates hovered between 15 and 20 per cent during the mid- to late 1990s.

15. There is a substantial literature on selective intervention. For a sampling, see A.H. Amsden, "A Theory of Government Intervention in Late Industrialization", in *State and Market in Development: Synergy or Rivalry?* ed. L. Putterman and D. Rueschemeyer, 25–38 (Boulder: Lynne Rienner, 1993).

16. For an application of these ideas to international competitiveness in the health sector of a CARICOM MDC, see chapter 9 in this volume.

Chapter 5

1. See John Williamson, "What Washington Means by Policy Reform", in *Latin American Adjustment: How Much Has Happened?* ed. John Williamson, 8–15 (Washington, DC: Institute for International Economics, 1990).

2. See, for example, Holger Henke and Ian Boxill, eds., *The End of the Asian Model* (Amsterdam: John Benjamins, 2000); and Norman Girvan, "Globalisation and Counter-Globalisation: The Caribbean in the Context of the South", in *Globalisation, A Calculus of Inequality: Perspectives from the South,* ed. Denis Benn and Kenneth Hall, 65–86 (Kingston, Jamaica: Ian Randle Publishers, 2000).

3. See, for example, Shahid Burki and G. Perry, *Beyond the Washington Consensus: Institutions Matter* (Washington, DC: World Bank, 1998).

4. See Christopher Clague, Introduction, in *Institutions and Economic Development: Growth and Governance in Less-Developed and Post-Socialist Countries,* ed. Christopher Clague (Baltimore: Johns Hopkins University Press, 1997), 3.

5. See Robert J. Barro, *Determinants of Economic Growth: A Cross-Country Empirical Study* (Cambridge, Mass.: MIT Press, 1997).

6. See Michael Porter, *The Competitive Advantage of Nations* (New York: Free Press, 1990).

7. In the context of the Caribbean region, for example, several countries in the Eastern Caribbean have formed an economic union, the Organisation of Eastern Caribbean States, and ceded monetary authority to the regional Eastern Caribbean Central Bank.

8. Countries that operate pegged foreign exchange systems with guarantees from the monetary authorities that foreign exchange will be available at the pegged exchange rate (open foreign exchange window) have reduced monetary policy options. In such systems increases in domestic money supply that do not correspond to increases in exchange reserves will lead either to a reduction in foreign exchange reserves or to an abandonment of the exchange peg. Countries determined to maintain their pegs will be forced to manage money supply levels prudently. Effectively, for such countries, elements of monetary policy become detached from ongoing political influence. For a discussion of the Barbadian experience in this regard, see chapter 3 in this volume.

9. Indeed, in the small developing country of Jamaica several members of the Jamaican police force are of the view that there should be a merger between the police and the

military, as reported by one of Jamaica's foremost criminologists, who himself has advocated the elimination of the Jamaican military force in its current form. See Anthony Harriot, *Police and Crime Control in Jamaica: Problems of Reforming Ex-Colonial Constabularies* (Kingston, Jamaica: University of the West Indies Press, 2000).

10. Examples include the Brazilian aircraft manufacturer, Embraer; the Mexican cement company, CEMEX, and from the developed world, the European aircraft manufacturing consortium, Airbus.

11. Japanese firms are often held up as examples of companies that were transformed into world-class competitors on the basis of being protected from competition. It is important to note that while Japanese companies were sheltered from international competition, they faced vigorous domestic competition. For an account of efforts by the Japanese government to develop the hardware and software computer industries, see Marie Anchordoguy, "Mastering the Market: Japanese Government Targeting of the Computer Industry", *International Organization* 43, no. 3 (1988): 67–88.

12. Jamaica provides an example of the combination effect of lax regulation and imprudent management practices in the financial services sector. In the aftermath of liberalization of the financial services sector, numerous banks and insurance companies were spawned, often combined in complex group structures, and in several cases with weak capital bases. In the insurance sector, in particular, the regulatory apparatus did not adjust to the changes in the structure of the industry. These entities were unable to respond appropriately to the movement from negative to highly positive interest rates, the reduction in inflation and a fall-out in the Jamaican real estate market. These changes, in the context of connected lending among member companies within financial groups, precipitated a financial crisis in Jamaica that eventually peaked at a cost of about 44 per cent of GDP. In the aftermath of this crisis, the Jamaican government has focused on significantly upgrading its regulatory oversight of insurance companies and other financial institutions.

13. The classic example of successful investment attraction by a small country is that of Singapore. In the late 1960s, Singapore's Lee Kuan Yew was encouraged to consider the attraction of foreign direct investment by Harvard Business School international business scholar, Raymond Vernon, as outlined in chapter 6 of this volume At that time many developing countries were concerned about the potential exploitation of their raw material base by foreign investors. Lee reports that, given Singapore's absence of raw materials, they felt no concerns about embarking on an aggressive programme of attracting export-oriented FDI. That country's success in this regard is now legendary. See Lee Kuan Yew, *From Third World to First: The Singapore Story, 1965–2000* (New York: Harper Collins, 2000); and chapter 6 in this volume.

14. See, for example, Louis T. Wells and Alvin G. Wint, "The Public-Private Choice: The Case of Marketing a Country to Foreign Investors", *World Development* 19, no. 7 (1991): 749–61.

15. As noted in chapter 4, a more recent success story of investment attraction in a small country is Costa Rica's attraction of Intel. This single investment is projected to increase manufacturing exports from Costa Rica by 50 per cent. Yet, the story of Intel's investment also indicates the challenges associated with other small developing countries attracting significant levels of export-oriented FDI. See Debora Spar, *Attracting High*

Technology Investment: Intel's Costa Rican Plant, Foreign Investment Advisory Service Occasional Paper, no. 11 (Washington, DC: 1998). See also chapter 6 for further discussion.

16. The issue of access to land by foreign investors, for example, has been of particular concern to the small islands of the Caribbean and the South Pacific.

17. For evidence on this point, see Joseph Battat, Xiaofang Shen and Isaiah Frank, *Suppliers to Multinationals: Linkage Programs to Strengthen Local Companies in Developing Countries,* Foreign Investment Advisory Service Occasional Paper, no. 6 (Washington, DC: World Bank, 1996).

18. For example, the thirty-six small countries with populations between 1 million and 4.9 million on which the World Bank reports have an average 1998 income level of US$5,509, which is somewhat, but not significantly, higher than the world 1998 income average of US$4,890. Of these thirty-six countries, seven are high income. On the other hand, the fifty-seven microterritories with populations up to one million on which the World Bank reports have an average income level conservatively estimated at US$7,444. Twenty-four of these territories are reported to be high income. Most are not independent countries. See *Entering the Twenty-first Century: World Development Report 1999/2000* (New York: Oxford University Press, 2000).

Chapter 6

1. See Raymond Vernon, "International Investment and International Trade in the Product Cycle", *Quarterly Journal of Economics* (May 1966): 190–207.

2. See Lee Quan Yew, *From Third World to First World: The Singapore Story, 1965–2000* (New York: Harper Collins, 2000), 56. Indeed, so valuable did Lee find the discussions with Vernon about the workings of contemporary economies and multinational businesses, he indicated that he "returned every four years to learn more from him" (460).

3. See, for example, Alvin G. Wint, "Liberalizing Foreign Direct Investment Regimes: The Vestigial Screen", *World Development* 20, no. 10 (1992): 1515–29.

4. See Stephen Hymer, *The International Operation of National Firms: A Study of Direct Foreign Investment* (Cambridge, Mass.: MIT Press, 1976); and Peter Buckley and Mark Casson, *The Economic Theory of the Multinational Enterprise* (London: Macmillan Press, 1985).

5. See, for example, Friedrich Schneider and Bruno S. Frey, "Economic and Political Determinants of Foreign Direct Investment", *World Development* 13, no. 2 (1985): 161–75; D. Lim, "Fiscal Incentives and Direct Foreign Investment in Less Developed Countries", *Journal of Development Studies* (January 1983): 207–12; Harry Grubert and John Mutti, "Taxes, Tariffs and Transfer Pricing in Multinational Corporate Decision Making", *Review of Economics and Statistics* 73, no. 2 (1991): 285–93; and Douglas P. Woodward and Robert J. Rolfe, "The Location of Export-Oriented Foreign Direct Investment in the Caribbean Basin", *Journal of International Business Studies* 24, no. 1 (1993): 121–44.

6. See Franklin R. Root and Ahmed A. Ahmed, "The Influence of Policy Instruments on Manufacturing Direct Foreign Investment in Developing Countries", *Journal of International Business Studies* (Winter 1978): 81–93.

7. See Douglas Nigh, "The Effect of Political Events on US Direct Foreign

Investment: A Pooled Time Series Cross-Sectional Analysis", *Journal of International Business Studies* 16, no. 1 (1985): 1–18; and K. Fatehi-Sedeh and M. Safizadeh, "Sociopolitical Events and Foreign Direct Investment: American Investments in South and Central American Countries, 1950–1982", *Journal of Management* 14, no. 1 (1988): 93–107.

8. See Jamuna P. Agarwal, "Determinants of Foreign Direct Investments: A Survey", *Weltwirtschaftliches Archiv* 116 (1980): 739–77; and Schneider and Frey, "Economic and Political Determinants".

9. See, for example, Leonard K. Cheng and Yum K. Kwan, "What are the Determinants of the Location of Foreign Direct Investment? The Chinese Experience", *Journal of International Economics* 51, no. 2 (2000): 378–400.

10. See Lim, "Fiscal Incentives and Direct Foreign Investment"; Grubert and Mutti, "Taxes, Tariffs and Transfer Pricing"; Woodward and Rolfe, "The Location of Export-Oriented Foreign Direct Investment"; Stephen Guisinger and Associates, *Investment Incentives and Performance Requirements* (New York: Praeger, 1985); and Robert Rolfe and Richard White, "The Influence of Tax Incentives in Determining the Location of Foreign Direct Investment in Developing Countries", *Journal of the American Tax Association* 13, no. 2 (1992): 39–57.

11. See Robert Lucas, "On the Determinants of Direct Foreign Investment: Evidence from East and Southeast Asia", *World Development* 21, no. 3 (1993): 391–406.

12. See, for example, Thomas L. Brewer, "Government Policies, Market Imperfections and Foreign Direct Investment", *Journal of International Business Studies* 24, no. 1, (1993): 101–20; and Sanjaya Lall, "Industrial Strategy and Policies on Foreign Direct Investment in East Asia", *Transnational Corporations* 4, no. 3 (1995): 1–26.

13. See, for example, Gerard E. Watzke and W.A. Mindak, "Marketing-Oriented Planning in Public Administration: The Case of the State Development Agency", *International Journal of Public Administration* 9, no. 2 (1987): 80–92; Louis T. Wells, Jr and Alvin G. Wint, *Marketing a Country: Promotion as a Tool for Attracting Foreign Investment*, Foreign Investment Advisory Service Occasional Paper, no. 1 (Washington, DC: World Bank, 1990); and Stephen Young and Neil Hood, "Designing Developmental After-Care Programmes for Foreign Direct Investors in the European Union", *Transnational Corporations* 3, no. 2 (1994): 45–72.

14. See John Dunning, "Explaining the International Direct Investment Position of Countries: Toward a Dynamic or Developmental Approach", *Weltwirt Archives* 117, no. 1 (1981): 30–64; and his "Toward an Eclectic Theory of International Production: Some Empirical Tests", *Journal of International Business Studies* 11 (1980): 9–31.

15. For a sampling of the voluminous literature in this area, see Dennis Encarnation and Sushil Vachani, "Foreign Ownership: When Hosts Change the Rules", *Harvard Business Review* (September–October 1985): 152–60; Nathan Fagre and Louis T. Wells, Jr, "Bargaining Power of Multinationals and Host Governments", *Journal of International Business Studies* (Fall 1982): 9–23; Raymond Vernon, *Sovereignty at Bay: The Multinational Spread of U.S. Enterprises* (New York: Basic Books, 1971); Louis T. Wells, Jr and Eric S. Gleason, "Is Foreign Infrastructure Investment Still Risky?", *Harvard Business Review* (September–October 1995): 44–55; Alvin G. Wint, "Liberalizing Foreign Direct Investment Regimes: The Vestigial Screen", *World Development* 20, no. 10 (1992): 1515–29.

16. See, for example, Raymond Vernon, *Sovereignty at Bay*; and Wells and Gleason, "Is

Foreign Infrastructure Investment Still Risky?".

17. See Rhee Yung Whee and Therese Belot, *Export Catalysts in Low-Income Countries: A Review of Eleven Success Stories,* World Bank discussion paper (Washington, DC: World Bank, 1990).

18. See United Nations, *World Investment Report, 1999* (New York: Oxford University Press, 1999).

19. See United Nations, *World Investment Report, 2000* (New York: Oxford University Press, 2000).

20. See Wells and Wint, *Marketing a Country.*

21. See Wint, "Liberalizing Foreign Direct Investment Regimes".

22. See Alvin G. Wint and Densil Williams, "Attracting FDI to Developing Countries: A Changing Role for Government?", *International Journal of Public Sector Management* 15, no. 5 (2002): 361–74.

23. See, for example, Cheng and Kwan, "What are the Determinants of the Location of Foreign Direct Investment?"; and James H. Love and Francisco Lage-Hidalgo, "The Ownership Advantage in Latin American FDI: A Sectoral Study of US Direct Investment in Mexico", *Journal of Development Studies* 35, no. 5 (1999): 76–95.

24. See Wells and Wint, *Marketing a Country.*

25. See, for example, Wells and Wint, *Marketing a Country*; Young and Hood, "Designing Developmental After-Care Programmes"; and Debora Spar, *Attracting High Technology Investment: Intel's Costa Rican Plant,* Foreign Investment Advisory Service Occasional Paper, no. 11 (Washington, DC: 1998).

26. See Louis T. Wells, "Revisiting Marketing a Country", in *Marketing a Country: Promotion as a Tool for Attracting Foreign Investment*, by Louis T. Wells, Jr and Alvin G. Wint, rev. ed., Foreign Investment Advisory Service Occasional Paper, no. 13 (Washington, DC: World Bank, 2000).

Chapter 7

1. For a discussion of this point in a Caribbean context, see Alvin G. Wint, *Managing Towards International Competitiveness: Cases and Lessons from the Caribbean* (Kingston, Jamaica: Ian Randle Publishers, 1997).

2. The average rate of growth of the Jamaican economy during the 1991–1999 period was 0.1 per cent. The 1994–1999 period saw an average growth rate of -0.7 per cent, and 1996–1999 saw the Jamaican economy experiencing four consecutive years of negative growth. See *Economic and Social Survey* (Kingston, Jamaica: Planning Institute of Jamaica, 1999). The rate of growth of exports of goods and services from Jamaica during the 1990–1998 period was 0 per cent. See World Bank, *Entering the Twenty-first Century: World Development Report 1999/2000* (New York: Oxford University Press, 2000). The Jamaican economy did return to a growth path in 2000.

3. In an interesting "subsequent event" to this study, in 2002 Lee-Chin became directly involved in the management of Jamaican enterprise. His AIC Group acquired the Jamaican government's 75 per cent shareholding in one of Jamaica's largest banks, the National Commercial Bank. The government's ownership position resulted from its intervention during the financial sector crisis. Lee-Chin moved quickly to consolidate the turn-around of this institution, and within a few months had recruited one of Jamaica's top international

bankers, Aubyn Hill, who held an MBA from Harvard Business School and came to the bank from a position as chief executive officer of the National Bank of Oman.

4. See Wint, *Managing Towards International Competitiveness*.

5. For an insightful perspective on the importance of leadership in long-lived enterprise success, see Jim Collins, "Level 5 Leadership: The Triumph of Humility and Fierce Resolve", *Harvard Business Review* (January 2001): 66–70.

Chapter 8

1. See Government of Jamaica, *National Industrial Policy: Growth and Prosperity – The Way Forward* (Kingston, Jamaica: Jamaica Information Service, 1996).

2. See *The Jamaica Stock Exchange 1999 Year Book* (Kingston, Jamaica: Jamaica Stock Exchange, 2000).

3. See Bennett Harrison and Maryellen Kelley, "Outsourcing and the Search for 'Flexibility'", *Work, Employment and Society* 7, no. 2 (1993): 213–35; and Robert Mackenzie, "Subcontracting and the Regulation of the Employment Relationship: A Case Study from the Telecommunications Industry", *Work, Employment and Society* 14, no. 4 (2000): 707–26.

4. See Jamie Peck and Nikolas Theodore, "The Business of Contingent Work: Growth and Restructuring in Chicago's Temporary Employment Industry", *Work, Employment and Society* 12, no. 4 (1998): 655–74.

5. For the seminal work on these challenges associated with contracts, see Oliver Williamson, *Markets and Hierarchies: Analysis and Antitrust Implications* (New York: Free Press, 1975).

6. See, for example, Les Worrall et al., "The New Reality for UK Managers: Perpetual Change and Employment Instability", *Work, Employment and Society* 14, no. 4 (2000): 647–68; Wayne F. Cascio, "Downsizing: What Do We Know? What Have We Learned?", *Academy of Management Executive* 7, no. 1 (1993): 95–104; Adrian Thornhill, "Downsizing, Delayering – But Where's the Commitment? The Development of a Diagnostic Tool to Help Managers Survive", *Personnel Review* 26, no. 1 (1997): 81–98; Elizabeth Morrison and Sandra Robinson, "When Employees Feel Betrayed: A Model of How Psychological Contract Violation Develops", *Academy of Management Review* 22, no. 1 (1997): 226–56; and Joel Brockner et al., "Interactive Effects of Procedural Justice and Outcome Negativity on Victims and Survivors of Job Loss", *Academy of Management Journal* 37, no. 2 (1997): 397–408.

7. See J.H. Boyett and H.P. Conn, *Workplace 2000: The Revolution Reshaping American Business* (New York: Plume Books, 1991).

8. See Boyett and Conn, *Workplace 2000*.

9. See, for example, Bill Gates, *Business @ the Speed of Thought: Succeeding in the Digital Economy* (New York: Warner Books, 1999); S.H. Appelbaum, M. Bethune, and R. Tannenbaum, "Downsizing and the Emergence of Self-Managed Teams", *Participation and Empowerment: An International Journal* 7, no. 5 (1999): 109–30; and C. Douglas, "Organization Redesign: The Current State and Projected Trends", *Management Decision* 37, no. 8 (1999): 621–27.

10. See M. Hammer and J. Champy, *Re-engineering the Corporation: A Manifesto for Business Revolution* (New York: Harper Books, 1994).

11. See Sumantra Ghoshal and Christopher A. Bartlett, *The Individualized Corporation: A Fundamentally New Approach to Management* (New York: Harper Business, 1997).

12. See, for example, M. Luoma, "Investigating the Link between Strategy and HRD", *Personnel Review* 29, no. 6 (1997): 769–90; Mark Huselid, "The Impact of Human Resource Management Practices on Turnover, Productivity, and Corporate Financial Performance", *Academy of Management Journal* 38, no. 3 (1995): 635–72; and Chris Brewster, Ariane Hegewisch, and Lesley Mayne, "Flexible Working Practices: The Controversy and Evidence", in *Policy and Practice in European Human Resource Management: The Price Waterhouse Cranfield Survey,* ed. C. Brewster and A. Hegewisch, 35–49 (London: Routledge, 1994).

13. See, for example, Robert Drago, "Workplace Transformation and the Disposable Workplace: Employee Involvement in Australia", *Industrial Relations Journal* 35, no. 4 (1996): 526–43; Ann C. Frost, "Explaining Variation in Workplace Restructuring: The Role of Local Union Capabilities", *Industrial and Labour Relations Review* 53, no. 4 (2000): 559–78; Harry Katz, *Changing Gears: Changing Labour Relations in the US Auto Industry* (Cambridge, Mass.: MIT Press, 1985); and Fred Pomeroy, "Workplace Change: A Union Perspective", *Canadian Business Review* 22, no. 2 (1995): 33–40.

14. See Frost, "Explaining Variation in Workplace Restructuring".

15. For a discussion, see Locksley I. Lindo, *Caribbean Organizations* (Kingston, Jamaica: University of the West Indies Printery, 1997).

16. See K. Carter, *Why Workers Won't Work: The Worker in a Developing Economy* (London: Macmillan, 1997).

17. See J.R. French and B. Raven, "The Bases of Social Power", in *Studies in Social Power*, ed. D. Cartwright (Ann Arbor: University of Michigan, Institute for Social Research, 1959), 150–67.

Chapter 9

1. See, for example, David Peters, *Health Expenditures, Services and Outcomes in Africa: Basic Data and Cross-National Comparisons, 1990–1996* (Washington, DC: World Bank, 1999).

2. See World Health Organization, *World Health Report, 2000: Health Systems – Improving Performance* (Geneva: World Health Organization, 2000).

3. For these estimates, see Boston University's Center for International Health, "Jamaica Health Sector Expenditure-Based Analysis" (1994, mimeo).

4. See Pan American Health Organization, *Jamaica Health System and Services Profile* (Kingston, Jamaica: Planning Institute of Jamaica, 1998).

5. See Ministry of Finance, "Estimates of Expenditure, 1999" and "Estimates of Expenditure, 2001".

6. See Ministry of Finance, "Estimates of Expenditure, 2001"; and Alfred A. Francis, "The Dynamics of Debt in the Jamaican Economy" (Department of Economics, University of the West Indies, Kingston, Jamaica, 2000, mimeo).

7. See World Bank, *Entering the Twenty-first Century: World Development Report 1999/2000* (New York: Oxford University Press, 2000).

8. See Medical Association of Jamaica, "Position Paper of the MAJ on the National Health Insurance Programme", November 1999.

9. See Jones Report, "Health Sector Pay Review Committee Report", March 1999.

10. See Coopers and Lybrand (Caribbean) Consultants Inc., and Government of Jamaica/Ministry of Finance, "Health Sector Pay Review Project Report", 1999.

11. See World Bank, *World Development Report: Investing in Health* (New York: Oxford University Press, 1993).

12. See Medical Association of Jamaica, "Position Paper of the MAJ".

13. See United Nations, *Human Development Report, 2000* (New York: Oxford University Press, 2000).

14. See Michael Porter, *The Competitive Advantage of Nations* (New York: Free Press, 1990).

15. See World Bank, *World Development Report: Investing in Health.*

16. See Gill Armstrong, "Jamaica Health Sector Review" (1994, mimeo).

17. See Yitades Gebre, *HIV/AIDS in Jamaica* (Kingston, Jamaica: Ministry of Health, 2001).

18. See Medical Association of Jamaica, "Position Paper of the MAJ".

19. See, for example, Stanley Lalta, *Review of Health Financing in Jamaica and a Survey of the Feasibility of National Health Insurance* (Kingston, Jamaica: Institute for Social and Economic Research, 1995).

Chapter 10

1. See Patricia Anderson, "The Changing Role of Self-Employment: A Review of the Jamaican Labour Market during the Nineties and Prospects for Growth" (paper presented at University of the West Indies Research Day Forum on Private Sector Perspectives on Economic Growth, University of the West Indies, Kingston, Jamaica, 18 October 2001). Anderson also notes that 33 per cent of the Jamaican labour force is self-employed, with the educational achievement level of self-employed workers increasing consistently throughout the decade.

2. See Hernando de Soto, *The Mystery of Capital: Why Capitalism Triumphs in the West and Fails Everywhere Else* (New York: Basic Books, 2000), 35.

3. Ibid., 33.

4. Ibid., 40.

5. Ibid., 190.

6. Ibid., 155.

7. See Joseph Battat, Isaiah Frank and Xiaofang Shen, *Suppliers to Multinationals: Linkage Programs to Strengthen Local Companies in Developing Countries,* Foreign Investment Advisory Service Occasional Paper, no. 6 (Washington, DC: World Bank, 1996).

8. For a classic elucidation of linkages between dual sector economies, see W. Arthur Lewis, "Economic Development with Unlimited Supplies of Labour", *The Manchester School* 22 (May 1954): 155–63.

9. See Battat, Frank and Shen, *Suppliers to Multinationals.*

10. See Paul Streeten, "The Social Dimensions of Development", in *Economic Development,* ed. Enzo Grilli and Dominick Salvatone, vol. 4 of the *Handbook of Comparative Economic Policies,* 80–98 (Westport, Conn.: Greenwood Press, 1994).

11. See de Soto, *The Mystery of Capital,* 169.

12. Ibid., 171.

13. Ibid., 175.

14. See World Bank, *World Development Report 2000/2001: Attacking Poverty* (New York: Oxford University Press, 2001), 121.

15. See Jonathan Morduch, "Between the Market and the State: Can Informal Insurance Patch the Safety Net?" *World Bank Research Observer* 14, no. 2 (1999), 187–207.

16. See World Bank, *World Development Report*, 121.

17. These programmes include Singapore's Local Industry Upgrading Programme, coordinated by the Singapore Economic Development Board; Taiwan's Center-Satellite Factory System, sponsored by Taiwan's Industrial Development Bureau; and Ireland's National Linkage Programme, established by a consortium of agencies led by Ireland's Industrial Development Authority. See Battat, Frank and Shen, *Suppliers to Multinationals.*

18. For a useful outline of the Grameen Bank programme, an indication of the extent to which it does benefit from government subsidies, and a discussion of why private sector institutions around the world have not rushed to follow this model, see Jonathan Morduch, "The Role of Subsidies in Microfinance: Evidence from the Grameen Bank", *Journal of Development Economics* 60 (1999): 229–48.

19. For an analysis of the Jamaica Exporters Association's noncollateralized lending programmes, including lessons for the successful administration of microfinancing to the export and other sectors, see Trevor Hamilton and Associates, "Evaluation of the Non-Collateralized Loan Scheme at the Jamaica Exporters Association" (October 2001, mimeo).

20. For evidence on this point, see Sudhanshu Handa and Claremont Kirton, "The Economics of Rotating Savings and Credit Associations: Evidence from the Jamaican Partner", *Journal of Development Economics* 60 (1999): 173–94.

21. See World Bank, *World Development Report*, 8.

22. Ibid., 25.

23. See World Bank, *World Development Report, 1991: The Challenge of Development* (New York: Oxford University Press, 1991).

24. See John Williamson, "What Washington Means by Policy Reform", in *Latin American Adjustment: How Much Has Happened?* ed. John Williamson, 8–15 (Washington, DC: Institute for International Economics, 1990).

25. For strands of this debate, see Holger Henke and Ian Boxill, eds., *The End of the Asian Model* (Amsterdam: John Benjamins Publishing Company, 2000); and Norman Girvan, "Globalisation and Counter-Globalisation: The Caribbean in the Context of the South", in *Globalisation, A Calculus of Inequality: Perspectives from the South,* ed. Denis Benn and Kenneth Hall, 65–86 (Kingston, Jamaica: Ian Randle Publishers, 2000).

26. See, for example, Shahid Burki and G. Perry, *Beyond the Washington Consensus: Institutions Matter* (Washington, DC: World Bank, 1998).

27. At the World Bank's headquarters in Washington, DC, is now displayed prominently the mission of the World Bank, which is to "fight poverty with passion and professionalism for lasting results". This new mission recognizes a need to mount a direct war on poverty. In part, it responds to critics of the World Bank's operations, as reflected in recent times in the report of the Meltzer Commission. This focus is also reflected in the subtitle of the World Bank's *World Development Report, 2000/2001: Attacking Poverty.*

28. See de Soto, *The Mystery of Capital,* 207, 211.

Conclusion

1. See Michael Porter, *The Competitive Advantage of Nations* (New York: Free Press, 1990).

2. Recall, from chapter 6, that Vernon's product cycle theory loomed large in the motivation of Singapore's foreign investment attraction drive. See Raymond Vernon, "International Investment and International Trade in the Product Cycle", *Quarterly Journal of Economics* (May 1966): 190–207.

3. An example is Brazil's Embraer, which, based upon Brazil's geography and the needs of the Brazilian military, developed a competence in the production of small commercial aircraft that was eventually parlayed into a competitive position in international markets in this industry segment.

4. Indeed, there are very few examples of small countries, of any income level, which have developed internationally competitive industries based upon the sophistication of home country demand. An interesting exception is Finland, where the multinational company, Nokia, developed a distinctive competence in communication technology based, at least in part, on the heavy demand in frigid, sparsely populated Finland for technology that would allow communication that did not require physical movement. In a manner well known in innovation life cycles, Nokia has been able to export its technology to a world that quickly came to see the virtue of such forms of communication.

5. See Robert Barro, *Determinants of Economic Growth: A Cross-Country Empirical Study* (Cambridge, Mass.: MIT Press, 1997). Barro points out, as noted in chapter 5, that many of the factors differentiating growth across countries typically lie within the purview of government action.

6. See Alan Rugman and J. D'Cruz, "The Double Diamond Model of International Competitiveness: The Canadian Experience", *Management International Review* 33 (special issue; 1993): 17–39.

7. See Lou Anne A. Barclay, *Foreign Direct Investment in Emerging Economies: Corporate Strategy and Investment Behaviour in the Caribbean* (London: Routledge, 2000), for an insightful and comprehensive analysis of the operations of multinational corporations in the anglophone Caribbean and the interactions of these firms with national competitiveness.

8. There are at least two reasons why these models speak past each other. The first is the preoccupation of the international business scholarly community with the activities of multinational corporations. Porter, who is not formally a part of this scholarly community, and would not feel a need to pay allegiance to the shibboleths of the community, only included multinationals as a by-product of his analysis, pointing to the fact that an overreliance on them would be likely to ensure that a country stayed in the factor-driven stage of development. The other reason that the Porter model was bound to lead to scholarly disagreement, however, relates to the "straining of intellectual credulity" evidenced when he implicitly includes, based on his research conducted in the late 1980s, countries as varied in levels of development as Niger, Jamaica, Australia, Canada and Singapore, for example, in the same factor-driven "stage of national competitive development". It is no coincidence that the first salvos of this disagreement were fired from a Canadian-based international business scholar.

9. See Devesh Kapur and Ravi Ramamurti, "India's Emerging Competitive Advantage in Services", *Academy of Management Executive* 15, no. 2 (2001): 20–33.

Index